With Every Step

A Son's Quest And A Father's Promise

Neil Cadigan

16

EasyRead Large

RHYW

Copyright Page from the Original Book

Published by Nero,
an imprint of Schwartz Publishing Pty Ltd
37–39 Langridge Street
Collingwood VIC 3066, Australia
email: enquiries@blackincbooks.com
www.nerobooks.com.au

The National Library of Australia Cataloguing-in-Publication entry:
Cadigan, Neil, author.
With every step: a son's quest and a father's promise / Neil Cadigan.
9781863957106 (paperback)
9781922231789 (ebook)
Cadigan, Andrew. Simpson, Chris. Fundraising—Australia.
Leukemia—Research—Australia.
361.70681

Cover and internal design by Peter Long
Cover photograph by Rik Gruwez

FSC
www.fsc.org
MIX
Paper from responsible sources
FSC® C009448

Printed in Australia by Griffin Press. The paper this book is printed on is certified against the Forest Stewardship Council® Standards. Griffin Press holds FSC chain of custody certification SGS-COC-005088. FSC promotes environmentally responsible, socially beneficial and economically viable management of the world's forests.

TABLE OF CONTENTS

To Andrew ('Cad'), and the indelible mark you left on so many.
To my family.
And to all those people who have lost a son or daughter too early.

Foreword

My son, Andrew 'Cad' Cadigan, was an ordinary Australian, known mostly to those outside his many friends and his family for being the third person to have walked solo around Australia, although he was the only one of these to have added Tasmania to the mainland states and territories. From late December 2010 to mid-June 2012 he paced just over 15,000 kilometres, averaging 43 kilometres per walking day (and an incredible 53 kilometres a day from Darwin to Sydney).

He did it in honour of a mate, Chris 'Simmo' Simpson, who had died seven months before Andrew's departure, age twenty-four, from complications associated with a disease called myelodysplasia, a rare pre-leukaemia condition. Cad relinquished his job as a carpenter/site manager and left with little preparation and no sponsorship, intending to fund his trek through the pending sale of his home. After deciding to dedicate the walk to Simmo, Cad elected to raise funds for causes related to Simmo's plight – firstly the Cancer Council of New South Wales, then the Leukaemia Foundation – and in the end raised around $65,000. He rarely accepted any donations towards his own costs.

Cad was endeared to thousands via brief meetings along his route or the almost daily video blogs he posted on his website and YouTube. Yet the sixteen months it took him to complete the course, including two months in Thailand to sit out the most torrential period of the monsoon season in Australia's Top End, had taken much more out of him than he articulated through his often witty blogs.

The way Cad withstood temperatures of over 40 degrees to walk more than 50 kilometres a day during the start of Australia's big wet was amazing, as was his crossing of the Nullarbor Plain.

Just four days after completing his walk, armed with the twenty-six handwritten exercise books that contained his daily diaries, Andrew left for Thailand. His aim was both to recover and to remove himself from potential distractions so he could write a book on his experiences, with my help. The idea originated in a book he'd read years earlier: *Giant Steps,* written by a former British paratrooper named Karl Bushby, who had attempted to walk from the southern point of South America to England.

Tragically, Andrew was fatally injured in a motorcycle accident in Thailand one month to the day after he completed his walk. He died twelve weeks later, after being returned to Australia.

At the start of the ten horrible weeks that my wife, Chris, and I spent in Thailand as Cad's condition swayed between probable death and a terrible life of permanent care, I vowed that I would write the book he was no longer capable of completing.

This is my fifteenth book, most of the rest having been as a ghostwriter for the autobiographies of others. It was by far the toughest to write. Yet for obvious reasons it is the dearest to me. It became a way for me to pay tribute to Cad, an ordinary bloke who proved to have something extraordinary in him.

Sadly, I only became aware of some exceptional aspects of Cad after his death, partly from the remarkable eulogies articulated by his closest mates (including a moving video tribute they put together for his funeral), but also from the many hundreds of people he met during his venture. These meetings were brief, but long enough for Cad to leave an indelible mark on these strangers. To them, his Oz On Foot trek defined him. To those who knew Cad well beforehand, it typified him.

As I sat at my desk compiling this book, often early in the morning or late at night, I felt like I was in my own cocoon, shut away even from Chris, whom I love dearly. I was writing these thousands of words as a memoir intended only for my family and Cad's closest friends. It was my way of telling them the complete story of his incredible walk, and of the terrible aftermath in Thailand right to his death back home. It was also, for me, a means of answering the many questions I couldn't answer to their faces – a way I could spit out all that was inside me, but having to tell it only once to a computer screen, and not continually to people in person.

Cad's incredible trek was made not just on the lonely highways across barren land, but also emotionally through the hundreds of pages of diary notes he recorded on his travels, and the many, many hours he had to himself to think about his life. It was new territory for him to document his inner thoughts as well as his daily experiences. His journals comprised some 450,000 words; much of it had to be condensed, and some was kept private.

This book contains many direct quotations from Cad's personal chronicles, in his unique and memorable voice. I removed an abundance of swear words but have retained some for the right emphasis, and I've occasionally made corrections for clarity and consistency.

Of course, the ending of the book is very different to what Cad and I had planned. Yet I felt I had to detail his terrible fate after the accident, both in order to truly complete his story and to give a loving father's narrative of a situation too many people have been confronted with.

My account of the very difficult months between Cad's accident and his death were largely written while Chris and I were in Thailand. I kept my own diary notes, which were the only means by which I could record and come to terms with what happened in those surreal, difficult weeks, as we endured the nightmare no parent wants to live. I often wrote as I sat by his hospital bed or in our hotel, which had been his. I had to get my thoughts and feelings out while they were raw, real and current, as I knew I would not be able to go there again. It was then that I also began reading Cad's handwritten diaries.

My hope for this book is that it is an interesting and inspirational insight into one man's unbelievable achievement in walking around a continent, often in harsh conditions. The ending of Cad's life was tragic, coming so painfully soon after his great conquest. Yet I am thankful that we had Andrew for thirty-one years, during which time he enriched our lives.

I do not want to suggest Cad was an angel without faults, vices or regrets – he did not always live his life as I had hoped he would, nor was he always the happy-go-lucky soul he often appeared. However, he had a most amazing inner strength and determination, an incredible threshold for pain, and a desire to go beyond the norms that restricted so many others. Most memorably, he had an ability to instantly endear himself to so many people.

He was a hero, no question.

Neil Cadigan

PROLOGUE

HAPPY FINISH, TRAGIC ENDING

14 JUNE 2012

The day had come. My son, Andrew Scott Cadigan, was on the Sydney Harbour Bridge, about to face a rousing welcome from family, friends, Leukaemia Foundation staff and a Channel Ten news crew after walking over 15,000 kilometres around Australia. His journey had begun two days after Christmas 2010 when I dropped him off and watched him stroll away, heading south down the Princes Highway pushing the modified pram he would name 'Redge' (after his beloved dog).

Here we were, 536 days yet seemingly a lifetime later. Andrew had survived. He'd changed. He'd grown. And he had signalled this day as the end of one life and the start of another.

My wife, Chris, and I were part of the 'A team' that stepped the last few kilometres with him down the Pacific Highway. My pride and emotion spilled over, and I could feel the tears welling in my eyes as we approached the small group waiting for him at the finish line. This was an extraordinary human achievement, the extent of which could only fully be understood by those closest to him, who were aware of the physical and mental torture he'd had to overcome. But for now, that was all forgotten.

Andrew was usually known as 'Cad', just as I am widely referred to as 'Caddo' instead of Neil. For a couple of kilometres as we paced up the hill from St Leonards and down the next towards North Sydney, Cad and Caddo inadvertently found themselves well in front of the ten others who wanted to be there for his final hard yards. It was one of the few times in a long while that Andrew and I were able to spend some time alone as father and son and just chew the fat. Mostly we touched on what it meant to be just the third person to have travelled around the country on foot solo (that is, without a support crew), and how it felt to have almost finished the daily grind that had seen him walk from Darwin to Sydney in just ninety-nine days, and from Townsville in only five weeks.

Cad had pushed his Chariot pram – one of those three-wheelers you often see young mothers jogging behind – which contained his food, water and camping essentials, through the toughest of conditions. He'd seen temperatures drop to just above freezing overnight, and trekked through torrential rain and almost plague-like intrusions of flies, locusts, mice and mosquitos. He'd also had to withstand excessive heat in the Kimberley, which had reached 45 degrees Celsius, with high humidity, defying what were undoubtedly life-threatening conditions at times to often walk 50 to 75 kilometres a day, his only company a solar-panel-charged iPod and iPhone, and occasionally the welcome company of passing travellers.

A man, a pram, two feet and a heartbeat.

Cad posted the first of what would become frequently viewed video blogs just south of Sydney Airport early in the afternoon of 27 December 2010. As I held the camera in a gusty wind, he announced that he was dedicating the walk – named Oz On Foot – to Chris 'Simmo' Simpson, a mate he'd lost to cancer at the age of twenty-four.

With Cad being typically disorganised and in a rush to get going, I had to drive him down to Blakehurst to embark on his first steps so that he could clear the heavy residential areas of southern Sydney before dark; we'd agreed that it would be our secret that his starting point wasn't actually the airport but an hour's walk down the highway. Almost a year and a half later, after he had decided to end the epic trek at another Sydney landmark, our famous bridge, his commitment to go strictly 'by the book' was so firm that I had to drop him back to that same spot on the Princes Highway, so he could backtrack to the bridge and ensure he did not miss one metre of the designated course.

That was Cad. The promise he'd made at Simmo's wake in May 2010 to dedicate his trek to him may have become an enemy to his physical and mental health, but it was also his driving force and ultimate test of character, loyalty and endurance, as well as the catalyst for a deep search inside his sometimes troubled soul. His mission became a vow not to quit on Simmo, himself or his goal.

But back to the finish. As we trooped as one unit – with Simmo's brother, Josh, and his parents, Wayne and Kim, among us – towards the shadows of the northern pylon of the bridge, I asked that we stop and get a group photo for posterity. Then Andrew and Josh lifted Redge up the stairs and we strolled the last short stretch to where my sister Alison, her daughter, Megan, Cad's other cousin, Luke, representatives of the Leukaemia Foundation and more friends waited at the centre point of the bridge's walkway. The Ten Network cameras captured Cad's final steps towards the cheering that awaited him.

He did a TV interview with Ten's Nick Lockyer, embraced his supporters (I noticed Wayne and Kim tearing up; Chris and I were too), and posed for photos. At last, his soul-testing sojourn had ended.

He placed his iPhone in its bracket on the handle of his pram, just as he had more than two hundred times before, and on the bridge recorded the last of his video blogs, which hundreds of people had regularly tuned in to – people from all parts of Australia and all walks of life, all of whom had been inspired by Andrew, even if they'd met only briefly en route.

I will never forget the words he spoke into the camera as he began his sign-off. It remains a chilling reminder of how uncertain and cruel life can be.

'Day 536, done and dusted,' he said. 'It's all over. The alarm clock has gone off; I've woken up from this nightmare. Day 536 ... But tomorrow will be day one: getting on with the rest of my life.'

18 JUNE 2012

It was a somewhat understated moment; well, tragically, it seems that way now. I pulled up at the drop-off zone of Sydney International Airport; as anyone who has witnessed the Gestapo-like attitude of the parking authorities there would know, it's not the place for prolonged farewells.

Andrew grabbed his two sports bags – full of the only possessions he would need for a while – and held out his hand to shake mine. We put our arms around each other and he said something like, 'Well, I'll see ya when I see ya, but I'll definitely be home for Christmas.'

I replied along the lines of, 'You take care. I'm proud of you, mate.' I might have told him I loved him too, which would have embarrassed him; blokes don't do that, he would have thought. He was never one to show loving emotion anyway, although he had told his mother he loved her when she farewelled him – the last time they would speak.

Then he was gone. He took a Thai Airways flight to Bangkok that he had only booked days earlier; until then he couldn't make up his mind whether to head overseas or reintroduce himself to life back on the Central Coast. In the end, he felt he had to get away and take stock.

While stuck in the Top End during the wet season, he'd taken himself off to Pattaya in Thailand, from late December 2010 through January and February 2011, to recuperate, build up some weight and put muscle on a body that had been reduced to 55 kilograms. And to regain some his heavily eroded peace of mind too, although he hid that well on the surface. During the final month of his walk he tossed up whether to return to Thailand, this time to Chiang Mai in the country's north, to rest and work on the diaries he'd handwritten almost daily during his trek, and which he had finally decided to turn into a book about his conquest.

He had some work lined up in Karratha, in Western Australia, a way he could rebuild his bank balance. While Cad had raised over $65,000 for the Leukaemia Foundation and the Cancer Council, he'd found it hard to accept even $10 in charity for himself, despite having used the money from the sale of his house to fund the walk and sustain him during such a long non-earning period. The pressure he'd put on himself to quickly finish the massive renovation of his home in beachside North Avoca and then head off indefinitely had essentially led to the end of his six-year relationship with his partner, Jaime, which was a great shame.

In the end, he'd decided to take a break, booking his ticket to Thailand the day after he walked back over the Sydney Harbour Bridge. He was initially only going to Thailand for three to four weeks, so he could do the Karratha job from late July, but his West Australian friends Jessica and Steve Browne said that if he arrived later and was ready to work – and he had a stronger work ethic than anyone I have known – the job would wait for him. So he was going to be in Chiang Mai for probably three months (he had booked a return flight for 18 August), transcribing his diaries and enjoying some travel into Burma, Laos and Cambodia. Well, that was the plan; Cad always had a plan.

As I drove him to the airport, after picking him up from his cousins' home in Marsfield, Sydney, where he'd stayed the night before, I was still musing about why he had to shoot through so soon. I wanted to spend more time catching up with him, as did his family and friends. But he had changed so much during his walk that he'd developed a fear of reverting to his old lifestyle on the Central Coast and being distracted from transferring his diaries to content for his book. It was time, he felt, to move on from the crazy image many had of him, and from his workaholic ways as a carpenter. He'd grown up, and he'd also grown his bucket list of things he had to experience and achieve. Travel was at the top.

Typically, all the way to the airport Cad was on his phone, returning texts or emails and fielding calls. Thus, we didn't have any deep and meaningful father–son chat, which was not unusual but is now a regret.

He'd first hit the Central Coast on a Sunday, ten days earlier. I hooked up the trailer and picked him and his pram up at Ourimbah after he'd finished, solo, his 'Triple Marathon Madness' – walking 126.6 kilometres without rest (that's the equivalent of three Olympic marathon courses), mostly in pouring rain, some of it with mates by his side. I could tell he was broken, physically and mentally. We had sold our house at Point Clare, also on the Central Coast, just a week earlier and were staying with our best friends, Mandy and Alan Shaw, so Andrew had elected to bunk with his grandmother at her retirement village at Point Clare, which 'Ma' had been looking forward to. Unfortunately, she was hit by her third bout of pneumonia in a year just days before Andrew reached the Coast and was in Gosford Hospital. So Andrew had her place to himself.

For the next week (which included four days of walking), being around him was like being on the edge of a whirlwind. But in between finishing his walk, appearing on the *Sunrise* breakfast TV program on Channel Seven the next morning, catching up with friends and family, including an enjoyable night at Central Coast Leagues Club with cousins, aunties and uncles and his beloved grannie, and spending his last night at his cousin Matthew's (and Lynn, Jessica and Paul's) home in Sydney, he'd departed.

And that brief airport goodbye was the last face-to-face conversation we had.

'See ya when I see ya.' It's another sentence that lingers tragically.

The next time I saw him was not a scene I had ever envisaged.

14 JULY 2012

It's the moment every parent dreads, the call in the middle of the night that chills your spine with fear. The call that you hear about on the news, but the one that is never going to happen to you.

For me, it interrupted my life just prior to midnight, six days before I was due to fly to London to work for the Australian Olympic Committee at the 2012 Games, an experience I was looking forward to. Three days later, Chris was to leave on a Pacific cruise with a good friend.

At the other end of the line was a woman who identified herself as being from the Department of Foreign Affairs and Trade (DFAT) in Canberra. She said she'd been trying to get hold of me for hours. My missed call log indeed confirmed calls at 6.45pm and 6.50pm, when I was away from my phone, and then again at 10.10pm, just twenty-five minutes after

I'd gone to bed with the phone sitting on the bedside table. That I had not heard it shows how deeply I could plunge into a good sleep ... well, back then, anyway.

It was a call I feared I might receive during the first year of Andrew's Oz On Foot walk, especially after he had described the many times he came within centimetres of being hit by road trains on the lonely highways of Western Australia and the Northern Territory. I had woken in the night a few times during his journey dreaming that something dreadful had happened. But I wasn't expecting it now, not while he rested and sank his teeth into preparing his diaries for this book.

When the DFAT rep called, she had no idea whose unconscious body was lying in a hospital in Chiang Mai. She first asked me if I knew of anyone travelling in Thailand, and I said, 'Yes, my son.' Then she asked my name and my son's name. I frantically asked what had happened and she requested I hold on for a moment, obviously checking her computer records to find Andrew's details and that he was indeed travelling in Thailand. She then explained it appeared that Andrew was in the Maharaj Nakorn Hospital with a broken leg and very serious head injuries, and was in a coma.

The department had received a call from an Australian man whose son, travelling in Thailand, had asked him to call DFAT and explain that an Australian in Chiang

Mai was in hospital and in a bad way after being involved in a motorcycle accident. I'm still not sure of the whole sequence, but someone had extracted the phone number Andrew had listed as 'Dad' in his mobile; that was the department's only clue as to his identity. He had only some cash and his phone with him, having left his wallet in his hotel room.

The DFAT woman had no more information but said she would try to put me in direct contact with the hospital to talk to a doctor. I was struggling to make sense of all of this. I knew the situation was dire but I still couldn't fathom how serious Andrew's condition might be, and just assumed that if he was alive, he'd recover. The call ended with her saying she would call back when she had the doctor on the line.

Our goddaughter Emma was asleep in the next room; we'd been living at the Shaws' house keeping her company while her parents, Mandy and Alan, were overseas. Chris was at Swansea, fifty minutes' drive north, staying overnight at her parents' place with her sister, Lynne, and our niece Jessica, who was heading to London for a couple of years. How was I going to break this to Chris?

I rang, and my mother-in-law, Maureen, answered the phone. I apologised for the late hour but asked her to get Chris to call me back, as Andrew thad been involved in an accident. Probably two minutes later Chris called, and soon Lynne was driving her back to the Central Coast.

The next few hours were a bit of a blur. I remember talking to the doctor in Chiang Mai, who explained that Andrew's right leg was broken and he had severe head injuries. They had removed half his skull (which was never replaced) and done an emergency operation. I struggled to comprehend his accent, but he was telling me that on a scale of one to ten, Andrew's head injury was a ten. I kept asking, 'Okay, could he die?' but the doctor would not answer. I guessed that meant yes.

By 5am our bags were packed and we drove to Sydney. I'd been unable to book a flight because of issues with the Thai Airlines website, though once we got to the airport they were fantastic in helping us. We boarded a 10am flight and arrived at Chiang Mai at 9.30pm our time (6.30pm in Thailand).

By then I'd rung our daughter, Nicole, who lives in Brisbane, and my sister Alison, asking her to inform the rest of the family what had happened (I was due to meet her, another sister, Robyn, and my mother for breakfast that morning), I'd also called Cad's best mate, Matt Delaney, and asked him to tell Andrew's friends. For the entire flight we were anxious and uneasy. It all felt so surreal, so unbelievable. Unable to sleep, I made myself watch a movie just to reduce the tension inside me. We hadn't really fully considered, nor did we even want to, what we might hear or see when we got to our destination.

We went straight to the hospital. From the moment we walked into the Intensive Care Unit's trauma ward, the horrible truth confronted us. We debated whether the only white-skinned patient in the ward could possibly be our son, so unrecognisable was his face. Our lives, and Andrew's, had changed forever.

This was not how the Oz On Foot legend was supposed to end.

1

CAD

How should I describe Andrew 'Cad' Cadigan? Certainly he was a very likeable larrikin. He had a mischievous smile and a golden heart inside a rough-diamond exterior. He could endear himself to royalty as readily as he could to an Irish backpacker, a neighbour, the 'grey nomads' who so affectionately took to him on his travels or the knockabout tradesmen he encountered on worksites. I bet Cad could have matched every one of them in dropping the 'f-bomb', which forever attracted the ire of his mother.

Cad was a talker and a doer, someone who felt compelled to do what he said he would. He so often had a grand plan, a funny scam or a dream, or was embroiled in one of his many schemes for making a dollar. He worked hard and he partied hard, but just about always he had an goal in mind.

He was a cuddly and warm child, born in Tasmania during a brief period when we lived there, but from ten months old grew up on the Central Coast of New South Wales, about an hour's drive north of Sydney. There he attended Point Clare Primary School, then St Pat's at East Gosford.

When Andrew was nine, we left on an adventure to Wakefield, in Yorkshire, England, where I worked as general manager of the local rugby league club. I still have the clip of the Channel Ten coverage in Australia that refers to the snowy-haired Andrew leading the 1990 Australian Kangaroos onto the field to play Wakefield Trinity.

On our return to Point Clare, Andrew went to St Edward's College at East Gosford. He and school didn't have a particularly warm relationship, although Cad did often attend six days a week. Normally, the Saturday visit was in the company of his 'partner in crime', Todd Bailey – on detention.

He became more mischievous and restless as he got older, before being diagnosed with ADHD in early adolescence. From there we encountered some tough years when he was rebellious and often distant. He left school at fifteen after completing Year 10, but fortunately had his mind set on being a carpenter. He became an exceptionally good one, which was no surprise; he had built a two-storey tree house at age twelve, and a skate ramp that filled an entire section of our yard at fifteen.

But don't think he was any intellectual fool – he went on to prove he had an exceptional mathematical and logical mind, and he retained a great interest in and knowledge of world affairs and many other subjects.

Cad almost didn't finish his apprenticeship because of his decision to spend a winter in the Snowy Mountains, snowboarding and working as a 'dish pig'. His calling to be the leader of men, or more accurately the village idiot, was obvious when he got one of his mates to bring a second-hand three-seater lounge down (formerly belonging to his sister, Nicole, and her partner, Glenn) and stretched the sport of snowboarding into snow-couching down one of the steepest slopes – everything was caught on film. Fortunately, he returned to his trade and TAFE and became a carpenter with one of the best names on the Central Coast. He obviously inherited that skill from Chris's side of the family, not mine; like my father before me, I'm much better at destruction that construction.

Cad left home at seventeen, and his later teenage years were certainly difficult ones when it came to our relationship. Chris worried terribly about him and his lifestyle. Let's not beat around the bush: like so many of his generation, his life from then included binge drinking, crazy behaviour and social drug use. He was no angel or model son (and I'm sure I was no model father either), but he was a good one of whom I was generally very proud, and whom I loved immensely, no matter how difficult at times he could be. I felt we had a strong bond. He had a love for and connection with his family greater than he knew how to express.

While Cad was a genuine, popular and extremely loyal friend or relative, there were two sides to him: the happy-go-lucky life-of-the-party mate to all and sundry, and then the stress-head who frequently put too many demands and expectations on himself, always at full throttle and with a deadline, a plan, a scheme or a dream. And too often it threatened to wear him down.

Cad loved travel once he got a taste for it while living in the United Kingdom from 2005–08 with his partner, Jaime, with many mates from home at close hand. He travelled to forty-five countries – short of his stated goal of seeing a hundred countries – and studied Mandarin and Spanish. (In fact, he became fluent in Spanish by the end of his walk after hours of audio lessons.)

After starting out in the United Kingdom building pergolas for a landscaping company, he joined Fit Out UK, a firm that fitted out large retail stores. There he climbed from a tradesman to job foreman to regional manager by the age of twenty-seven. That period was a great example of his personal drive; he was paid by the hour and, under pressure to complete store refits in the shortest period of time, he often worked 100- to 120-hour weeks.

Another well-known part of his character was his bizarre get-rich-quick penchant. I'll never forget when he bought his first ute, suitable for loading his tools as a carpenter, and he would head around suburbs collecting junk thrown out for council pickups, only to stack them at our place (he was living elsewhere).

Later, he'd sell the goods at garage sales, making several hundred dollars each time.

The scheme I liked best was when he potted a thousand chilli plants in his backyard, which he planned to sell at markets or on the roadside. But either a resident possum or birds would get into his crop, so there was no great harvest or profit.

While sport has always been my life, Andrew leaned towards other activities, although he did play soccer, cricket and rugby league briefly. Skateboarding (at which he was brilliant) and, for a while, bodyboarding were his passions, along with stretching the boundaries whenever he could; thus his nickname, 'Cannonball Cad'. That became the title of a *Jackass* -style video he released in 2004 (the full title was *Cannonball Cad: Bored Individuals),* a compilation of a couple of years' worth of recordings of his crazy stunts, like jumping off bridges into water with an umbrella as a parachute (and one time while riding a bike), licking an electric fence (twice for good footage) or any similar stupid dare that he was silly enough to accept. He organised a gala premier at the historic Avoca Theatre and filled it, then ran off a thousand DVDs, about a third of which stayed in my garage unsold!

His other passion became tattoos – another area where father and son differed. His first was done at age seventeen, with a letter of approval from his parents. He was only six months short of being of legal age, and we knew he would have worn us down anyway. I don't know how many tatts followed – I'd guess fifteen, and just about each one had a story. Some were inked during his Oz On Foot trek, but none on his arms or neck.

The thing that was always stable about Cad was his remarkable work ethic, and his ambition to achieve something and really experience life.

When he was twenty-one, Chris and I asked him if he wanted to take half-ownership of an investment property we decided to buy in our suburb of Point Clare, with the aim of him renovating it when it suited us all. After we'd rented it out for eighteen months, he moved in to live there while doing the work section by section and adding a second storey. He did a magnificent job with the help of some tradesmen mates – after a rather unusual start. I went around after a couple of weeks to check on the progress, only to find that the whole back of the house had been converted into an inside skate ramp with two half-pipes, and an outside bleacher for spectators!

Cad left for England as soon as the house was finished, and when he returned three years later, with much of his UK earnings in the bank, he was determined to buy a house of his own. After acquiring a place at North Avoca, not far from the beach, Cad did a second magnificent major renovation, on top of working tirelessly in his busy building job, where he was rarely 'on the tools' but a site manager for Carpentry Construction. That was yet another time in his life when I begged him to slow down with 'what's the hurry, son?' style talks, but, conversely, I admired his incredible determination and resilience.

An example of his truly amazing determination came in 2009, when he took up an invitation from his mother's brother, Ken Knight, to enter, as a two-man crew, the 111-kilometre Hawkesbury Canoe Classic paddle race from Windsor to the Hawkesbury River. It's a gruelling event, much of which is conducted in the dark from a Saturday evening through to the Sunday morning. Ken, an experienced canoeist, suffered a shoulder injury two weeks before the event and had to pull out. After unsuccessfully trying to coerce his best mate, Matt Delaney, into joining him, Cad decided to compete by himself in a totally insufficient and unsuitable kayak (without a rudder) owned by Alan and Mandy Shaw, and with about a month of inadequate training (he'd never paddled prior to then). Ken and I served as his support crew. In an amazing show of his determination and resilience, he endured pain, a pitch-black night and greater struggle than other competitors experienced for sixty-five kilometres and nine hours before being towed back to Wiseman's Ferry totally exhausted. I'd never seen him so drained, nor seen him concede to a challenge like that, but Ken and I were in awe of how he had continued for so long.

Generally, if Cad made a commitment to others or had a goal to reach, he had to fulfil it. And he always seemed to have somewhere to go and something to achieve. His walk around Australia became one of those 'must do' events. However, I must admit that Cad was the last person I expected to become a charity fundraising champion; I'd never seen that in his nature.

Who knows what path he would have tried next, armed with the obvious maturity and peacefulness about himself after his walk that wasn't there before? Like so many conundrums that were part of his character, we'll never know.

2

THE PROMISE HE HAD TO KEEP

Andrew had long thought of throwing himself into a memorable trek. And it wasn't some fanciful notion that he would tell others about but never get around to doing. That's one thing about Cad that impressed, or horrified, people: he would announce he would do something and invariably do it, whether some crazy stunt at a party like a drinking challenge, or more respectable pastimes like making sure a house was built to impeccable standards, or honouring any commitment he made to do a 'love job' for a friend or family member.

The first I knew of his yearning for a long walk was when he told Chris and me he was going to walk the Great Wall of China; he had even started learning Mandarin. But after the 2008 Beijing Olympics, getting a visa to travel to China became a difficult exercise, with tourists having to document where they would stay on every night of their trip. Plus several parts of the wall had been closed, some due to damage and others in an effort to preserve what was left. He reluctantly dropped that plan.

So the challenge became traversing across or around Australia, and not just in any conventional way. He mused on becoming the first person to cartwheel from coast to coast; other ideas were pushing an orange with his nose from one side of the continent to the other, or crossing the nation on a pogo stick. Then there was a more achievable method for entering the *Guinness Book of Records* (he even emailed them about this): crossing the country using the greatest number of non-motorised means – walking, running, cycling, uni-cycling, skateboarding, on a pogo stick, crawling, walking forwards and backwards. At some stage the plan became a more sensible task of walking Australia's circumference.

When Cad and Jaime stopped in central America in September 2007 on their way home from three years in England, Cad read Karl Bushby's book *Giant Steps* and was gobsmacked. Bushby, a former British paratrooper and red beret, had left Punta Arenas in Chile, the southernmost point of South America, in November 1998 with the intention of walking home ... to Hull, England. This meant walking north to Alaska and then to Russia across the treacherous Bering Strait, the 93-kilometre stretch that is frozen and thus navigable for only a small part of each year, when temperatu.mres are around minus 80 degrees Celsius. It took almost seven and a half years for Bushby to achieve his first objective, reaching then crossing the strait by foot to Russia. Since then, he has been unable to clear Russia because of visa issues; his trek, called the Goliath Expedition, remains incomplete.

Bushby's story became the stimulus for Cad's own epic journey. After Christmas 2008, he had six weeks without work in the building industry so he decided he'd walk from Sydney to Brisbane as a conditioning run. He lasted a day and a half, making it from Manly to Bateau Bay on the Central Coast, when he could not shirk the sharp pain in his left knee and painful shins. The fact he'd done little preparation was an obvious hindrance (and characteristic Cad!). He went to a sports medico and was told he had 'runner's knee' and needed to rest and do specific stretches.

And what did he do? Cad asked if my second-hand mountain bike was roadworthy enough for a long-haul trip; he was going to ride from the Central Coast to Cairns, a casual 2350 kilometres. So after making a bracket to bolt a plastic storage box to the rear of the bike, he set off and rode to Cairns in under five weeks, before catching a plane home (after my unsuitable bike had snapped the bracket and had to be repaired first day in).

However, the walk remained on his radar, but first he wanted to complete the renovation of his home at North Avoca. From mid-2009 until December 2010, mere weeks before his Oz On Foot expedition began, he almost exhausted himself by combining full-time work as a carpenter/site foreman with a complete rebuild of his house, sparing not enough time to relax with Jaime and friends and family. But the result was a beautiful home.

Cad had no exact plan or departure date, and the classic hike around the country remained an idea, a bucket-list experience, until his mate Chris Simpson passed away six days after his twenty-fourth birthday, in May 2010. Then it became a promise.

'Simmo' was one of the young blokes who mixed with Cad around Killcare and the neighbouring suburbs where he spent much of his late teens and twenties. They always got on very well because they were quite alike. Simmo was just one of many mates in Cad's group, but they became closer just before and during Chris's illness. Their fates were destined to intertwine.

Andrew was shocked by Chris's death after a twenty-nine-month battle with aplastic anaemia and myelodysplasia syndrome (MDS), which is a pre-leukaemia blood disorder. Simmo came home from a trip to Bali in December 2007 feeling crook on the stomach and thought it was a case of 'Bali belly'. After it didn't improve, he went to a doctor, who told him it was most likely a gastro ailment. Not satisfied after continuing to feel off-colour, Simmo went to another doctor and was ordered to have blood tests. He was diagnosed with aplastic anaemia and underwent immunosuppressive drug treatment (ATG) in May 2008.

His parents, Wayne and Kim, and older brother, Josh, were tested for suitability as bone-marrow donors, and Josh was found to be an almost perfect match. But a week before Josh was scheduled to donate, a further bone-marrow biopsy detected that Chris's condition had developed into MDS. In extreme cases like his, the only cure is a successful bone-marrow transplant, and Josh wasn't 100 per cent compatible.

A donor from Hamelin in Germany was found, and Chris underwent a transplant on his twenty-third birthday. Unfortunately, it was not successful. A year to the day later, on his twenty-fourth birthday, doctors transplanted marrow from a Tasmanian donor but Chris died six days later from complications. It was such a sad thing to happen to a wonderful family.

At the wake, Cad was talking to his mate Matt Hansen and Chris's girlfriend, Jamie (amazingly, Chris's and Andrew's partners had the same names, just spelt differently), when it hit him. He'd had the idea of an epic walk in Karl Bushby style, and the opportune time to do it would be when he'd finished the house renovations, so why not do it as a memorial to Simmo while raising money for cancer research? He told Matt and Jamie what he was going to do.

Josh Simpson remembers Cad coming up to him and explaining how he had it in his mind to do a 'walking mission' around Australia, and asking if Josh thought it would be okay with the family if he dedicated it to Chris. Josh thought it would be perfect – adding a cause to a dream. Cad shook hands with Josh, and the idea became a commitment he would live up to.

It became Andrew's new mission. As Josh emotionally stated on Cad's testimonial video, he definitely was the mission man.

Later, he decided he'd try to raise money for a charity appropriate to Simmo's plight, and he settled on the Cancer Council. Cad became quite passionate about this – and even more so when he switched his allegiance to the Leukaemia Foundation.

Unsurprisingly, in the ensuing months – as Cad ran himself into the ground with his daytime job and night shifts that often went after midnight (including most weekends), and with frantically carrying out his renovations – undue stress was put on his relationship with Jaime. Andrew was often not the most enjoyable person to live with when stressed, and this period certainly made him that. In his eyes, everything would be alright once the house was completed and he'd got the Oz On Foot walk out of his system, but Jaime, who had been living with him for nearly six years, wasn't so sure. She broke off the relationship a couple of months before he left – and, to be frank, I could understand why. After living in a virtual building zone for about fifteen months and watching Andrew work day and night for most of the past few years, she had been asked to spend a year away from him as he embarked on his trek. They talked of reconciliation on and off over the next few months but it didn't happen.

After a frantic and exhausting last push to finish the renovations and a tough period emotionally, living alone in the dream four-bedroom home that he'd just created, Cad put the house on the market a few weeks before he left. A week before Christmas 2010 he hosted the extended Cadigan family at his place, a great day on his beautifully built and landscaped outdoor entertaining area. On Christmas Day it was down to Sydney for lunch with Chris's side of the family; Cad was always close to his cousin Matthew Ruff, and they were in good form together that afternoon. His intention was to leave the next day with his second-hand Chariot pram, bought on eBay from someone in Adelaide less than two weeks earlier.

Typically for Andrew, the build-up to this momentous day was cyclone-like and his preparation too brief; in fact, he'd done no testing with the pram, and to my knowledge had not walked so much as five kilometres as a warm-up for the 15,000-kilometre journey. But he was leaving on this one-man expedition that none of us, himself included, could fully anticipate.

I was anxious, concerned about what Cad might encounter, knowing he would be charging full-bore into it. Most likely, he'd become his own worst enemy because of impatience and his underlying belief that he was bulletproof. My main worries were that he might be hit by a truck, be mugged at night in the middle of nowhere, or disappear into the vastness of the Nullarbor Plain. But I also knew he'd ridden to

Cairns without incident and was as determined, resilient and industrious as anyone I knew.

Armed with a big heart and imbued by the spirit of Chris Simpson, but still fragile after his separation from Jaime, Cad was leaving, no matter what. A man, a pram, two feet and a heartbeat ... and a game plan of working it out along the way.

3

OFF AND WALKING

Andrew was due to leave on Boxing Day but was still fussing around making last-minute adjustments to his pram, buying food for his first few days and generally stressing out. So, rather than leave late in the day, he decided to get going the next day, 27 December 2010. I hooked the trailer onto my car, loaded up the pram and drove for over an hour from our Point Clare home to Sydney Airport; Cad thought he'd start and finish at a landmark location.

He left with a mix of excitement, trepidation and anxiety, because everything to do with the trip had been a rush and more of a mission than it should have been. He had less than $200 to his name but both his car (acquired only five weeks earlier, when he had to hand in his company vehicle) and beautifully renovated home were up for sale to fund the journey.

Because he and Jaime had left the door open to reconciliation, he'd committed only to walking to Perth, via New South Wales, Tasmania, Victoria and South Australia, meaning he would be away for around six months. But always in his mind was the urge to still trek the whole continent, as he had originally planned to.

Our first stop was a byway next to the airport, where Cad did his first of about 250 video blogs, which was short and sweet and delivered with his usual laconic colloquialisms. It was there that his journey – and his amazing story – truly began.

DAY 1, 27 DECEMBER 2010
BLAKEHURST TO LOFTUS (10.5KM)

'G'day. My name's Andrew Cadigan. Just leaving Sydney Airport on my way to Perth. This is day one, pretty crappy weather – it's been gale-force winds all morning, just died off a bit now. First and foremost, I'd like to say I dedicate this trip to my mate Simmo, Chris Simpson, who tragically passed away this year at the age of twenty-four, and that's why I plan to raise as much money as I can for the Cancer Council of Australia on this trip.

'A bit about the trip. I haven't planned it too well: I only got me pram about a week ago, chucked some shit in there and I'm away. Don't really know how long it's going to take or which way I'm going to walk. All I know is first stop Tassie, then heading over to Perth, and who knows, I might even keep walking up to Darwin. So anyways, without further to-do, I better keep going. I've had a pretty slow start to the morning – I was actually supposed to start yesterday but fashionably late as usual. Anyways, catch you tomorrow.'

So began what became much-followed video blogs, which are now treasured as a lasting memento of Cad's life, a live digital archive of an experience that, for many people, came to define him. (The videos can still be viewed on the website he set up for the walk, www.ozonfoot.com.au.)

We had to agree to a little white lie that day: it was so late by the time he did the blog that he would have been walking in the dark by the time he cleared the metropolis, so we drove down the Princes Highway, with his pram sitting in my trailer. We stopped just past Tom Uglys Bridge over the Georges River, had fish and chips and he was away.

I drove north towards home but just had to turn around and go past Andrew, taking in my last vision of him for I didn't know how long, and beeping as I doubled past. He would have thought his old man was a real dork but I didn't care; I wanted to keep that scene in my mind.

Cad's first on-the-road entry in his diary, in the satirical style we became accustomed to, was written from his first campsite, at Loftus Oval on the edge of the Royal National Park. It included this: 'I felt very surprised I didn't feel excited [beginning the walk], or anything for that matter, it was like I was just off to work or something. Started to get arsehole chafe about 5 kilometres into it, stopped and lubed up my arsehole in a bus stop, cars driving past would have thought I was playing with myself with my hands down my pants.'

Maybe that was not entirely out of place with the place he decided to set up camp that first night. The bush next to the oval was supposedly a well-known rendezvous for homosexual men; seeing some 'suss' blokes lurking, Andrew chained his pram to his tent and set up an alarm system when he went to sleep. An electronic alarm that gave out a piercing sound was fixed to the end of a line that was attached to a wheel on his pram at one end and to a zipper on the fly of his tent at the other. If the line was moved, the alarm sounded. 'If the pram goes, I go with it,' he wrote.

He was woken at 1am by the flashing blue lights. 'It was coppers or firies, they were on their walkie-talkies in the car park at the other end of the field,' he diarised. He blogged next day with traditional Cad wit: 'Thank Christ day one's over. I'm down at Loftus cricket oval, and I tell you what, there's a bit of dodgy brothers going on here ... There's blokes lurking in the bushes and cars turning up every five minutes, going in there for five minutes at a time. I don't know if they were poo-punching or drug dealing, but suss as. I slept with one eye open and my knife next to my sleeping bag.'

DAY 2, 28 DECEMBER 2010 LOFTUS TO STANWELL PARK (26.4KM)

If the fear and mystique of his first overnight camp was enough to put Cad on alert to expect the unexpected, he was in for more alarm during his first full day of walking – and an event that affected him quite deeply. He thought he was the catalyst for a fatal motor accident.

He wrote that he 'felt excited this morning, was singing away to my iPod' when, two hours into his day's walk, he was on the median strip waiting for a break in the traffic to cross the Princes Highway and heard a loud crash. He turned to see a motorbike had ploughed into the back of a four-wheel drive vehicle, which was the first in line at a red light. 'I don't reckon he even saw it because I didn't hear any brakes. It was obvious he was gawking at me. I felt bad, especially when I saw all the coppers and shit flying past about twenty minutes later. I just took off, I couldn't look at this guy, he was all bent up, I'm pretty sure he was dead.'

Andrew called me not long after to talk about it. He was obviously upset, saying, 'I think I just caused a fatal accident; I feel terrible.' I tried to reassure him that if that was the case, it was the rider's responsibility to concentrate on the road and he couldn't blame himself. Only now, as I write this, the irony of this hits me, considering how Andrew died.

Andrew had papered to the front of the pram a simple sign that said 'Oz on foot.com – for cancer' and had thought he would direct anyone who wanted to donate to his cause to go online. However several people stopped to donate money on Day 2, but at that stage Andrew hadn't considered taking donations on the road but only through the website's online mechanism. Days later he decided to order receipt books from the Cancer Council and take advantage of the many opportunities that he realised would come.

Later in the day he met a stranger, but a very interested one, in Mandy Verdich, who told him she was planning to walk from Sydney to Perth with the same Chariot pram and her kelpie dog. 'Spin-out ... wish I had taken Redge,' he wrote. I guarantee his blue cattle dog/bull terrier cross couldn't have kept up the pace and would have been too big a handful. Mandy, who had cycled from Perth to Sydney years earlier with a friend, joined him that evening for an hour and gave him a light fold-up chair, which came in very handy until he left it at a roadhouse in Western Australia.

Cad followed what he had been told was the law and walked into the face of traffic when there was no road shoulder, but found it 'scary when a car comes ripping around the corner coming at you'. He got used to it but there were still plenty of scary moments.

That night he camped at a picnic area and amused a European family who were having an early evening feast when he rocked up to the tap next to them and lathered up for his first Oz On Foot 'shower', before explaining to the bewildered family what he was doing. As they left, the mother came over to his tent and left him some 'yummy cakes'.

DAY 3, 29 DECEMBER 2010 STANWELL PARK TO NORTH WOLLONGONG (26.4KM)

Andrew wrote in his diary that he was trying to live off $10 a day and spent $30.20 on a three-day shop. At that stage he had $133.60 to his name; he was desperately trying to get a buyer for his home; he hadn't worked for over a month while he spent day and night finishing his renovations. He was also hoping to get $1200 for his old Commodore wagon, which he'd left with me to sell. He knew I was there to 'sponsor' him if he asked (I'd already offered) but, typically, he wanted to be self-sufficient if he could.

During a two-hour break in the middle of the day, Cad recorded that he was exhausted after matching the previous day's distance of 26.4 kilometres (he refused to go backwards in daily distance until he was regularly walking 30 kilometres a day). Little did he contemplate then that he would often double or triple this daily odometer before too long.

DAY 4, 30 DECEMBER 2010 WOLLONGONG TO KIAMA (37KM)

Only four days in and Cad had already distinguished his pet hate: taking the time to say hello to people as he walked by only to get no response or, worse in his eyes, a strange stare that he reckoned said, 'What do you want, you freak?' The fact that he had several earrings, lip and tongue piercings and one in his chin, plus heavily tattooed legs and was pushing a pram, obviously led some people, particularly older ones, to judge this book by its different, perhaps hobo-looking, cover. He swore at one middle-aged lady who ignored his greeting and regretted it instantly, but he was sick of people not bothering to acknowledge him.

He should have become used to it over the ensuing months, but he never accepted it. He also started his habit of taking the pram into any store he entered as he didn't want to let it out of his sight in case it, or something inside, was stolen. This caused more stares. Cad described the look: 'It's like a mix of intrigued, dumbfounded, amused, curious and "what the fuck" rolled into this blank expression.'

A reporter from the *Illawarra Mercury* newspaper approached him out of the blue and did an interview, sending a photographer out later to get a snap – Andrew's first on-the-road media coverage.

Cad got inventive and found what looked like a good spot to camp at the rear of a church. He thought he'd do the right thing and knocked on the door to ask the priest and was given the go ahead. He then realised to the rear was a camping ground, and one loud-mouthed resident whose van was up against the fence kept him awake for hours. He saw the irony: 'I now know how my neighbours feel when I rock up maggot at 3am when the pub shuts and drink til the sun comes up – karma. I suppose that's why all the P-platers hurled abuse at me all day as well. It's funny how things come around eventually, even if it takes over a decade.'

DAYS 5–6, NEW YEAR'S EVE 2010 AND NEW YEAR'S DAY 2011 KIAMA TO BOLONG (32.8KM), THEN A REST DAY

Cad chatted to a few people in the town of Kiama, including a long talk with one gentleman, who mentioned that he worked for the National Rugby League. Andrew asked if he knew me and it emerged that he was talking to Paul Heptonstall, welfare and education manager at the NRL. Small world. At the time I was working as operations manager for rugby league's player agent accreditation scheme and often used a desk next to Paul's when in the city between appointments.

In Gerringong a local walked up and asked Andrew what he was doing, then donated $10. Suddenly it was contagious and donations came from others in the café. He had $150 by the end of the day ('I don't think that will happen again,' he wrote). Further down the road along Seven Mile Beach, a couple of locals, Dick and Frankie, asked him into their home for a cold drink, sandwiches and a shower; Cad was taken aback by their hospitality. Fortunately, it was one of many such gestures he would encounter over the next eighteen months.

That evening Adam Martin, who was his best mate at primary school, and his partner, Natasha, drove four hours to see in the New Year with Cad and camp the night in a bush clearing.

DAY 7, 2 JANUARY 2011 BOLONG TO BEWONG (37KM)

The big event of the day was the tantrum Cad had when his straw hat kept blowing off every time a truck or caravan whizzed past, an embarrassing 'show' witnessed by a cyclist, who stopped to ask if he was okay. It was a spat that saw him badly scratch his $190 sunglasses. At least he had a win with a three-day shop at Nowra that cost only $21.35. Despite hating oats and tuna, they had become his daily staples. 'I've fully stopped eating for pleasure or enjoyment, just to try to quench my eternal hunger,' he wrote. 'I shovelled peanut butter sanga after sanga in my gob today like they were going out of fashion but I was still starving all day.'

Cad decided to name his rig 'Redge' after his dog – 'because it is always trying to run away from me'. His love affair with P-plater drivers continued when one threw a fifty-cent coin at him from a window. A bigger find was a computer bag on the roadside that Andrew assumed was empty until he hurt his toe when he kicked it. Inside was a Mac-Book laptop computer that worked fine.

As Andrew said on his blog, this wasn't consistent with the odd array of items he'd noticed on the roadside so far: 'Top of the list, ockey straps, followed by kids toys, followed by CDs, which I just can't help checking, which normally entails me clambering up or down a muddy embankment to get to, the occasional dildo and a few bottles of urine thrown in for good measure.'

DAYS 8–10, 3–5 JANUARY 2011 BEWONG TO BATEMAN'S BAY (102.3KM)

Cad had his first taste of 'fame' when a lady at the driver-reviver station treated him like a celebrity and gave him a free bacon-and-egg sandwich. He was wearing an Australian Olympic wet-weather tracksuit top (one of mine from the Beijing Olympics) and was asked if he was an Olympian – 'too funny'. Mandy from Stanwell Park and her husband, Mark, turned up and gave him an array of gear for his travels – 'everything but the kitchen sink – legends!'

Cad had worked out that the best way to try to locate the owner of the MacBook was to email everyone in the owner's contacts and it worked: he received a call from Richard, who lived a couple of hours south; he told Cad the computer had been stolen from the back seat of his car when he was having a coffee in Nowra. He found Andrew later that day and was happy to donate $100 to the cause as a reward.

Cad's diary entry that day was prophetic: 'Was sore all day from the big day in the hills yesterday, I can't wait to have a day when I'm not in pain although I honestly reckon that may never eventuate.' It certainly didn't.

That pain was relieved somewhat by my phone call, telling him I'd sold his car for the $1200 he wanted. 'WOO HOO!!! Fish and chips for lunch tomorrow, might even break the bank with a prawn cutlet and crab stick.' He shared his culinary critique with hundreds on his video blog: 'I nearly had an erection when I saw the crabstick.'

Less orgasmic was the next line of his diary: 'I've got to stop farting in my tent, it's like a gas chamber, must be the tuna and pasta.' He added (not related, I assume): 'Nearly passed out today. I got some wicked head spins and felt light-headed for about an hour and a half and had to stop and lay down for half an hour – weird!! I was getting bad visions of me hitting the deck and my pram rolling onto the road and getting cleaned up by a car.'

He woke at 9am next day to voices and leapt out of the tent with only his undies on, to be confronted by a group of young girls on horseback, with two women who were obviously their instructors. He had camped in the middle of their riding track. 'They were debating whether to pass ... I yelled out "good morning" and jumped back in to throw on some shorts. I said hello again as they warily passed but the ladies looked straight ahead as if I was invisible while the girls didn't stop giggling.'

Coyness wasn't an issue with Joanne, sister-in-law of his new friend Mandy, who worked at the local pharmacy at Batemans Bay. Andrew was on a $50 donation dare from Mandy if he could get Joanne to show him the turtle tattoo on her arse; 'She's as mad as a gum tree full of galahs,' he wrote of Mandy. Joanne was expecting him, as were the other girls in the pharmacy who passed the hat around and bought him some chocolate. 'Jo showed me her tattoo, it was a tiny little thing.'

As he passed McDonald's on the way out of town, a woman with her family asked if she could buy him lunch. 'I said thanks but I've already eaten. What was I thinking, I've got to get on board this freeloading shit. I don't know what the go is, I've always had a problem with getting a hand, or handout, unless it's from close friends or family.'

While Cad was filling his water bottles at a service station, a bloke in his sixties introduced himself as Owen and offered him a roof over his head for the night and a shower at his place further down the road; it was to become the first of many such overnight stays courtesy of generous people along the route. 'He was a nice old bloke, probably late sixties, he had a face of sun and hard work with deep crows-feet and a big old smile – probably what I'm going to look like when I'm done.'

It's hard for me to record the following diary entry, considering Andrew's fate, but I have to in order to provide an insight into his character. 'Not long after I was walking in the shoulder into the traffic when a white station wagon crosses the white line and starts driving towards at 100+ kays, narrowly swerving back into his lane at the last minute and gave me a toot on the way passed. I turned and flipped the prick the bird. It gave me quite a scare and got my heart beating. I started thinking if that was someone who had fallen asleep I wouldn't have reacted in time and I'd be dead, but I still reckon when your time's up your time's up, so there's no use worrying about that shit.'

On reaching Owen's, he was presented with his own three-bed guesthouse in the back paddock of a 100-acre property that Owen shared with wife Trish.

After dinner and a few beers, Cad and Owen were off to the shed to see Owen's potty and chainsaw collection. 'The potties were all hanging off his rafters – what a character! This bloke's too funny, what a nice guy, I've had a smile on my face the whole time and my cheeks hurt.' A great photo of Owen's range of bed pans and potties, hanging from the shed ceiling, was posted on Cad's website next day.

DAY 11, 6 JANUARY 2011 RUNNYFORD RD TO BERGALIA (35KM)

A reporter and photographer from the *Canberra Times* were driving past and stopped Cad for an interview and to take a snap, Cad's fourth media encounter in a week, which he was delighted about, hoping it would help the donations. But what made his day even more was when he encountered a Spanish woman and he successfully communicated in her language. 'I picked up the accent and said *"habla español"* [you speak Spanish?] She asked me the same, I said *un poco* [a little]. I managed to tell her in my pigeon Spanish that I'm walking from Sydney to Perth for cancer and it will take me about six months and it's about 5000 kilometres and that I had travelled a lot of Spain. She told me that I have good Spanish and her English is terrible. I said goodbye and have a good day. I walked up the road with a massive smile on my face, WOW! I was so surprised I remembered all that having not spoken a word for over eighteen months, now I'm keen as mustard to get into my Spanish lessons I put on my iPod.' It was another insight into the many talents and interests of Andrew Cadigan.

The first of many running repairs over the ensuing months was required later in the day when the pin on the front axle of the pram snapped; luckily he was able to get a lift back to the nearest town of Moruya and pick up a new one, and a spare, from a bicycle shop.

Once back on the road Cad came across a tree that had been hit by lightning, sparking the first of many journeys back into his life that would become regular occurrences during long, lonesome stints on the highways. 'It triggered this vivid random memory I didn't even know I had of me and my sister sitting in the back of the olds' car, driving through suburbia in a storm, and seeing a tree on fire that had just been hit by lightning. It was really weird, don't know where that came from?'

DAYS 12–13, 7–8 JANUARY 2011 BERGALIA TO NAROOMA (33KM), THEN A REST DAY

Andrew camped just behind the rear roller door of the fire station in Narooma, but worried that if there was a fire in the middle of the night he'd be woken and probably in trouble if in the way of the fireman facing an emergency. The irony was that he woke to relieve himself and zipped open the tent, forgetting he had set his 'alarm'. He eloquently described the event this way: 'Woke up in the middle of the night half asleep with the urge to drop the kids off and forgot the alarm ... It was ear-piercing, I couldn't believe how loud it was for such a little key ring. The cord had ripped clean out of it so I couldn't push it back in to shut it up. I'm standing there with it cupped in my hands trying to muffle it, trying not to wake anyone in the houses nearby. I ended up having to smash it into the corner of the brick wall, it took six big hits and wailed my hand in the process – what a debacle!!'

DAYS 14–15, 9–10 JANUARY 2011 NAROOMA TO TATHRA (77.6KM)

After climbing the rising, winding highway south of Narooma, Cad decided to leave the Pacific Highway and head along the coastal scenic route from Bermagui as the rain pelted down. It was breathtakingly pretty and there was far less traffic on that road than the highway. A local called Judy invited him to pitch his tent on a property she was staying at, overlooking the ocean on a headland with wonderful views.

Cad made it to Tathra in the driving rain and heavy winds, and he was shivering uncontrollably as he crossed the Bega River with the wind whipping straight of the ocean. He was in a café having a cup of tea to warm up when three young guys approached and invited him to the pub. That was the start of an eventful night with the locals (one of many others to come) that Andrew could only remember the first half of come morning. 'They had geed the new owner Mark up to sort me out with a bed ... he came out for a chat when I arrived and gave me a $100 donation. The boys were all mad dogs and were buying me beers quicker than I could drink them. They called their mate who had seen me in Batemans Bay and had told the boys about me. He rocked up for a few and turned out he worked for the same Fit Out company in the UK [which Andrew had worked for in 2005–06].'

They ended up moving on to the comfortable home of Toby, who was wheelchair-bound, where the boys started mixing cocktails. Cad was soon very much the worse for wear. But he insisted on sleeping outside in his tent despite an offer of a bed and the fact he was hardly in any condition to work out the intricacies of its construction. On his blog next day he explained his undoing as he moped on his air mattress: 'It was a pretty big night ... I remember spewing, I've got bark off me everywhere so I've obviously come a gutser but don't remember that ... it's 9.30 and I'm still rolling around in the tent so I won't be walking today.'

DAYS 16–17, 11–12 JANUARY 2011 TATHRA TO KIAH (67.4KM)

Well, he did walk, about half an hour after posting his sorry video blog. A potato-chip sandwich perked him up a little, but not nearly as much as the sight of a beautiful blonde girl called Nina, who was riding past on the other side of the road. The young woman was the first of many European backpackers he would meet, all with their varying tales. 'She stopped to ask where I was going, I yelled out Perth. She crossed over for a chat, a beautiful blonde Austrian girl with amazing green eyes. She was bumming at some property around here and sleeping in a hammock, she was a feral hippie chick and was covered in dirt, didn't look like she had had a shower in a while. She was riding to Tathra for a look and still had a long way to go, she had no water so I gave her a drink. She gave me a scabby piece of kangaroo skin that she had cut into the shape of a love heart and had written in pen on the back – "all you need". She said it can be my good luck charm. She gave me $10 which made me feel bad because she was on a shoestring budget.'

Cad reached Eden at about 2pm the next day, just as it started to pour, and headed for the Westpac Bank, which doubled as a real-estate agent, to deposit the loose change and notes from his donations; it amounted to $752. This was also the momentous day that he agreed on a sale price for his North Avoca home. He was soon to be free of debt and have a kitty to fund his walk, which was a massive relief just over two weeks into his mission.

DAYS 18–19, 13–14 JANUARY 2011 KIAH TO MALLACOOTA (71.6KM)

The dead blue-tongue lizards had by now become dead red-bellied black snakes, which unnerved Cad. And persistent march flies became his bane, forcing him to walk with a pine needle branch in each hand to keep swatting them away. 'Stopped at a rest area for a bite and a couple of blokes pulled up on those silly sit-down bikes with every bell and whistle imaginable,' he wrote. 'They were as queer as a row of pink tepees and looked like idiots in their lycra get-ups. They were riding to Sydney and had been on the road for a week, and had two left. I thought, You're kidding, aren't you? I nearly walked it that quickly.'

He was hoping to have a day off the next day, but with food running short he had to press on. He set up camp at dusk and was instantly attacked by march flies that he reckoned were as big as $2 coins. 'They felt like they were taking chunks out of me, it was painful. I wound myself up in such a panic, it was like nothing I'd ever experienced. I finally got in my tent and waited until dark so I could cook but the mozzies were at me. My shirt was still wet with sweat and stuck to me so I was getting flogged on my back, then the icing on the cake came in the form of hoppy-joes, and hundreds of them. I must have disturbed a nest. I got bitten on the leg and as I jumped around in pain I kicked a heap of dirt and sand into my dinner. I lost it, I went ballistic and carried on like a psycho. I gave up, left everything where it lay and crawled into my tent, sweaty and physically and mentally exhausted. I've got no clean clothes because they all got wet and smell. I give up and go to bed a broken man, not before smearing Bushmans all over my zippers; last thing I need is another hoppy-joe bite in the middle of the night.'

I'll let his diary notes describe the start to the next day: 'Woke up and could hardly find the energy to move. I was in no hurry because I could hear the flies waiting for me outside, it sounded like I was in a helicopter. I finally crawled out of the tent about ten to the worst onslaught yet. I put my putrid-smelling long-sleeve shirt on, wrapped another around my neck, covered myself in repellent and made a run for it. I stopped up the road to try and eat breakfast but could only manage a banana and muesli bar on the run because they were that bad.'

He'd crossed his first state border, from New South Wales to Victoria, and decided to head into Mallacoota for the weekend. It's a quaint little fishing village, but 24 kilometres off the highway to the east, via a winding, hilly road. 'Dad had told me it was worth heading in and was an easy walk; he was full of shit [about the easy walk].' Making it harder was rain that got heavier as the day went on. He settled into the caravan park, not happy with paying $27 for an unpowered site, but at least he could have his first hot shower for nineteen days. He headed to the pub for a feed and a couple of beers and decided he'd spend the weekend in the town and rest up, and maybe throw a line in and catch some fish.

DAYS 20–21, 15–16 JANUARY 2011 REST DAYS, MALLACOOTA

A passer-by outside the local noodle bar had suggested Andrew try to raise money at the Saturday markets. He bought a sheet of cardboard and made a sign that said 'walking from Sydney to Perth for Cancer Council, donations welcome' and was given permission to use a spot at the markets near the entrance, where the entering pedestrian traffic would be hard-pressed not to notice him. After an hour he'd received nothing until a local called Nancy came over and dropped $50 into his straw hat. He had $200 when he decided to finish up early afternoon.

Next day Andrew fished, unsuccessfully, for a few hours. He was soon bored and thinking about what his mates were doing back on the Central Coast, while sitting on the wharf 'like a lonely dog with no home'. The first, but certainly not last, onset of the solitude of his task was evident. 'I got lonelier. If I feel like this is now how am I going to feel down the track?

I thought about the last couple of hours hanging out with oldies [in the caravan park] and trying to sound half-educated and not swear, it's just not me. I wish I was hanging out with the boys being myself, but I'd take the oldies any day of the week rather than being alone. I went and got my diary and buried my head in it with my iPod on ... went back and read my book, I was bored senseless, all these happy families around weren't helping. I became reclusive and didn't want to talk to anyone ... I got another offer for lunch and steak for dinner but declined both; I don't know what my problem is about accepting food from people.'

DAYS 22–25, 17–20 JANUARY 2011 MALLACOOTA TO CANN RIVER (185KM)

Andrew snared a lift back to the Pacific Highway (saving him 24 repeated kilometres), where he resumed his walk south. About 20 kilometres down the road a policeman stopped and tried to convince him to get a lift over Mt Drummer, as there was no hard shoulder, it was very windy and he was concerned about Cad's and the motorists' safety. Andrew asked politely if he was ordering him to do so but the policeman said he could only advise. Andrew, not wanting to 'cheat', said he'd walk and was told to jump over the guardrail if he came close to colliding with ongoing traffic.

He quickly found out that the copper wasn't just being a nark. 'I start the climb and wonder what he is on about but soon see as there is a guardrail tight to the line on one side and a ditch on the other. It's too dangerous to walk around the blind corners on the inside so I find myself running from side to side whilst dodging traffic. It's dodgy as and I have to listen for the cars because it's too late by the time I can see them. A couple of trucks passed leaving inches between us. I was a happy camper to reach the top.'

After lunching with a French backpacking couple at the bottom of the mountain, Cad broke the cord to his headphones while swatting another killer march fly, so had to walk for days without music. Instead he daydreamed, about everything – 'sex was the top of the list!' – and was away with the fairies enough to forget to get off the road a couple of times and was almost run down.

Despite following his mate Adam's suggestion of putting honey on his oats, it didn't make them any more palatable and he continued to always feel famished. 'He's full of shit, they still taste crap. I'm still starving all day every day, and I ate three peanut-butter sangas, an apple, orange, three muesli bars, and a whole box of Shapes for lunch!'

He came across two blonde women, an American and an Aussie, who were on a bicycle tour, and they were soon exchanging experiences. 'They were cool, they turned out to be the same chicks who rode past the other day when I was having something to eat, one of them had blown a tyre and they had to hitch back to a bike shop and then ride the leg again. She tried to fix it with duct tape but it just blows a big duct tape egg out of the hole. I told her to use a bank note next time, which another cyclist told me after it had happened to me [during his 2008 ride to Cairns].'

He stopped at Orbost to do some banking and buy food and replacement earphones, and camped the night at Wombat Creek, reaching Lakes Entrance the next afternoon. Just short of town he was passed by four cyclists who seemed to be in a hurry. They were there when he stopped at KFC for lunch so he introduced himself to Indi, Simon, Locky and Ben, bike couriers from Melbourne who had caught a flight to Sydney with nothing but their courier bags and had a week to return home. They invited him to have a drink with them at their 'local' in Melbourne when he got there, an offer he would take up, which sparked a great friendship.

He decided to pay for the luxury of a camp spot and shower block in Lakes Entrance, and that was just as well: 'Had a shower to find I'm covered from head to toe in pimples, maybe I need to start showering more.'

DAYS 26–28, 21–23 JANUARY 2011 LAKES ENTRANCE TO BAIRNSDALE (37KM), THEN TWO REST DAYS

Andrew had arranged to meet Justin, a mate he'd worked with in the United Kingdom who was now living at Albury, to spend a night out in Bairnsdale. He arrived late Friday and couldn't find accommodation at the caravan park or the first four pubs he passed. Resident Ross saw him sitting in the gutter on the phone outside of his home and offered Cad a cuppa; Andrew thanked him but said he had to find somewhere to stay the night. Next thing he was offered a free bed and dinner of a seafood salad, which he gladly accepted.

The following day Cad checked into a motel (on his old man's credit card as he didn't have one!) and Justin rode his motorbike from Albury to join him for a big night, which ended with Cad losing his motel key and having to wake the owner to get in at an ungodly hour, then sleeping past check-out time next day. So he booked an extra night and had to pay $50 for the lost key, making it an extremely expensive weekend (again on my credit card!). He did a shop for the next few days and afterwards had $1 in his wallet and $1 in the bank.

DAYS 29–30, 24–25 JANUARY 2011 BAIRNSDALE TO TRARALGON (118.2KM)

Andrew didn't sleep well, and woke up sweating after having a dream about breaking his back (he'd had back troubles for years from lifting heavy materials). He woke again at 5am with severe back pain and spent an hour trying to stretch it out. 'My back has been giving me more grief than my legs so far,' he wrote. 'I was hoping it was going to get better now I'm off the tools but it's getting worse.'

He'd walked the 67 kilometres to the centre of Sale with an hour of light left and so 'decided to have a crack at the 70-club', clearing town and pitching his tent in the dark beside a farm driveway; he had done 71.2 kilometres for the day. He woke up feeling really well: 'surprised I wasn't tired or sore from yesterday, I must really be getting match fit now.' Yet within a few hours his feet were sore and he decided to take Panadol Forte for the first time since leaving Sydney. 'It was only the other day that I was daydreaming that I could walk around Oz without taking a single painkiller, I was kidding myself.'

He made it to Traralgon, where he had arranged to hook up with Steve, another former colleague from Fit Out UK. He was part-owner and manager of what Cad described as a flash motel where he stayed that night, Steve's wife, Melissa, having only just arrived home after delivering their first child a week earlier.

DAY 31, 26 JANUARY 2011, AUSTRALIA DAY REST DAY, TRARALGON

It was a quiet Australia Day for Cad, who usually would have hopped into the grog, and maybe two-up, in true Aussie spirit. Instead, Steve took him for a tour of the town and the open-cut coalmine and power station. 'It blew me away, I'd never seen anything like it,' he wrote.

Cad later borrowed Steve's car to do some shopping (I'd deposited some money into his bank account) and watched DVDs in his room. There were several Canadian helicopter pilots and mechanics staying at the motel for the summer, paid guests of the Victorian government while on standby with a chopper in case of bushfires. Typically, Cad picked their brains over a few beers. 'It was interesting learning about the chopper and how it can suck a backyard pool empty in seconds. What's with Canadians and moustaches?'

DAYS 32–35, 27–30 JANUARY 2011 TRARALGON TO ST KILDA (167KM)

Cad conspired with his cousin Matt Ruff, a plumber, to solve the problem of pulling into parks in desperate need of water only to find there was no handle to the tap. Matt sent him a tap handle, which would have been handy except Cad only got to use it once, in Launceston, and left it there by mistake.

Contributions from a local named Lynda, Matt's mother, Lynne, and Cad's other aunty, Alison, saw him collect enough to buy new shoes. Chris and I bought the next two pairs after those wore out, and from then I was able to get a couple of pairs from Nike, a couple from the Parramatta Eels, where I was doing media consultancy work, and another pair from Peter Wynn's Score sports store (Peter is a mate of mine). We got him through the walk (nine pairs used) without him having to dip into his own pocket. It's hardly big sponsorship, I know, but it typified the basis of Andrew's support – all a bit piecemeal.

With no pedestrians allowed on the motorway into Melbourne from the east, Cad had to zigzag on the service roads, winding through sheep farms and power stations before reaching Moe just on dusk. There he threw up his tent on the grass at the first service station he came to, in full sight of the pumps and main road. This wasn't the least bit conducive to a good night's sleep.

Next morning a regional TV news crew arrived, arranged by one of the locals who'd met Andrew the day before, and he was as nervous as a kitten doing his first on-camera interview. 'I was so nervous, my first TV interview,' he wrote. 'I hope I don't come across as an idiot.' He must have come across well enough; donations spiked the next day with many plus-$50 contributions, several from people whose families had been touched by cancer.

By the afternoon he'd decided to ignore the signs banning pedestrians on the motorway, fed up with the meandering service roads. After he reached Dandenong on the city's southern outskirts, Stevie Parkin, a mate from the Central Coast and another former work colleague from the UK, took him back to his place in Brunswick, a northern Melbourne suburb, for a night of laughs and liquor. He didn't get back to the drop-off point until 11am but still knocked out over 36 kilometres to St Kilda Beach, where he joined the large throng in the cool water of the bay before catching a tram back to Stevie's.

DAYS 36–37, 31 JANUARY–1 FEBRUARY 2011 REST DAY IN BRUNSWICK, THEN A FERRY ACROSS BASS STRAIT TO DEVONPORT

Cad was brilliantly hosted by Stevie and his partner, Sarah, over the next two days, but he admits he stretched the friendship when, after borrowing Steve's beard trimmer, he ignored the warning not to prune his pubic region (if Stevie reads this he will be horrified!). 'I couldn't help myself and mowed the green and trimmed up the fairway. I probably wouldn't have if he didn't say anything – HA HA HA!'

Cad was on the lookout for a good tattooist for some ink-work after deciding he'd add, when he returned to Melbourne after completing his Tasmanian leg, to his already extensive array of body work. He decided on Korpus Tattoo in Brunswick and booked in Jaclyn Rehe to have the first fleet ship *Endeavour* tattooed on his leg. Jaclyn was to see much more of him.

After catching a train to the city and walking four kilometres to the port, Andrew had to go through all sorts of bother with security before being allowed to take his pram on board. 'One halfwit suggested sending it down the long stainless steel chute with the other bags. I took one look and said, "You have to be kidding – you wouldn't believe how fast it rolls, you will kill someone." All this fuss because they were so sure it wouldn't fit down the escalator. I said, "Let me have a look at the escalator, I'll tell you if it will go down, I've just walked it here from Sydney." I took one look, assured them it would go, then they still had to hang onto it with me. Got to the boarding ramp only to have some other tool freaking out, asking me if there were kids in there – he felt the need to call his supervisor as well'.

After locking himself out of his room and lining up for thirty minutes to get assistance so he could get back in, it was off to the dining hall, where he caused a raft of whispers at the 'Tower of Pisa' pile of food he loaded onto his plate, so keen was he to get some value from the $27 being asked for one serving from the buffet. 'I really was taking the piss, all to the amusement of the oldies in the line, who all felt the need to make remarks like, "Geez, you must still be growing."'

In the morning he woke in the state of his birth, Tasmania. It wasn't to be a pleasant reunion.

4

A PAINFUL RETURN TO HIS BIRTHPLACE

I'm not sure why Andrew decided to add Tasmania to his itinerary. I thought it was because he was curious about the state in which he was born, in April 1981, during a twenty-month stint I had as a journalist on the *Launceston Examiner.* He'd never seemed particularly inquisitive about his link to the state and had never wanted to return previously, and while there he didn't even stop to look at the home he lived in on Trevallyn Road, right near the beautiful Cataract Gorge, despite me giving him the details. Yet I'm glad he saw the state and town in which he was born, and where he learned to speak his first words. And I know he was too.

Nicole was ten months old when we arrived in 'Lonnie' in June 1980, days after the end of an ill-timed six-week journalists' strike that saw me having to appeal for handouts from a union trust fund to pay the mortgage on our first home in Seven Hills in Sydney's west. We drove the Mazda 929 sedan I'd bought from my eldest sister, Robyn, freshly fitted with a new towbar so I could cart a second-hand trailer with our remaining possessions (from memory, a washing machine, dryer, television and cot, plus clothes) to a place I had only seen for two very wet days on a weekend, and Chris had never set eyes on.

A mate from my cadet journalist days at the *Parramatta Advertiser,* Peter Dwyer, had moved to the *Examiner,* and I felt we could do with a break from working two jobs to pay off our home loan and get out of the hustle and bustle of Sydney for a while. It was a big gamble and lifestyle change for Chris and me, both in our early twenties with a young baby, leaving the security net of good friends and family behind.

Unbeknown to us at the time, Chris was a few weeks pregnant with Andrew when we left the mainland. He was born at Launceston Maternity Hospital and I have vivid memories of the overnight/early-morning event and being locked out twice after I had to vacate to the waiting room, the first time while they prepped Chris and the second because of a change of shift. Both times the nurses had forgotten I was outside and I had to ring a doorbell to be let back in. Then, without any previous notification or request for permission, a maze of medical students rushed to the room (the doctor was late arriving) as Chris delivered our only son.

It was a wonderful period of our lives in a pretty place that gave us some friends for life, and I got to play a few cricket games with future Test legend David

Boon at Launceston Cricket Club (I was definitely a lower-grader but was called in to fill up the numbers in first grade on a handful of occasions). As a reporter for the local paper, I often travelled with the Tasmanian Sheffield Shield side that included future internationals Boon, Roger Woolley and Peter Faulkner (father of current international James Faulkner).

Amusingly, the *Examiner* recognised Andrew's now-distant association in a front-page story on his mission, published during his Tassie trek, that began with 'Former Launceston resident Andrew Cadigan...' Spending the first ten months of his life there conveniently made him a 'former resident'? Geez, I laughed, especially as former colleague (and great bloke) Martin Gilmour was the editor.

But it was not to be an enjoyable homecoming. Cad hit a physical wall that left him in writhing pain halfway along the Midland Highway, forcing him to abandon his walk for three weeks.

DAY 38, 2 FEBRUARY 2011 DEVONPORT TO DELORAINE (51.3KM)

On board the *Spirit of Tasmania* for the Bass Strait crossing, Andrew shared a cabin with a Canadian man. Much to the chagrin of his roommate, Cad was up before the captain's wake-up announcement at 6am, and he also reckoned the Canadian would have been unimpressed with his farting and tossing (and snoring, no doubt) all night.

He was off the boat at 7am but had to wait two hours in Devonport to do an interview and photo with *The Advocate* newspaper. During that period, he made his compulsory visit to the local bakery, where he was given a surprising greeting. 'I walked in with my phone charging on my motorbike battery and [store owner] Judy freaked out big time: "That's not a bomb, is it?" she uttered. I think she was serious. I suppose it does look a bit suss with the digital reader and regulator taped to the side with wires hanging off it everywhere.'

He enjoyed the change of scenery as he headed east – potato crops and apple orchids – but not the many dead possums he had to dodge. After ten hours' walking he experienced his first touch of Tassie hospitality when a woman pulled over to give him a bag of raspberries dipped in chocolate. 'They were exquisite. She had seen me walking up a big hill and said it looked like hard work, so went and bought them and brought them back.' It was chocolate raspberries and a banana sandwich for dinner as he'd forgotten to get fuel for his cooker (the security staff had made him empty it when he boarded the ferry).

DAYS 39–41, 3–5 FEBRUARY 2011 DELORAINE TO CAMPBELL TOWN (129KM)

After a cold night, Cad was up early and made good time to Launceston. He recorded his first glimpse of his birthplace: 'Made it to the big hill that descends into Launceston about eight o'clock. I got a good view of the town and surrounds, and it wasn't at all what I'd imagined. It was surrounded by big hills and was much bigger than I'd expected.'

At 9pm he set up camp in the dark at an oval on the edge of town after completing a 60-plus-kilometre day. When he woke next morning he saw a blackberry-covered fence as far as the eye could see: 'Breakfast is served! I shovelled them in until I felt sick and then cut the top off a water bottle and filled it for later.'

He'd planned to spend a couple of days in Launceston to get to know the place on the way back to the port at Devonport at the end of the Tasmanian trek, so for now it was a big shop to last him the four days he planned it would get him to Hobart and a quick exit. During this process, he decided to look at the nutritional information on everything he bought for the first time in his life. 'I nearly flipped out to read that a single muesli bar has more energy and carbs than a bowl of oats. To think I've been forcing that slop down my throat every morning. I came to the conclusion that nuts are the best all-rounder but they're not bloody cheap!' The rep from Tassie Forest Waters was in the store and she took a shine to Cad, giving him fourteen free bottles of water. He was loaded to the max as he climbed the big hill south out of town to hit the Midland Highway.

He set up camp at a rest area next to the South Esk River near the north-eastern town of Perth after a long 61-kilometre day. As he settled in an old English gentleman walked past, having just finished fly-fishing. 'I asked him if he had caught anything and he said, "I've caught two trout in three years," and he said if he caught his third I could have it for breakfast. With those odds I wasn't holding my breath! He got a massive tangle within minutes, blamed the fading light and left. I was asleep before the sun was.'

Next day his troubles began. When he stopped for lunch he had 'a hardcore shooting pain up both my shins. It was that bad I should have stopped but wanted to get to the next town of Conara.' He took some Panadol Forte and reached the village at 6.30pm but it was tiny and had no shops. He thought that if he was going to have a rest day he wanted to be in a large enough town so decided to battle on for another 11 kilometres to Campbell Town.

'That turned out to be the longest 11 kilometres of my life. I got a couple kilometres up the road and realised that I was fucked up. Both sides of the road were lined by water-filled ditches and barbed-wire fences so I started thinking about going back, but backtracking is never an option. I became desperate and had my eyes peeled for somewhere to sleep. I saw a "heavy vehicle checking station 1 kilometre" sign and thought I was in luck, but when I got there it was nothing more than a bitumen driveway next to the road. I stopped to rest and things started to become dire, I was in the worst pain I'd been in for a very long time and was thinking, "What have I done?" I ate the other two caps [painkilling capsules] my mate gave me, which I knew wasn't a good idea after the six Fortes I'd just eaten.

'A cracker rainbow emerged and the painkillers kicked in; all the traffic seemed to disappear and rays of sunshine were poking through the clouds, it was all quite surreal. Next thing it got dark and my hands went numb and I wandered straight into the oncoming lane, only for a minibus and trailer to swerve, narrowly missing me. It snapped me out of my zonked-out surrealism and back to a world of hate and pain. I stopped and shifted everything heavy right up the front of my pram so I could slouch a lot of my body weight onto the handlebars and just shuffle my feet along. I had never felt so relieved to reach town. There was only a café/pizza place left open so I went in to order. The young bird said, "Sorry, we are closing," but the chef out the back could see by the look on my face I was in all sorts and said he would make me one.

'I sat there, head in my hands in disbelief, until she brought out my pizza. I asked if there was anywhere to camp and she put me onto a paddock down the end of town where all the caravans park. I ate as I shuffled along in the dark, and a car stopped to give me my first donation for the day. I made it to the paddock and camped against the neighbours' fence away from the nomads. I was out to it within minutes of getting the tent up and I couldn't even manage to finish a pizza, which was the worst sign yet.'

DAYS 42–46, 6–10 FEBRUARY 2011 LAID UP IN CAMPBELL TOWN

The extent of his shin soreness hit him between the eyes, literally, when Cad rose to relieve himself next morning. Going to take his first steps he fell flat on his face and had to pee while on in his knees. He hobbled into town to find a chemist, only to discover it was closed on Sundays. He limped the kilometre back to his free camp on the south end of town on the Midland Highway, next to a convict-built bridge over the Elizabeth River. It would remain his home for almost a week.

He immediately searched for calf-muscle stretches on YouTube to relieve the pain and spent an hour doing them before applying icepacks to each leg. Later, he hobbled back to town to go to the toilet and had to rest in the park for half an hour before he could get back. He knew he was in trouble and didn't move for the rest of the day, with Norman, the Irish wolfhound from the neighbouring property, keeping him company through the fence. 'It's the biggest dog I've ever seen, and is the same size as the two miniature horses he is running around with. They all play together, chasing each other up and down, it's hilarious.'

Despite the rest and plenty of anti-inflammatory tablets he hadn't improved and knew he had to get to the Campbelltown hospital on the Monday and, unable to get a lift with any of his fellow campers or hitch a ride on the highway, he had to walk all the way. After initially being told he would have to wait four hours to see a doctor, the receptionist and nurses recognised him from the *Examiner's* front-page article published that day and fitted him in when the doctors returned at 2pm. It was a waste of time and considerable effort; he was told by the doctor that he had shin splints and there was nothing for it but rest, and Cad had to convince her to at least give him more painkillers and anti-inflammatories.

He perked up when a seventy-five-year-old nomad from Western Australia came over for a chat and had him in raptures with his many yarns. 'He was a funny old bloke and all he talked about was trying to root this bird or that one, and he was going to Amsterdam soon and was going to try to root some bird there. He rides around living off his pension and eats sardines and crackers every single night for dinner. I cut the top off a water bottle for a cup and went halves in a longneck with him while he told me stories; he was on his third lap of Oz.'

Next day Andrew went into one of the three antique shops in Campbelltown and bought an old potty for $20 and sent it to Owen near Batemans Bay to add to his collection. 'It cost a fortune to send but it's cool cause he is the biggest mad dog I've met so far.'

I'd offered to shout him a couple of nights at a pub but he reckoned he couldn't justify $65 a night, so he went back to his free camp and iced his legs every hour until 8pm, but there was little improvement.

A local girl, Sahra, came over and invited Cad to a barbeque that evening at her house and he was more than happy to have some company. He met the family she was staying with who ran Coopers of Campbell Town, a saddler and the local stockists for R.M. Williams gear. Sahra (who wrote to us a beautiful letter after Andrew's death) was a policewoman in Sydney who'd left the service and was working in the Tassie town as an apprentice chef. They struck up a great friendship.

Just to top off Andrew's predicament, next day the local policewoman arrived at the field Andrew had camped on and gave him his marching orders; the council had complained that the area was set down for caravans and campervans only, not free campers. 'I said, "I can't walk so what am I meant to do?" She said, "Sorry, I know what you're up to but I'm just doing my job."'

DAY 47, 11 FEBRUARY 2011 CAMPBELL TOWN TO TUNBRIDGE (28KM)

Andrew had no choice but to bow to his eviction notice and hobble on in pain towards Hobart. He made it to historic Ross ten kilometres down the Midland Highway and rested, surprised that his legs weren't too bad. It was a false dawn; ten kilometres further and he was in severe pain and decided that was enough for the day. But the road was lined with barbed-wire fences protecting properties, with every gate padlocked, so he couldn't find a place to camp and had to endure another seven kilometres before he found the next laneway.

'Seven long painful kilometres later I got off the road and threw my tent up, ate a can of spaghetti and crawled in to die. My legs were as bad as when I reached Campbell Town so I knew I'd be hitching to Hobart in the morning. It was the coldest night by far and I woke up a shivering mess. I didn't dare get out in the rain to get more clothes so just tucked up into a ball, pulled the end of my bag closed and shivered myself back to sleep.'

DAY 48, 12 FEBRUARY 2011 HITCHED FROM TUNBRIDGE TO HOBART

With the back of his solar panel bearing the message 'Hobart Hospital', it took Andrew an hour to attract a lift from Don and Jill in an old Mazda 929 station wagon, which was just capable of fitting Redge in between suitcases. Let's just say he had an interesting discussion about religion with devout Christian Jill for most of the way before departing with a Bible in hand; after their generosity, he had decided he could not upset her by declaring he was an atheist. He was extremely appreciative that they detoured to the hospital.

Cad thought maybe Jill had convinced God to smile on him when, after little over a minute in the casualty ward, a hot young blonde nurse fetched him. The doctor gave him the news that his problem was muscular (shin splints, as he expected) but he needed more than the week's rest he'd just been forced to endure and, she claimed, to halve his intake of anti-inflammatory drugs as the quantity he was consuming was not healthy.

After finding a hostel and loading himself up with vitamin supplements, hoping to help his legs, Cad didn't hit his bed until 5.30am after drinking and talking endlessly with a gathering of backpackers, most of who were in Tassie for cherry-picking work, including Dutchman Dennis, who he would come across again, and a girl from Taiwan, Alia, who had the hots for him, according to Cad's diary notes.

DAYS 49–53, 13–17 FEBRUARY 2011 BAILED UP IN TASMANIA

Cad went up-market and spent $120 on a hotel room for the night and went out with Alia and her friends for the afternoon. 'Turns out I'd jagged the annual wooden boat festival and it was going off like a Jewish foreskin. There was a big stage with a band, stalls and exhibitions, boats of every shape and size lining the piers, street performers and people everywhere.' He came across another walker at the hostel, a twenty-three-year-old student from Canberra who days earlier had had to be evacuated by helicopter from the south-west ranges in Tassie in bad weather.

Down in the dumps at not being able to walk, Andrew hit the social scene instead, and his spirits lifted when the money for his house sale came through – he was cashed up and no longer had to live as frugally (although he placed a large percentage of the funds in a fixed-interest account).

A mate, Adam Martin, and his partner, Tash (short for Natasha), were in Hobart a couple of days later for a wedding and they caught up. Enriched with diet hints from Adam and a local health store proprietor, Cad had stocked up with all sorts of protein powders and supplements, hoping they would help his legs handle the workload he had planned for them. In the end he learned that stretching down at the end of the day was just as important as stretching before he walked; taking vitamin C and magnesium tablets was also crucial.

After four nights in Hobart, Adam drove him back to Launceston to spend the two nights he'd had planned in his birthplace. Still unable to resume his walk, Andrew had decided to head to Melbourne to rest up, keep an appointment at a tattooist and then complete his walk to Hobart when he was fit enough. They did a trip, with Dutch backpacker Dennis joining them, to the Bay of Fires in the north-east. Cad couldn't believe how beautiful it was, 'like something out of the Caribbean'.

DAYS 54–62, 18–26 FEBRUARY 2011 BACK TO MELBOURNE

Andrew decided to fly back to Melbourne from Launceston, the pram and his gear packed into a bike box, and was surprised that it all weighed 45 kilograms,; that meant he'd regularly been pushing around 70 to 80 kilograms on the highways once he added food and water. It also meant he was facing $15 per kilogram for the extra 25 kilograms ($375), but one of the airline staff had read about his walk and squared it off at $100. From Tullamarine he caught a cab straight to the tattooist, only to realise thirty minutes into the ink job that he had left a bag at the airport carousel! He called the airline to rescue it.

Andrew had arranged to stay at the share house of Indi, one of the bicycle couriers he'd met at Lakes Entrance, and spent the next nine nights in Melbourne, which gave him twenty days' break from his walk. He visited a physiotherapist, who told him she didn't think he was suffering shin splints but muscle tear; he had a couple of sessions, which helped, and was referred to a podiatrist, who told him he had collapsed arches and fitted him with orthotics for his shoes and gave him some stretching exercises to follow.

More time was spent at the tattooist than caring for his injured legs, however; he had three sessions with Jaclyn and booked in to get a topless mermaid added to the extensive artwork already along both legs (including a sketch of the famous ship the *Endeavour,* and a workman's boot to signify he was giving up 'the tools' as a carpenter), which would mean he'd have to get back to Melbourne from wherever he was on that date – yet another distraction that contributed to his walk taking a lot longer than it could have. The fact that he had to keep his newly created tatts out of the sun and also try to keep his legs in decent order saw him let go of $300 for two pairs of Skins compression tights to walk in. Paying that much probably hurt as much as his leg pain!

DAYS 63–66, 27 FEBRUARY–2 MARCH 2011 RETURN TO TASMANIA, TUNBRIDGE TO HOBART (133KM)

Andrew made his second Bass Strait crossing on the *Spirit of Tasmania* and originally planned to catch a bus to Launceston then another to Tunbridge to pick up his aborted walk. But it was Sunday and he'd made a commitment to return to Melbourne for the Friday night fundraising 'alley cat' riding challenge organised by the bike couriers to fund him a new pair of walking shoes, and the bus would take too long. Instead, he was able to arrange a hire car for the next morning; the manager, aware of his story, was good enough to provide him with a ute for three days at no charge.

He drove to Tunbridge via a stop at Launceston to shop, and another at Campbell Town to say hello to Sahra. He convinced one of the Tunbridge locals to let him park the ute in his yard for a couple of days and was back into stride, just hoping that his legs weren't going to rebel once they realised what they were in for again. 'I had a massive stretch, taped my feet like the physio showed me, had something to eat and was finally away. I had mixed feelings about being back on the road after a spell – half of me was stoked and the other half was over it. I just cruised all afternoon, I didn't want to come a gutser first day back – again! I just took normal steps all day. I had got into a habit of over-striding, thinking I could cover more ground quicker, but the physio told me it was a big no-no, along with sprinting down the back of hills.'

He camped just short of Oatlands and it was the coldest night he had experienced since he'd left home, requiring him to wear three layers of clothes as he slept. It was raining when he woke, and freezing despite it being the last day of summer. Welcome to Tasmania! But he had to get on the road.

'My hands were cold from the get-go and it wasn't long until they were stinging like crazy. I had that many layers on I was sweating my arse off up the hills, but didn't dare take any off because the howling southerly just cut straight through you. I couldn't take it anymore, it got to the stage where I couldn't even touch the aluminium handlebars because they were that cold. I stopped and cut the sleeves off my woollen jumper and tied the ends together with cable ties to make mitts – what a relief!!'

After a stop in Oatlands, the weather turned even nastier with hail coming in sideways and turning the ground white, then it was sunny, then dark clouds would roll in again. Nevertheless he knocked out 39.5 kilometres before making Jericho. He found a spot a few hundred metres up a steep dirt road off the highway and camped, and if he thought the night before was cold, this spot was infinitely chillier. He slept in every piece of clothing, plus his rain gear, and was still shivering. He spoke to a local the next morning and she said if he'd wanted to pick the coldest place between Launceston and Hobart, he just had.

He walked well into the next night, in heavy rain, so he could get to the outskirts of Hobart and camp for the night then get to the city centre next day and bus it back to Tunbridge the next afternoon to pick up his borrowed ute and drive to Devonport. For some stupid reason, considering he needed to nurse his legs back into the routine, he walked until 3am after deciding to reach the city centre that night, making it a 69-kilometre leg.

'I crossed the River Derwent at Bridgewater and had to hang onto my hat and solar panel, the freezing wind was howling up the river so much. I got onto the highway and had a few eerie kilometres in the dark. By the time I reached lights and civilisation again I thought I might as well go for gold and reach Hobart tonight. I finally reached a servo that was still open at about midnight and had a couple of Mars Bars and a Coke to try to wake up a bit. I grabbed four bags of ice and went and lay in the car wash across the road to get out of the wind and ice my legs. I had two bags under and two bags on top of my legs for half an hour until they were numb, it was freezing.

'I climbed a killer hill at about 2am and finally caught sight of Hobart below, what a relief. My knees started to hurt and I shuffled down to the main roundabout.

I decided to head a park and I wandered around for a while before throwing the tent up behind a building near the war memorial. Made myself have a stretch in the rain and finally got in my bag after 3am, a broken man.'

DAY 67, 3 MARCH 2011 BACK TO LAUNCESTON

Despite running late for his bus back up the highway, Cad couldn't resist stopping in for another of the lamb shank pies ('this time with chutney') that had impressed him so much a couple of weeks earlier ('with an egg and bacon pie thrown in for the protein').

He made the bus for Tunbridge and picked up the hired ute, but after hearing from the *Mercury* newspaper, he drove 105 kilometres back to Hobart for a photograph and interview (yet another example of being his own worst enemy). On the way back up the Midland Highway he stopped at Campbell Town for a pot of tea and a plate of homemade brownies with Sahra before finally arriving in Launceston, where he'd arranged to stay with the daughter of people he met while laid up in Campbell Town. Let's just say his last night in Tasmania was a long, liquid and eventful one!

DAY 68, 4 MARCH 2011 TO MELBOURNE

Cad was up at 6am and drove to Devonport, stopping on the way to book a ferry ticket. One of the boat's staff organised a free cabin for him, and while he waited for departure in a deckchair Cad was amused to see the bloke sitting alongside was reading the story about him in the *Mercury.* 'I went to say, geez, he's a good-looking bloke, but I didn't bother.' He slept all day except for a lunch break, abusing the one-serve buffet rule again, this time with a bonus plastic bag of bread rolls that he took back to the cabin.

He had just thirty minutes between docking and the start of the 'alley cat run' organised by the courier cyclists in his honour, which was six kilometres away, so had to jog. 'I made it to the river and was weaving in and out of the hordes of people. Everybody was staring, laughing and yelling shit like "run, Forest, run!" or "Go, Benny Cousins!" – must have been the Skins? I had to drag the pram backwards up a full flight of stairs at the St Kilda Road bridge and then legged the last couple of kilometres to the museum. I ended up killing it and got there in under forty minutes through traffic.'

About twenty cyclists raced and, without prior notice, one of the cyclists, Lane, asked Cad to say a few words and present the winner's prize. 'Next thing Lane dropped the "now Cad wants to say a few words" bomb on me. I froze like a shit in a dead cat's arse and blurted out a couple of words, thanks for coming and handed it back to Lane. He said, "He's not usually a man of few words," but to check out my website and see what it's all about.'

Cad's Tassie ordeal was over. He'd added a 345-kilometre stretch from Devonport to Hobart to his around-the-mainland sojourn, but it had taken thirty days since he first crossed the Bass Strait, instead of the planned nine. It involved three ferry crossings, a flight, bus rides, hitchhiking, six days of pain stranded in Campbell Town, several nights partying hard in Hobart and Melbourne, hours at a tattooist – which put a large hole in his cashed-up pocket after selling his house – and he'd made many new friends.

Two days later, with new shoes in which to place his orthotic soles, he was back to life on the bitumen ... until his next diversion, less than two weeks away.

5

MELBOURNE TO CEDUNA

After a day and night in Melbourne to socialise (Andrew went hard, as usual) with the new crew he'd met en route, Cad encountered problems getting out of Melbourne's environs. As he could not walk on the freeway he had to improvise, which meant taking to the Federation cycle path and sleeping in wetlands the first night. The next day – due to being misled by Google Maps, he claimed – he ended up in Melbourne Water land next to the highway but had to skull-drag his rig through long grass, over logs and barbed-wire fences he'd flattened, and breaking padlocks on gates with rocks to avoid a 10-kilometre and two-hour detour. With a tender leg (due to his fresh tattoos) adding extra pain as he scratched and scraped his way through thick overgrowth and temporary fencing, he was determined to live up to the one rule that was non-negotiable on his trip: 'Backtracking is just not an option.'

So it was tough going until he made it to Geelong, where an old friend interviewed him on his local radio show, put him up for the night in Torquay and drove him back to Geelong to resume his journey south towards the Great Ocean Road, which he regarded as the most striking scenery he encountered on his around-Australia stroll.

The countdown had begun also to his thirtieth birthday – or 'reaching the dirty thirties', as he put it. He'd planned to return to mate Kaine Dobbs' wedding to Lucy a week before his birthday and have a premature birthday bash on the Central Coast, but that also put pressure on him reaching Adelaide for his birthday on 9 April; he was hoping to have a decent celebration in a major city.

Then it was to the western edge of South Australia for his longest respite before taking on the Nullarbor Plain, the challenge he'd been warned about since he first started discussing the walk.

Let's pick up the story from Geelong.

DAYS 70–72, 6–8 MARCH 2011 PORT MELBOURNE TO BELLBRAE (107KM)

After an interview with the *Geelong Advertiser* newspaper, Cad hit the road in a new pair of Asics shoes he'd bought for $200 in Geelong, only to almost immediately have a difference of opinion with a road gang that was not going to let him walk through the highway roadworks. He let go with a typical Cad tantrum after initially being stopped, only for the foreman to utter, 'Are you finished now?' before explaining he'd escort him around the works and show him a short cut. 'Talk about making myself look a dickhead!'

No sooner had he got over that than we had a blue on the phone over something I had failed to do for him, leaving him to diarise: 'It made me realise if I want anything done, I have to do it myself.' It was an attitude he carried with him for many, many more weeks every time something didn't go to plan.

DAYS 73–74, 9–10 MARCH 2011 BELLBRAE TO SEPARATION CREEK (66KM)

Next day he came across a Spaniard named Aitor, who had left Egypt on his bicycle two years earlier. He'd cycled through Asia, down the Stuart Highway from Darwin and was en route to Melbourne, from where he was going to fly to Auckland. 'He was flat broke and needed to get a job fruit picking for a few months before he could ride back to Asia and beyond. I asked him if he has been getting out and having fun, he said no way – one beer is like two meals for him. I didn't dare tell him I just spent $2000 [on tattoos].' He was one of a surprising number of travellers from all parts of the world using all sorts of modes of manual transport that Cad would encounter around Australia.

Andrew made it to Lorne at 8.30pm, wet from the intermittent rain and freezing cold. Next morning, he came across a farmer from south of Perth who told him how much he would enjoy the Nullarbor, a stint he had been pessimistic about. 'He was the first person to say that I'm going to love the Nullarbor and that all the rest areas are full of people and he reckoned heaps of people will stop to see if I'm okay. He said there aren't really any stretches bigger than 200 kilometres. Sounds like I've got nothing to worry about; everybody I speak to has been saying how crazy it's going to be and have been stressing me out.'

The mood darkened, however, when Andrew, feeling satisfied after banking $350 for the Cancer Council, was harassed by a Lorne local, and not for the last time he plunged into a verbal battle. 'When I came out there was this big guy in his forties waiting for me. He was all worked up and barked, "Is this yours?" pointing to the pram. Yeah, I replied. Are you going to try to walk that to Apollo Bay? I said I am going to walk it to Apollo Bay! I don't know where this tool came from, I gathered he had seen me down the road and charged around looking for me until he saw my pram. He starting blurting things out like if he was the police he would put a ban on me so I couldn't walk on the road, I didn't let him get too much more out before I started with, "Well, guess what? You're not the police and it's not illegal to walk on the road."

'He just kept saying, "Let me finish, let me finish," and I just kept interrupting him. It was going nowhere fast and I'd heard enough so I put my earphones on and told him to keep his opinions to himself and walked off while he was still crapping on. He decided to follow me, barking into my face the whole way across the courtyard, "You're going to kill yourself and you're going to kill someone else," ra ra ra. PING! I'd heard enough – to be honest, I don't know how I managed to cop it for as long as I did before I snapped. I started screaming at him, causing an even bigger scene in front of everyone at a café.'

There's probably no need to document Andrew's tirade, but suffice to say the man complained about his language before Cad restrained himself and walked away. 'That was probably one of the top ten angriest moments of my life, my heart was pounding and my head was racing ... he was crapping on about how he had my website and he was going to ring all the media and the cancer organisations and tell everyone what a bad person I am. I started stressing and thought maybe the Cancer Council will drop me, then I thought, 'Well, good if they do – in seventy-four days on the road I haven't had so much as an email from them.'

Indeed, he received very little contact or support from the Cancer Council, despite raising over $25,000 for them; that was why by the time he reached Perth he'd decided to switch his allegiance to the Leukaemia Foundation, with whom he struck up a terrific relationship and who were there to cheer him on when he passed the finish line. The Leukaemia Foundation, through the lovely Nina Field, also supported Chris and me after Andrew's accident, with several representatives attending his memorial service. Andrew never heard from the Cancer Council during his walk, nor has his family since.

Always a sponge for information, Andrew was fascinated to learn about William Buckley and the Aussie saying 'Buckley's chance' during that day's walk. He wrote: 'The Great Ocean Road is pretty off its head, hairpins winding around headlands, cut into the cliffs as far as the eye can see. It really is breathtaking. I stopped at a lookout to eat and read a plaque about William Buckley, who escaped a convict settlement in 1803 and was living in a cave below the lookout. As winter set in, he wasn't in a good way and decided it was time to turn himself him. On his way back to the settlement he was rescued by the Wathaurong Aborigines, whom he lived with for the next thirty-two years. He eventually popped out at some farm at the age of fifty-seven and was pardoned by the Governor and made head Aboriginal interpreter. He married and lived out his days in Hobart until seventy-five. And that's where the saying "you've got two chances – Buckley's and none" comes from. I must have said "you've got Buckley's" over a thousand times in my life.'

DAYS 75–76, 11–12 MARCH 2011 SEPARATION CREEK TO LAVERS HILL (71KM)

For those who knew that Andrew never drank tea or coffee before he embarked on his walk, this was a red-letter day: the day he consumed his first full cup of coffee, at a place called Kennett River. 'There were tourists galore and half a dozen buses pulled up. I went into the shop and Sue, Keri and Chris were expecting me [motorists had advised them a walker was not far away]. They were nice ladies and gave me $60 between them and handed me a cappuccino. I was going to ask for a tea but they had already made it. I was surprised that I actually enjoyed it – I think that was the first cup of coffee I ever have actually finished. I've been missing out. It's funny how you hate something your whole life then all of a sudden you like it.'

Cad, for the first of many times, found the humidity unbearable next day but kept pacing the highway until he came to Lavers Creek, altitude 500 metres. There he was invited by the local policeman, Laurie, to bunk at his place and enjoy a meal at the pub – copper's shout. Laurie introduced Cad to the pub population and suddenly his hat was full of coins and notes.

Soon after, he found himself in a compromising position with an English girl. Before you get the wrong idea, let him explain: 'Matt and Jenny came over with an odd request for Jenny to piggyback me while she pushed the pram. She was a redhead from Slough in the UK and had tattoos on her arms; she lives in Melbourne and works for Triple J doing the jmag. Matt was an old local who lives in Tasmania now, playing footy. She explained that she has a website called "Hey Man Now You're Really Living" and she is doing something different every single day for a year and blogging it. I was only too happy to oblige.

'Me and Laurie went over and got the pram, I jumped on her back and she pushed us both along out the front of the pub while Matt took pics – how random! Matt told me later that it's bloody killing him trying to help her think of new things to do every day; he said he had been racking his brain for something to do tonight.' A great photo was posted on Facebook and the Oz On Foot website.

DAY 77, 13 MARCH 2011 LAVERS HILL TO PORT CAMPBELL (58KM)

Cad had been looking forward to viewing the Twelve Apostles, the remarkable rock formations off the windswept coast, but was not as impressed as he'd expected to be. 'I was actually a bit disappointed – I've seen some pretty cool shit over the last few years, from the Colosseum to the Grand Canyon to the Giza Pyramids, and they just weren't cutting the mustard. It's funny how you build things up in your head and they never quite meet your expectations.'

Despite the howling wind, he recorded this day as his best to date for donations, with the Great Ocean Road crawling with tourists. That was the day's good news. The bad news was that it wasn't until he was seven kilometres off course that he found he was walking away from Warrnambool and not towards it, and had to break his golden rule of not backtracking. After being attacked by two dogs, an eventful day finished with him camping in the centre of an Aussie Rules field, after first considering pitching the tent in a graveyard.

DAYS 78–80, 14–16 MARCH 2011 REST DAY, THEN PORT CAMPBELL TO TOWER HILL (77KM)

Cad loved the scenery but not the winding and steep road, which made his safety a little treacherous at times. 'It was really cool scenery today, the road ran along the orange and yellow cliffs, at times close enough to see the sandy coves below; there were no trees, just shrubs everywhere. I guess this is what the Nullarbor is going to be like. I stopped at the Bay of Islands lookout and this one was spectacular, for me it was better than the Apostles, it was a big bay guarded by limestone pillars jutting out of the ocean at the mouth. There were dozens of them in all shapes and sizes stretching up the coast.'

Andrew recorded a meeting with a man who had been touched by cancer; it was one of many such meetings he diarised, stories that obviously affected him deeply. 'I got back out on the road and K. Saddler had stopped to have a chat, he was very interested in what I was doing because he had recently lost his four-year-old grandson to brain cancer and was planning to do a charity walk from Brisbane to Cairns, leaving on the same date and at the same time as when he passed away. He told me all about it and said that they kept smashing him with chemo time and time again for a year before he died, it left him so unhappy that he decided to travel around Australia to try to clear his head.'

Cad banked $1100, which showed how lucrative the previous few days had been. He picked up a pair of orthotic soles from the post office that had been posted to him from the podiatrist he'd seen in Melbourne, and as he unwrapped them he found an envelope with a $60 donation inside from the podiatrist, along with a note that said to break them in for fifteen minutes a day ... Buckley's chance!

Instead, he knocked out a 52-kilometre day, the start of him getting back into his routine eleven days after leaving Melbourne. That night he couldn't pass up the chance of ticking from his bucket list the experience of sleeping in a cemetery. 'I stood at the gate unwinding all the wire keeping it locked and then pushed the big, rusty, creaking thing open, it was a scene straight out of a B-grade horror movie. I set up camp next to James Patrick Casey, who died at twenty-nine on 25 April 1916; I don't believe in ghosts, when you're dead, you're dead. I set up in the dark because there was a house nearby and I didn't want them to think there were kids mucking around and call somebody.'

DAYS 81–84, 17–20 MARCH 2011 TOWER HILL TO PORTLAND (90KM); PORTLAND TO LOWER GLENELG NATIONAL PARK (115KM)

As he was leaving Portland, four young women passed him and he heard one say 'that's him'. 'One of them came running back with a $50 donation and then the other three followed. I started telling them what I was up to and they said they knew and had been watching my blogs. One of them had just gone and tried my hash brown on a cheeseburger trick, too funny!! I can't believe someone tried it after I crapped on about it.'

This was the day he heard the Lynyrd Skynynd song 'Free Bird' for the first time (I am surprised it was in his music library considering the song was nearly released in 1973, on an album I bought as a teenager). It soon became something of a theme song for him (and an anthem I played over and over, trying to get a reaction from him when he lay unresponsive in hospital). 'I had a good afternoon singing away at the top of my lungs, "Free Bird" by Lynynd Skynynd came on my iPod shuffle, the lyrics really caught my attention. They seemed so fitting for my walk and what was going on with Jaime. I must have listened to it ten times in a row.'

Cad woke with a plan: to walk 65 kilometres today, 55 kilometres tomorrow and 100 kilometres the next day. He trooped through dense pine forest, crossed the border into South Australia and walked well into the night to make Mount Gambier, 32 kilometres into South Australia. He became agitated at high-beam headlights blinding him, and when drivers did not turn them off he would give them 'the bird'. A car stopped and turned back towards him; Cad thought he was in for a confrontation, so took out a knife he'd packed for self-defence and picked up a large rock. 'The car turned down a side street and left me standing there shaking with rage. It was lucky for both of us because they would have needed a new windscreen and I would have either ended up in the cop shop or bashed and left lying in a ditch. I calmed down and started thinking, "You need to chill out." I was in such a rage – what if I had done something stupid with that knife? I only got it out for show but it was a bad idea; no more getting the knife out when I've got the shits.'

He made it to Mount Gambier at 10.15pm, low on food and water. 'I'd had enough for the day and wanted to crash but there were drunks stumbling around the streets and P-platers cutting laps up and down the main street yelling shit at me, so no way I was sleeping in town.' He cleared the town by nine kilometres and at 12.15am thought he would attempt his first 100-kilometre stint, but the clouds soon closed in and it started pouring. He hastily set up camp on a track off the highway and spent more than half an hour, in driving rain, deafening thunder and lightning trying to set up shelter. He fell asleep exhausted at 2am, the wind almost blowing his tent out of the ground. He'd walked 74 kilometres, a record to date but one that would be broken two days later.

DAY 85, 21 MARCH 2011 MOUNT GAMBIER TO TANTANOOLA (25KM)

Next day he didn't wake until 10am, 'blistered, sore and wet through. But I decided to stop being a pussy and gave myself a kick up the arse and got out in the rain and started packing up.' He climbed out of the tent to find he'd camped on someone's front yard, so bad was his visibility, and saw the elderly resident peering at him. He walked over to explain. Soon after he was inside having coffee, zucchini soup and homemade bread followed by zucchini chocolate cake with Judith and Brian, retired schoolteachers who had invited him to have a break at their home.

He made Tantanoola by mid-afternoon, walking into the pub to be greeted by five surprised locals at the bar. A woman he'd met on the road earlier said she'd arrange a room at the hotel but there were none available, so next thing he has been shunted across the road to the home of 'Cuddles'. A middle-aged man who had not long before split with his wife, Cuddles had little furniture so Cad sat on an esky chatting to him. He was in bed at 10pm and set the alarm for 2am so he could embark on his 100-kilometre stint that the weather had interrupted two days earlier. Cuddles arranged a mate who had a regular freight run to pick him up the next afternoon and give him a lift to Mount Gambier, from where he could catch a bus and train to Melbourne for a flight to Sydney for Dobbsy's wedding.

DAY 86, 22 MARCH 2011
TANTANOONA TO CONMURRA (80KM)

Determined to make the magical 100-kilometre mark before being picked up by Cuddles' mate, Cad was on the road at 2.30am in the drizzle, his feet blistered and sore, probably from the new orthotic soles. Thousands of white snails filled the streets, swishing underneath his shoes. He stopped for a coffee ten kilometres into the day at a twenty-four-hour service station at Millicent, chatting to a couple of early risers while watching thousands of black crickets jumping around everywhere. 'One lady who was dropping off the newspapers asked me a heap of questions like "Aren't you scared some axe murderer is going to pull up", ra ra ra. I thought, "Thanks, love, just what I want to hear before I go back to wandering around in the dark."'

For no stated reason in his diary, he'd decided to walk without headphones today and did a walk, jog, walk, jog pattern until 1.30pm before collapsing on the roadside. 'Every inch of me was ailing. I lay there for a couple of minutes and then made myself get up. I knew this exact moment was coming and I had said to myself out loud this morning that when the time comes when you're absolutely fucked and think you can't go on then you have a choice, a choice between giving up and being a dog or being a mad dog and having a go. I decided to be a mad dog and started hobbling up the road. I had done 70 kilometres and decided that I would only be remotely happy with at least 80 kilometres or it just wasn't worth putting myself through all this pain. I had about three hours before my lift but it still wasn't going to be easy. I put my headphones on and said out loud what was the point of no music, you idiot. I put 'Free Bird' on full bore, fired up and started to jog. I was yelling, "Let's do this, fuck 80, it's 90 or nothing!" I jogged until I was fucked, then went back to a power walk to catch my breath and then I'd start jogging again.'

Cad was devastated when Cuddles' mate pulled up at 3.45pm (he'd expected him at 4.15 to 4.30pm) as he was hell-bent on getting at least 80 kilometres on the clock, a personal best, after realising he wasn't going to reach the magical 100 kilometres. He thought he'd fallen short when he dropped a pin on the Google Maps app on his phone – he'd been walking for thirteen hours – but he'd snuck in by half a kilometre. He dropped Redge at Judith and Brian's before Cuddles' mate Chris dropped him in Mount Gambier. There he found a hotel near the highway, ate big, burst the blisters on his feet and filled them with peroxide, then went to bed dreaming of a bender back on the Central Coast.

DAYS 87–94, 23–30 MARCH 2011 TO MELBOURNE AND THE CENTRAL COAST, THEN BACK TO CONMURRA

This period involved a bus from Mount Gambier to Warrnambool and a train from there to Melbourne, where he spent $500 on a suit and $200 on shoes for the wedding and a lot more on a tattoo of a topless mermaid from his new favourite tattooist, Jaclyn. Flight home on the Friday (25 March), a trip to the Olympic Stadium that night with Matt Delaney and me to a Parramatta NRL match, and catching up with his cousins and uncle from Wodonga, Josh, Regan and Ken. Breakfast with family then the wedding next day, a long thirtieth birthday bash with friends on Sunday (thirteen days before his birthday). Much of Monday was spent sleeping and recovering, ready for a flight next day and back to the grindstone. He also spent time with Jaime, and talked about what the future might hold. He flew via Melbourne, where he had the topless mermaid tattooed on his leg.

After picking up his rig from Judith and Brian's, he was back on the road, trying to hitch a ride to where he had been picked up five days earlier. As it approached sunset, and despite holding out a $20 note then a $50 note as enticement for someone to take enough pity on him to pick him up, he gave up and camped just off the roadside.

DAY 95, 31 MARCH 2011 CONMURRA TO KINGSTON (29KM)

He nabbed a lift with three people and a Rottweiler in a beat-up old red ute, the driver advising him the giant dog didn't like people! 'I could tell the thing looked like it wanted to kill me as I put Redge in the back while Keith [a fellow passenger] held him. I sat in the back trying to keep my head out of the masses of spider webs that had accumulated in all the corners, while Keith stuck his two cents in about anything and everything while he drunk his cans of beer and smoked durries.' The trip home for a mate's wedding cost him eight days, and a lot of money; it was commitments like this that he paid for in November and December when enduring oppressive conditions in the country's harsh north.

He was back to the lonely grind, and it hit him hard. And he went through this mind challenge every time he went from enjoying company and having fun, wherever it was, to lonesome Oz On Foot life. 'I got out and looked around, nothing in every direction. Not a single tree, house, car – nothing but dry grass paddocks and a handful of sheep – welcome back to the middle of nowhere! I sat around pretending to stretch, rang the boys, had something to eat, rang a few more of the boys, basically just trying to delay the inevitable as long as I could until I made myself get up and start walking. My feet were pissing me off so I stopped and took my orthotics out, then I stopped and put them back in, then out then in then out then in! I stopped every two minutes to scratch my itchy legs from my new tattoos, then I stopped to put sunscreen on, then again to put zinc on. Then my balls were driving me crazy because I'd shaved them and the regrowth was itchy. I stopped to moisturise them, then stopped to try tattoo cream, then I cracked the shits and stopped to take my Skins off. I was getting nowhere fast – I really didn't want to be here. I thought about starting again in the morning but there was no choice as there was a barbed wire fence running down each side of the road as far as the eye could see in either direction. I made myself snap out of it and start walking.'

The following diary entry that night is the real-life example of the conflict within Andrew that he took to the grave: the choice between the secure and rewarding life of a husband, father and worker that, however, would mean a life that would not satisfy the adventuring test-the-limits, aim-for-more personality that was deep within his character. He mulled over it for weeks and weeks, having spent some time with Jaime during those few days back on the Central Coast.

'I needn't have bothered listening to music, it was drowned out by the thoughts of my spinning head. Mainly Jaime – I knew this would happen. I must have planned out my entire future until death 100 times over until I came up with two scenarios. It basically came down to do I want to get married or not; if I did, I guess I probably couldn't choose a better chick, keep in touch, maybe catch up every capital city. Go home, get married, have kids, buy a block of land, build a shed on it to make furniture out of until I make enough money to build a house on it and spend the rest of my days growing old accumulating shit that I can't take to my grave with me. But I don't think I want that anymore. Maybe I want to keep having fun, keep travelling, keep adventuring, climb Everest, live life to the full – after all, you only get one life. Do I want to spend the rest of it working my arse off? But then is it only a matter of time until I want the first option and then it's too late – I'm an old man and I missed my chance. I just wish my brain would just shut up, this shit was on loudspeaker all day non-stop, nothing I could do would switch it off.'

Four young blokes pulled up in an old station wagon and asked where Cad was going. When he replied,

'Sydney,' they told him he was going the wrong way. They were sheep shearers and he was invited to bunk with them at their quarters seven kilometres up the road. He accepted and arrived while they were in town for dinner. When they returned, he picked their brains, as was his way, and heard how they received seventy-five cents a sheep and could shear 600 to 800 a day. It's a wonder he didn't decide he wanted to be a sheep shearer!

DAYS 96–97, 1–2 APRIL 2011 KINGSTON TO TILLEY SWAMP (67KM)

Andrew treated the next 143 kilometres before the next town, Meningie, as a practice run for the Nullarbor. After washing clothes at a laundromat and doing a small shop at Kingston he was into it, loaded up with twenty-four litres of water and a new aim: to spend no more than $10 a day, except for any equipment repairs. He walked until 6pm and was about to find a place to camp when a couple pulled up and offered him shelter in their shearing shed on their 8000-acre sheep and cattle property, and to attend a barbeque at a neighbouring property. He wished he hadn't. When he returned from dinner to his quarters the stench in the shed was overbearing, and the noise of a generator and hordes of mosquitos saw him get little peace. 'I cracked it and set my tent up in my boxer shorts on the grass outside.'

On his walk back to the highway next morning Andrew had to confront five bulls sitting by a gate, which he passed without taking his eyes off them, very dubiously for someone who had twice run with the bulls at Pamplona in Spain. 'There were two medium-sized trees within running distance if they charged. I was going to be up the top of one of them quicker than you could say stuff this!'

Soon after, Cad met a young Australian guy riding from Adelaide to Melbourne on his pushbike – the only person he came across all day. 'He had that much shit on his bike and trailer it wasn't funny. I asked him how many kilometres he was doing a day and he said the biggest was 70 and now it was 30 to 40 – I was disgusted! He said he walked every step of the Adelaide Hills and he normally rides for five to ten minutes and then gets off and walks for five to ten mins to give his arse a rest, and stops riding mid-afternoon because he thought people drove worse in the afternoon and it was too dangerous.' Andrew told him of his first bike tour from the Central Coast to Cairns, over 2300 kilometres in thirty-eight days (an average of 62 kilometres a day) with no preparation. The man had taken nine days from Adelaide to get to this point, whereas Cad planned to be there in six days on foot. 'I hope he felt like a big girl, adventure is about pushing yourself, having a go and going through a bit of pain. He was a good bloke and we chatted for a while but I left shaking my head.'

DAYS 98–100, 3–5 APRIL 2011 TILLEY SWAMP TO POLTALOCH (111KM)

About 10 kilometres out of Salt Creek, Cad was confronted by three hydrogen-fuelled Mercedes cars – and nineteen convoy vehicles – as part of the 'F-Cell World Drive', 32,000 kilometres in 125 days, from Germany back to Germany, to prove the technology was viable. They skipped between continents in 747 jets! Christian Maier, who was in charge of a production team documenting the whole trip (along with press journalists and photographers), invited Andrew to do a guest spot, filming him from different angles walking down the highway and doing an interview that can be seen on YouTube. It was crazy how, in the middle of nowhere, he came across the remarkable convoy and their worlds overlapped, and then, in the blink of an eye, they continued on their whirlwind four-continent jaunt while he was back to his slow, painful, solitary trek.

He was to come across similar experiences (but not as spectacular as this) over the next months. The next day he met Colin, a sixty-two-year-old who was on the last leg of his 17,000-kilometre round trip from Melbourne on a bicycle with a trailer.

Andrew was well into the Coorong wetland wilderness and was taken by the scenery. 'The Coorong has opened up to this massive lake 1–3 kilometres wide and as long as the eye can see, with large sand islands poking out everywhere covered in grass and shrub. There was a real small red grassy shrub that blankets the landscape, with green knee to waist high shrubs poking out through the red. It was pretty cool. The dunes that separated the Coorong from the ocean were huge and more like a mountain range, also stretching as far as the eye could see. They were covered in vegetation and only small patches of the yellow sand were left exposed.'

As he camped that night with hundreds of curious mozzies, he received an email from someone who advised him he'd made it onto Wikipedia in the list of people currently walking across Australia and that he would be only the third person to have walked around Australia solo (he'd thought he'd be the second). He was able to get the email address from the web page of one of those previous solo trekkers, Colin Ricketts, who lived at Mount Barker, near Adelaide, and wrote to him in the hope he could arrange a meeting. Colin replied, and Cad became excited about seeing him and hearing of his experiences.

Next day Cad decided to try his luck at seeking some sponsorship (I took over the role weeks later) and was able to snare a new sleeping bag and mattress, free, from Roman.

DAYS 101–103, 6–8 APRIL 2011 POLTALOCH TO ADELAIDE (183KM)

Cad received a call from Colin Ricketts, who'd raised $150,000 on his around Oz epic in 2005, and arranged to meet up the next night. 'He's a legend and does know what it's like,' he wrote. 'He said he was pushing around 100 kilograms and kept snapping axles. I can't wait to meet him.'

I clearly remember the next day when I was trying to post a photo on Facebook for Andrew but, being a Facebook novice at the time, I was having trouble. I called him for some help and we ended up having a terrible argument. Cad recorded in his diary that he woke in a great mood but I was in a bad mood and that got his back up. Anyway, we ended up arguing and I hung up on him. He recorded: 'My blood boiled so quickly it wasn't funny. I stewed over it all day and texted him and told him I wouldn't ask for another thing and to basically fuck off.'

Reading these words in Andrew's diary as I sat by his bed while we were in Chiang Mai, I felt terrible. This is what I wrote in my own diary at the time:

'It reminds me of how busy I was at the time, trying to combine my job as operations manager of rugby league's player agent scheme, media advisor to Parramatta Eels and being right on deadline to finish a book on State of Origin. I was working sixty-five to seventy hours every week and had realised I wasn't spending enough time with Chris and just didn't have the spare hours to be chasing PR for Andrew, despite feeling guilty that I wasn't providing the support he needed. I didn't realise none of his mates were helping him out. He was out there in the middle of nowhere doing it tough, and I turned my back on him because of my workload. Working my arse off just doesn't seem important now, but family is. I was stressed and tired and short-tempered, wanting to finish the origin book and get some of my life back. I wanted to later join him for a few days, but he needed me right then. Only now do I realise how much it hurt him.'

Cad made it to Mount Barker at 8.15pm, and Colin, who'd arranged for him to stay at a caravan park, was there to meet him on the edge of town. 'I jogged it while Colin was following me in his maroon sedan with the hazard lights going, it was a pretty funny sight,' he wrote. 'He showed me a cabin and I had a shower – which felt great, the first one since the sheep shearers' shed [six days earlier] – while he went and grabbed a pizza, garlic bread, drink and gelato. What a legend.

'We chatted about everything – not so much about equipment or anything like that, more about the media and raising money and general stuff. He is still writing a book but he decided to do his walk coffee- and alcohol-free; he's gunna laugh if I ever write a book. He planned his trip for nearly two years and had MLC as his major sponsor and they gave him $15,000 for expenses. He had help from friends and family, and I told him I was spewing my friends and family were not more involved. He said you can't expect anything from anyone, and people have to want to help you.

'He didn't camp out much; he stayed with a lot of people he met along the way. He took a book with him and got a lot of people to write down their details and a message in there. I said it was a good idea and I should do it. Next thing it was one o'clock. I thanked Colin again for the pizza and asked if he had paid for the cabin or if it was free, he said it was free.'

The next day Andrew found that Colin had in fact paid for his cabin – 'cheeky bastard!'

DAYS 104–105, 9–10 APRIL 2011 ADELAIDE

Cad did an interview for the *Adelaide Advertiser,* caught up with Dutchman Dennis, who he'd met in Tasmania, and hit the town with plenty of other backpackers from his hostel for his thirtieth birthday celebration. He had a great pub-crawling night and posted his birthday video blog while blind drunk – not remembering he did it until he checked his phone the next morning!

Next day Colin Ricketts called to meet up with him and passed over a book with 'Oz On Foot' and

'Cannonball Cad's Guest Book' written on the cover. 'What a nice guy,' Cad recorded.

DAYS 106–110, 11–15 APRIL 2011 ADELAIDE TO SNOWTOWN (167KM)

This was an uneventful stretch. Cad was offered a bed at Largs North, seventeen kilometres out of Adelaide, by a worker at the bike shop who provided new tyres and did repairs for him. Further along, he encountered some rain and – for the first time but not the last – a mass of mice when he camped. He reached Snowtown, best known for the 'bodies in the barrels' murders in the 1990s, when eight bodies were found in barrels of acid in a disused bank, taken there from elsewhere, which led to four men being convicted of murder.

DAYS 111–112, 16–17 APRIL 2011 SNOWTOWN TO PORT PIRIE (82KM)

For those who became regular viewers of his video blogs, Day 111 is renowned for the instructive routine of how to lube one's testicles and bum to avoid chafing – a classic bit of Cad humour.

His blog the previous day revealed he'd walked 53 kilometres and struck some body bother: 'It's very surprising; I have been walking in agony all day – no, it's not the blisters or the shins, it's mango rash. And I've got it bad, AKA scrot rot, otherwise known as chafing, I've got it all up under my nuts, top of my legs, in my crack. I've been walking around with my hands in my cheeks trying to give my arse a bit of relief all day. I blame the Skins, they just lock all your gear in, you know, and friction does the rest. Anyway it's nothing a bit of 3B won't fix up and I'll have another big day tomorrow.'

Next day was another classic post, done with his cheeky look into the camera and him acting out his instructions just out of shot: 'So yesterday I was telling you about the old 3B cream; liquid gold this, it's worth more than its weight in gold. Me mate Stevie P put me onto it – if there's one man who knows what I'm going through it's him, he's quite partial to a bit of mango rash himself. Anyways, they say prevention is better than the cure so let's get the old Skins down there [as he removes his pants just out of sight of the camera] – it's a morning ritual but I didn't have a go yesterday thus the problems I had yesterday afternoon. You start off with a small amount and give it a good rub up under the Jatz Crackers, normally come back with a good second spadge; it's just like buttering your toast, really, you don't want to miss any bits or it's gunna result in dry corners, and problems. And last but not least, a good healthy serve up the old crack there – don't be afraid to get involved, people. Have a good old go at it; it's going to save you for the day. So that's it ... with that we're away ... a bit of excess there, we'll get rid of that [he wipes more on his arse]. Skins up, we're into it.'

He wasn't as humorous late in the day when, while walking in the dark near the centre of the road, as there was little traffic, a young blue-singleted driver of a white Commodore decided to be an idiot and accelerated, crossed the broken lines on the road and came with centimetres of knocking Cad over. It wasn't the last, or closest, call he encountered with errant motorists.

DAY 113, 18 APRIL 2011 REST DAY, PORT PIRIE

After our telephone argument, Cad had decided to follow up a PR agent he'd been put onto, Sarah Rice, who quickly arranged a series of with local media interviews for him in Port Pirie. Discussions with Sarah a few days later revealed that she'd worked with me in the Australian Olympic Committee's media centre at the 2008 Beijing Olympics. What a coincidence!

Cad wasn't so impressed with the Cancer Council, from which he'd had no contact and battled to get a return phone call from. He had a progressive total for his fundraising on his website and every time someone donated online the tally would increase. He would deposit donations he received on the road into a nominated account but they would sometimes not show up on his tally, and he could rarely get an explanation or reconciliation of the money. In the end he would deposit money into my account and I would post the amount online with the credit of 'donations on the road', to ensure they were correctly recorded.

DAYS 114–116, 19–21 APRIL 2011 PORT PIRIE TO PORT AUGUSTA (94KM)

Donations picked up, a direct result of the media coverage, especially on television. Cad listened to his Spanish lessons while enjoying the change in scenery, with the Flinders Ranges nearby and the landscape of wheat fields turning to bushy scrub.

He did more interviews at Port Augusta, including one for *The Transcontinental* with reporter Elise (described as 'a hottie' in his diary), who stumped him when she asked what were the three most random things he had seen. He could only think of the sex toys he'd found on the side of the road (why didn't he recall the laptop computer?); 'I don't think she'll put that in.' She didn't, but I liked his quote about warming to the task after 115 days: 'I guess I'm like a saddle that takes a while to be broken in.'

DAYS 117–120, 22–25 APRIL 2011 PORT AUGUSTA TO COWELL (182KM)

Day 117 was Good Friday. Cad's Easter plan was to walk over 180 kilometres through Whyalla to the next decent sized town, Cowell. The local MP, Lyn Breuer, stopped to donate $50 and said she had read about him in the newspaper. After 50 kilometres he'd had enough and pushed up a dirt track, crossed a railway line and camped in the dark, only to find he'd picked a spot that was covered in thorns (I can imagine how many f-bombs were let off!) and quickly moved his tent.

He reached Cowell on Anzac Day, a day Cad would always celebrate with two-up and a few too many beers, but he was too late for the two-up session. So he had an ale and headed off to have a shower, only to find the caravan park was full (although he was granted a free shower), so he trooped off to the local oval to free camp for the night with a group of grey nomads. It was back to the Commercial Pub, where he was soon talking to some local oyster farmers. Typically, a thousand questions from Cad and many beers later, and he had been invited to work on the boat with them the next day.

DAY 121, 26 APRIL 2011 OYSTER FARMING IN COWELL

Cad woke up feeling rough from his long session at the pub but was back into it mid-morning when Gary and Terry took him across the bay to their oyster lease and had him stacking oysters onto the boat. They went back to shore to open the baskets and pour the oysters into a big steel tub. 'I worked up a sweat and was feeling sick from not eating or drinking enough after a hangover. When it was done I had a sticky inside at Gary sorting out the various sizes as they ran along the conveyor belt and through tunnels and all ended up in different sacks, it was pretty cool.'

DAYS 122–125, 27–30 APRIL 2011 COWELL TO PORT LINCOLN (161KM)

The day started with goodbyes and a visit to the bank, where the $860 deposit took his total to $10,700, making Oz On Foot the Cancer Council's biggest online fundraiser (it still is, at $25,456), then a visit to the chemist to try to get some relief for his 'scrot rot'.

Sarah had suggested Cad do a YouTube 'best wishes for your wedding' blog for Prince William and Kate Middleton, who were being married in two days' time. He felt it was a stupid idea but Sarah thought it would lift awareness and might get a run around the world. So he did, and it's a scream (www.youtube.com/wat

ch?v=aArlJTszGJc); 'I thought I'd put fair dinkum and hooroo in – Poms love that shit, don't they?'

Cad was walking in the rain about 30 kilometres out of Port Lincoln when locals Lofty and Chris pulled over to donate and offered him shelter in their shed for the weekend. When he limped into town like a drowned rat, in agony from the chafing, rash and blistered feet, he called Lofty, a retired fisherman. Arriving at their place, he found Lofty and Chris waiting for him in the driveway. They even offered him a fold-out bed in the rumpus room rather than the back shed – 'absolute legends!' It wasn't just the lamb shanks and vegetables for dinner that night that lifted Cad's spirits enormously, or the magnificent house overlooking the bay, but how Lofty and Chris went out of their way over the next few days to show him their town and treat him fondly. It created an instant friendship.

DAYS 126–127, 1–2 MAY 2011 TIME OFF IN PORT LINCOLN

Port Lincoln is best known for its fishing, tuna particularly, and for the fact that Australia's greatest staying racehorse, three-time Melbourne Cup winner Makybe Diva, has links to the town through its owner, local tuna fisherman come good Tony Santic; there is even a statue of the great mare along the waterfront. When Chris and I stayed there on our 2006 around-Australia trip we loved it, and Andrew came to share our affection for the town.

I remember talking to him while he was there, and he seemed keen to invest in real estate there when the walk was finished; from his diaries I found that had come from discussions with Lofty. Lofty and Chris took him sightseeing, out for meals and generally played the perfect hosts. He went to a doctor to seek relief for his rash, topped up his food and water supplies, bought new tyres and did repairs on the pram, banked more money and restocked his energy and motivation. The doctor diagnosed his problem as a parasite and put him on a course of penicillin, telling him to rid himself of the underwear he'd been wearing and not to walk in Skins.

That prompted a trip to a St Vincent's store, where Cad bought six shirts for $6; 'two were funny old man's shirts'. Soon after that he acquired long pyjama pants to match, making him quite a sight along the highways of South Australia and the Nullarbor in his new 'uniform'.

DAYS 128–134, 3–9 MAY 2011 PORT LINCOLN TO STREAKY BAY (294KM)

When leaving Port Lincoln, Andrew was approached by a guy who said he was a freelance television journalist. After discovering Andrew's mission he arranged to meet him on the road next day with a film crew to do a story, which he claimed national television would pick up. He arrived on cue next day and Cad spent an eternity walking up and down the road for filming and answering questions, and was then filmed setting up camp and cooking that evening. It was great to have someone go to such effort, but to my knowledge nothing ever appeared on the box.

As Cad approached the roadhouse at Sheringa he was confronted with the cynical Aussie humour of owner Mark and two mates sitting out the front. 'Need some fuel, do you?' they smiled, pointing at his pram. Cad replied that he did, as a matter of fact, for his cooker.

While Cad went inside and asked for the copies of the Port Lincoln newspaper that he'd called ahead about, asking Mark's wife, Kath, to put them away for him, Mark read the article. The wisecracks continued: 'Sold your house to do this, eh?' Yeah. 'And your car?' Yeah. 'What about the missis?' Yeah. 'That's the smartest thing you ever did ... at least you don't have to pay maintenance. You brought the kids with you, though, eh!'. Kath and Mark's mates burst out laughing again. Cad sat down for a natter before he continued the journey; 'they were a funny bunch,' he later wrote.

The scenery changed further over these days to more barren expanses and sand flats. As he settled into his tent after dinner he heard country and western music but couldn't pick where it was coming from. Soon after came constant rifle fire, which he found unnerving: 'I was waiting for a stray bullet to come through the tent.'

Next night he hit Streaky Bay after his six-day leg from Port Lincoln, where he cooked up a 'hell feed' of sausages, onions, carrots and potato. Looking at his video blogs, he seemed well there – except for his uniform of pyjamas and orange high-vis vest – as he braced himself for the leg that he'd been anxious about, the Nullarbor. He had a day off to wash, shop and rest then headed out on the 102-kilometre three-day path to Ceduna, the last town before the Nullarbor.

DAYS 135–141, 10–16 MAY 2011 STREAKY BAY TO CEDUNA (102KM), THEN FOUR REST DAYS

Ceduna, the last outpost before the Nullarbor, was where Andrew took stock and stocked up. He had to organise several food parcels to be taken ahead (he commandeered some fellow caravan park residents to act as honorary couriers) and meticulously mapped out the distances between each roadhouse and what food he would require. He went to the post office soon after arriving and gathered the new shoes, Leatherman utility tool and plastic containers I'd sent, an iPod full of new songs from Narelle, one of the crew he'd befriended in Melbourne, especially to help get him across the Nullarbor, and a book and stickers for the pram from Colin Ricketts.

While at Ceduna he met Ivan from the Isle of Man, who was riding his bicycle with a trailer around the world on a shoestring budget.

The assignment in Ceduna was to do some running repairs on Redge, put together his food parcels, sleep, rest and prepare for the 1200 kilometres until the first town past the Nullarbor: Norseman.

6

THE NULLARBOR

The Nullarbor. It's where I feared Andrew had run into big strife, the first time I panicked and became concerned about his safety. Basically, he went missing – well, that's certainly how it appeared for the one person – me – who had the job of tracking him and posting his location on the Oz On Foot website every few days.

The stretch from Ceduna to Norseman, across Australia's famous Nullarbor Plain, was the leg of his trek that I was most worried about, for a reason I can't explain. Maybe it was because I knew how isolated, and cold, it would be, particularly if he left the main road to camp. Plus, I had been warned, when Chris and I drove the same route, not to pull over if we encountered anyone from the remote Indigenous communities trying to stop us along the highway, pretending they had broken down – that they were just after money. That's exactly what we did encounter, but kept driving. Also I'd heard of men heading out of the communities for all-night drinking sessions and becoming quite aggressive. Since he left Sydney, the Nullarbor had been on my mind.

I would have liked to have kept as close a track as I could of his progress, but this was difficult as he would only have phone coverage and could thus only send me his position or contact me every four or five days, at best. As it turned out, he didn't have any phone reception for thirteen days after leaving Eucla. Cad had put together a rough map, or master plan, of his walk from Ceduna to Norseman – 1200 kilometres on the knocker – and listed the locations where he would have food parcels dropped off, and the distances and days between each roadhouse; this was our only guide to where he might be during this period.

The trouble was, as he found to his great frustration after a few days, that his calculations of distances between roadhouses (one of which no longer even existed) were incorrect in places; he blamed the inaccuracy of Google Maps. The fact was, however, that he hadn't done any detailed preparation until he reached Ceduna, and then he'd only used his smartphone for information. A more preventable reason was that he'd decided to 'blitz it' and walk far quicker and further than he had planned, including a 100-kilometre day on 28 May, to mark a year since Chris Simpson's death.

His mud map, which he'd posted on Facebook, showed that he would walk the 1200 kilometres along the Eyre Highway from Ceduna to Norseman in twenty-eight days, including four days off; that's an average of 50 kilometres of walking a day, which is a very fair effort. By the time he passed through Caiguna, about 750 kilometres into the Nullarbor trek, he had no network coverage and could not make contact with anyone.

Initially, I wasn't too concerned about the lack of contact as I knew there was a reasonable amount of traffic on the Eyre Highway, although no facilities in between the roadhouses, which were up to 200 kilometres apart. But coinciding with my gathering anxiousness were calls from some of his friends asking if I knew where he was. I didn't. So, sitting at the NRL office while working as the player agent accreditation scheme operations manager with Paul Heptonstall next to me – who, coincidentally, had met Andrew just a few days into his walk – I started to call the roadhouses to try to piece together Cad's movements.

I had no idea he'd walked 100 kilometres in a day for Simmo (he only posted the blog for this day, and others, when he reached Norseman weeks later), or that he'd had only one day off – well, he walked five kilometres that day before collapsing with exhaustion. So I referred to his mud map and called Cocklebiddy, Caiguna and Balladonia roadhouses, asking if they'd seen Andrew. At Cocklebiddy they said he'd passed through the previous week, picked up his food parcels and kept going; they thought it was on the Thursday about lunchtime. But those I spoke to at the other roadhouses (who, while I was on the phone, would ask others working there or truckies having meals if they'd seen Andrew) had no memory of him, and this was the following Friday, eight days later. Caiguna was 107 kilometres past Cocklebiddy, and Balladonia was 51 kilometres further west again, so even with a day off he should have been there by then; certainly he should have been well past Caiguna.

I called Fraser Range Station, a further 91 kilometres to the west, and they hadn't seen him either. I was stumped; he had to have passed through one of those places. I started to wonder if he'd met some strife.

I knew it was very cold. I knew he would have been bush bashing to get off the road to camp, and it may have been easy to have a fall as there were hidden caves aplenty. I knew he was the middle of nowhere and if he let out any cries of distress there would most likely be no one to hear him. He should have absolutely been sighted at Caiguna or Balladonia – who could not notice a young bloke strolling along in with a pram, wearing pyjama pants and an orange high-vis vest?

A woman at the Balladonia roadhouse, who could sense my concern, was very good and said she'd ask, as they called in, the road train drivers coming from the west if they'd seen Andrew en route, which was a relief.

An hour later I headed towards home in my car, with an overnight trip to Western Australia on my mind. About fifteen minutes later the woman from Balladonia called and said another staff member had told her that Andrew had indeed come through a couple of days earlier and picked up his food parcel, and one of the truckies had seen him the next day safe and sound. The panic drained from me instantly. As it turned out, he made it to Fraser Range Station the following day, had his first full day off in three weeks, and was four days ahead of the schedule he had sent me!

Typically, when he hit civilisation at Norseman – sixteen days since he'd last posted a video blog or been in contact with anyone – and found there had been dozens of frantic calls and texts, he wondered what all the fuss was about. 'Just coming into Norseman – that's the Nullarbor done and dusted; 1200 kays in twenty-five days, better than a poke in the eye with a blunt stick,' he said on his video blog. 'I've harped on before about some boxes in life that you want to tick over and over again, like beer, pizza and sex, two of which I'm going to get now – not sure if there is a pizza shop in town for the third. I tell you, the old Nullarbor is not in that category, I won't be ticking that box again. Boring as bat-shite. I thought I would be all excited getting into town but I guess I'm more proud, like a young bloke who's just wet his iron for the first time. But anyways, inundated with emails and voicemails and text messages and comments from people who were concerned for my safety these previous two weeks when I have been out of reception. It's nice to know I'm loved and missed, people, but c'mon, I'm a big boy, it's not like I didn't get off the primary school bus. I don't want to sound ungrateful or anything but ... anyways, I have a hot date with a sparkling redhead at the pub. See youse tomorrow.'

That was our Cad. However, that cheeky vision of him, the first for some time, hid the ordeal he had put himself through during the previous three weeks since he'd left Ceduna.

DAY 142, 17 MAY 2011 CEDUNA TO PENONG (69KM)

Before he left Ceduna, Cad did his biggest shop so far: seventy cans of tuna, ten jars of pasta sauce, five boxes of Weet-Bix, fruit, chocolate, muesli bars, crackers and more were divided into eight food parcels, to be dropped at the Nullarbor roadhouses by a convoy of retirees who were heading to Perth for a navy reunion. Just on sunrise on 17 May 2011 he finally set off west into the vastness on his Nullarbor excursion.

It was just before 7am as he hit the road and the breaking day was freezing (4 degrees Celsius overnight). Wearing a thermal vest, T-shirt, flannelette long-sleeve shirt and woollen jumper, Cad instantly hit a gusty headwind, which was to be his biggest enemy for the next three weeks. Usually a dry north-wester, it was regularly 30 kilometres an hour into his face and sometimes double that.

Shortly after leaving Ceduna a helicopter hovered above him; at first he thought it was the police (he had advised the local constabulary of his pending departure) but the passenger opened the door and waved to him. Next day they were back, and this time they landed. Peter and Adrian, who had the job of maintaining the electricity wires along the Nullarbor, came over to chat and donate $50, saying they'd checked out his website after seeing it on his pram the day before.

Soon after Cad thought he was about to be mugged by two suspicious characters, who parked their ute well ahead and were walking towards him; one had pulled his hoodie over his head and the other spread metres to his left. 'I thought, right, it's on. I picked up a decent rock and started planning my next move. The guy to the left was smaller so I thought I'd peg the rock at his head and I'll go straight in with a mid-heel kick to the bigger guy's knee and try to drop him. My heart was pumping. As they got closer I could see they were alright, although I shouldn't have assumed that, and dropped the rock. It was Terry and Pierre from Quebec in Canada; they were driving from Melbourne to Perth and gave me $5 and asked if they could walk with me.'

The pair, university students, was putting together a film about their travels and taped their conversation as they walked. They'd driven past earlier while the helicopter was hovering, thus Cad hadn't noticed them;

they said they thought it was the police checking Andrew out.

They were the last people Andrew spoke to that day, despite walking until 7.30pm. His left knee hurt and he was suffering after cutting dead skin from his feet while in Ceduna, exposing pussy blisters underneath; the tenderness this created was a real problem on the first day of this leg.

DAY 143, 18 MAY 2011 PENONG TO WEST OF BOOKABIE (61KM)

After posting his video blog in Penong, Cad walked past a window sign that said: 'Last shop for 1000 kilometres. Warning: remote zone ahead.' He also quickly learned that the next thousand kilometres would involve dodging road trains, and the fact there was no road shoulder made that even more inconvenient with Cad having to push onto the dirt when faced with one (he was still walking into the oncoming traffic).

The convoy from Ceduna that was carrying his food parcels came past, beeping and waving. Soon after a Taiwanese cyclist, riding from Perth to Melbourne carting an oversized trailer, stopped for a chat and advised of an 'old guy' walking about 400 kilometres ahead. Andrew had been hearing about the man for a week or so and set himself the task of trying to catch him. 'The Taiwan guy reckons he only does 40 kilometres a day, so it's possible,' he wrote.

Andrew never did catch him, but later found out the man was Mike Pauly, a seventy-one-year-old arthritic who from 1 March to 26 June 2011 walked from Melbourne to Fremantle, an average of 30 kilometres a day. Mike had done the walk in reverse two years earlier and was obviously an inspirational character, and the more he heard about him, the more Andrew admired him. So many mistook Andrew for Mike, and would tell him they'd heard him on 'Macca's program' *(Australia All Over* with Ian McNamara, a popular national ABC Radio Sunday-morning program), and Cad had to do all sorts of explaining to convince people he was someone else. He spoke to Mike by telephone when he arrived in Perth but they didn't get the chance to meet.

DAY 144, 19 MAY 2011 WEST OF BOOKABIE TO YALATA (70KM)

Cad had asked his newfound friends to drop his first food parcel to what he recorded on his map as 'mobile'), presumably a Mobil roadhouse east of Yalata. He was alarmed to find on this day, while talking to a road gang at the Nundroo roadhouse, that there was indeed no such place and that the Yalata roadhouse had also been closed for years (since 2006), which meant it was 150 kilometres before the next outpost of any sort, apart from a one-man police station that was all that remained on the highway at Yalata. Cad was desperately hoping his friends had dropped his food at the police station, otherwise he faced two days without adequate food and water.

The workmen warned him not to go to the Yalata community, two kilometres from the highway, as the people there were in mourning and would be drinking; in other words, he might be heading into conflict. The headwind picked up to a good 40 kilometres an hour, adding to his feeling that this wasn't going to be a good day, although by mid-afternoon, like a switch had been turned off, the wind dropped to nothing.

So Cad was on a mission to make the Yalata police station by midnight, which would make it a 75-kilometre day. He kept walking in the pitch black, the monotony broken only by the occasional passing vehicle. He was spooked by a bonfire that he guessed was a kilometre off the road, and later by voices in the darkness.

Suddenly a beat-up old white station wagon appeared from behind him and slowed to a halt just in front, then slowly drove off. He knew they were local Indigenous youth as he'd witnessed this for three days, although in the daytime. They kept riding the brakes before stopping at the bottom of a hill about 300 metres ahead, where several men got out of the car, a scene he could just make out in the moonlight that had emerged from the clouds an hour before. I can only imagine how frightening it was to be truly in the middle of nowhere, on foot and confronted by this situation.

'I thought, here we go,' he wrote in his diary. 'Then they started yelling and screaming. I could make out a crowd of people in the moonlight beside the car and then someone started kicking into the car and there was a lot of yelling and screaming in Aboriginal. I shit myself and quickly turned off my lights and took off my high-vis. I stood in the dark for a while watching and listening and decided it wasn't safe to walk past, so I somehow managed to push Redge up a steep sandy bank on the side of the road and into the bush while I scouted around and found a way through the scrub into a clearing. I kept my light off and really couldn't see because the trees blocked the moonlight. Once in the clearing it was better, I walked through spider webs and was shitting myself that I had spiders on me.

'I was dripping wet now as the dew was really heavy, the fog was closing in and water was dripping off Redge. I pitched the tent in the dark and stretched, I didn't dare turn my light on in case I was spotted. They were just below and I could hear them carrying on all night. I was starving but couldn't cook so I had my last two cans of tuna over crackers. It was midnight before I tried to go to sleep.'

DAYS 145–146, 20–21 MAY 2011 YALATA TO NULLARBOR ROADHOUSE (99KM)

When Cad emerged from his tent at 8am he could not believe the thickness of the mist blowing in; it was like it was raining horizontally, with water dripping off his beard. As he walked up the highway he could smell a fire that appeared to be still smouldering and heard voices in the bush. He passed a sign at the junction of the road to the Yalata community which read: 'Danger, keep out, no cameras, no alcohol.' Plenty of alcohol had been consumed outside the community's boundaries.

Five kilometres further on Andrew reached the abandoned Yalata roadhouse (and had phone coverage for half a kilometre) and scouted for his food parcel with no success. He noticed the police building at the western entrance and found a line of dongas (used as police cells, he guessed). The policeman was talking to a man Cad assumed was a community leader, and Andrew interrupted to ask if any food had been dropped off; the policeman replied in the negative, quite uninterested, and said to call the Nullarbor roadhouse. Andrew did so and found that it was there – and a further 95 kilometres away.

The policeman seemed aloof as Cad tried to explain his situation: 'He really wasn't concerned that some idiot was about to go trundling off into the bush with no food. I suppose it's nothing new, he would get walkers and riders coming through here weekly, I was just another idiot passing through would have been what he was thinking.'

So to last 100 kilometres and the two days it would take him to get to the Nullarbor roadhouse, Cad had a can of spaghetti, two chocolate bars, two muesli bars, some pasta and cereal but no milk (and no baby wipes or toilet paper). The headwind became 'ferocious', which inspired him to do his video blog on Day 146 as a silent film. Flicking from page to page of the exercise book in which he recorded his diary, in the howling wind, Andrew posted this message: 'These/#@*?ing/headwinds and hills are/#@*?ing/really starting to/#@*?ing/piss me off!!'

Any vegetation more than knee high had disappeared, which gave him no cover from the wind, and he had intermittent rain all day. He walked well into the night, although only completing 40 kilometres, arriving at the roadhouse at 8.30pm – he had no choice with his food supply having been exhausted.

The experience caused him to write: 'I realised out there tonight that there is something about my brain that is different to just about everyone else. I never thought "I can't do it", never thought about giving up or anything like that. I just had to walk to that servo and that was that – I didn't have a choice because of the food situation but that didn't have anything to do with it. I was in agony, my blisters were killing and I was hobbling badly, wet socks made it worse. I stopped for a piss and saw I had blood all over the tops of my legs. I was shocked and horrified at the state of my testicles, they were raw, literally rubbed back and pissing out with blood. I had been walking in pain all night but didn't bother to check what was going on. I stopped and covered myself in Savlon cream. My legs and knees and hips were stuffed, my lower back was killing me and it was raining again but I just kept putting one foot after the other like I was going down the drive to check the mail – didn't faze me at all. I would have made a good soldier.' While I greatly admire his resilience and determination, if he was here now I'd rib him about giving himself such a rap when the seventy-one-year-old arthritis sufferer Mike Pauly was ahead of him and, as I found out, would have been in as much pain and did his entire trip in the same pair of sandshoes!

So fatigued had Cad become that he inadvertently crossed to the wrong side of the road and had a road train almost hit him from behind, causing him to leap from the bitumen a second or two before the truck reached him. The driver was among the truckies he encountered soon after at the roadhouse; Andrew apologised and explained the only reason he was walking so late was because he'd run out of food. He was soon chatting away to the truckies over dinner, and at least they told him his headlamp and high-vis vest 'lit up like a Christmas tree, which was good to know'.

DAYS 147–150, 22–25 MAY 2011 NULLARBOR ROADHOUSE TO EUCLA (197KM) – ENTERS WESTERN AUSTRALIA

Andrew's sleep was interrupted by mice getting into his food, and one even making it into his sleeping bag. It didn't put him in the best condition to battle the headwinds the next day that he estimated reached 60 kilometres an hour, literally pushing him backwards if he slowed too much. 'The wind didn't let up for a single second and was physically exhausting. My arms ached like they hadn't before and calves felt like they were going to pop. Every time I felt flat I kept thinking of Simmo today. Today would have been his twenty-fifth birthday and I posted on his wall this morning. I thought about his family a lot today and what a shit week for them having his birthday and anniversary of his death in the same week.'

As he camped that night his legs were too sore to touch but he badly needed sleep, which was difficult to get with dingoes howling near him all night. He knew he was sleep deprived next morning when he could walk only two kilometres into the driving wind before having to lie down or pass out. He laid there, his back on the rocky dirt, for about an hour before he was woken by raindrops on his face. He felt he needed sugar quickly so ate a chocolate bar and six biscuits, but more desperately he needed a day off. However it had been in his mind to walk 100 kilometres on the anniversary of Simmo's death, 28 May, and to do that he had to finish at a roadhouse so he could have a full day off to recover – that meant he was looking at finishing at Madura, three days past Eucla, his next piece of civilisation. This meant he was ignoring several lookouts over the Great Australian Bight that were so close to the highway on this stretch. Sightseeing was no longer a consideration, which was a pity.

That night Cad calculated that, despite the weather and his exhaustion, he had walked 377 kilometres on the first week of the Nullarbor section, which was his best effort since leaving Sydney.

The wind was so strong overnight he feared it was going to blow his tent out of the ground. Next day gave him some comic relief when he found a hula hoop on the side of the highway, which led to a funny video blog of him, quite impressively I might add, swinging the hoop around his hips and yelling, 'Hula-hooping on the Nullarbor, yeeew!'

He made it from Nullarbor roadhouse and crossed the South Australia–Western Australia border to Eucla in three days, starting the third in the dark on the treeless plain. Hours later, a Malaysian cyclist named Malvin who he'd met in Ceduna caught up to him and they chatted briefly, mostly whinging about the wind, before heading off; 13 kilometres further, at a rest area, he caught Malvin who was lunching with some young European backpackers.

Cad recovered his food parcel at Border Village, 11 kilometres east of Eucla, his final destination for the day, and was joined again by Malvin, who walked alongside and informed Andrew that he was averaging 7 kilometres an hour, a fair pace considering he was pushing up to 80 kilograms inside of Redge into a headwind. They camped next to each other and Andrew enjoyed the company; he had little for the next week.

DAYS 151–153, 26–28 MAY 2011 EUCLA TO PAST MADURA (182KM)

Cad had breakfast with two families he'd met the night before, and during conversation agreed to deliver a speech about his walk to the Perth primary school class of Sam, the son of Cathy and Neil Pitcher. It was a commitment he was to keep (and enjoy) and another friendship formed en route.

Next morning he'd set the alarm for 3.30am so he could get an early start and walk the 40 kilometres that would get him in the right location to be in bed early for a midnight start for his 100-kilometre stint for Simmo. It was important to him to stretch his willpower further than he ever had before on the anniversary of his mate's death and to finish at Madura, then send a video blog to be played at a fundraising tribute being held for Simmo on the Central Coast after a golf day that was coined 'Sink One For Simmo'. That part of the plan went awry; he'd had network coverage at all the roadhouses to Eucla and assumed that would continue, but he was to have no more reception until he reached Norseman, just over 700 kilometres away. He knocked over his 40 kilometres and was in his sleeping bag at 5.30pm. He wrote of the challenge he was about to set himself:

'I've got no feelings about tomorrow. I thought I'd be excited or nervous or anxious or something but nothing at all. I just want to get the hundred over and done with, and I'm never going to bother again unless I'm still walking next 28 May in which case I'll beat it. I'm not really up for 100 kilometres tomorrow physically but I'm doing it for Simmo so end of story. It's kinda not good doing it for Simmo because I know I won't stop until I hit that servo, broken leg or whatever, I'll crawl there if I have to. I suppose it's a good thing though because I'll never have a better incentive. If times get tough tomorrow I just need to think of him fucked up in hospital with tubes hanging out of him. I know my pain won't compare.'

Minutes after midnight he was dressed and ready for the assignment. After some cereal, a video blog and sparring with the thought of going back to bed, he packed up his tent and was finally away in the dark at 1.10am. He wore six layers of clothing, including thermal vest, raincoat and socks on his hands as gloves, yet he was still freezing. With his torch strapped to the solar panel on Redge and his headlamp on, he turned left on the Eyre Highway and embarked on the mission he called 'Sink 100 for Simmo'.

Every 10 kilometres he filmed the road signs for his blog. He'd walked almost 30 kilometres in the lonely darkness, while even the dingoes and snakes slept, before the sun joined him. He was halfway at 9am, right on target. With 40 kilometres to go his feet were in pain but the rest of his body was holding up surprisingly well. At the 70-kilometre mark his left knee was pinching badly every ten steps or so, which would make the leg 'go tingly and weak'. After 75 kilometres he was in trouble.

'I was whinging and making noises so I stopped. I ripped my shoes and socks off and lied on my back with my feet on the back of Redge whinging for about ten minutes. Then I got up and ate a can of spaghetti and my last two pieces of bread. I tried to rub my feet but couldn't touch them. I could see the blue bruising coming out on my left foot on the inside near my big toe. I pushed a few more biscuits into me and yelled at myself out loud – don't start whingeing now, get back into it. It took a while to get going but I found my rhythm again after a few kilometres.'

An old couple, Jack and Fran, who days earlier had stopped and given him a leg of ham and tomatoes, pulled over and took him from his painful seclusion, although they were oblivious to what he was going through. He liked Jack on account of him being the one much older person he'd met who swore more than Cad and his mates did.

As he hit the five kilometres to Madura marker at 5pm, Andrew pushed harder, inspired that the end was so close. His newfound zest was smashed when he was confronted by a hill he didn't think he had enough in him to conquer: the Madura Pass through the Hampton Tablelands, with blowholes and wonderful scenery nearby, but he wasn't in any frame of mind to explore it. He pulled out his iPod, put on the Beatles' 'Hey Jude' (I'm as surprised as anyone!) and powered forward.

He stopped under a streetlight in Madura, which at that moment was like being in the bright lights of Las Vegas after having won big on the roulette wheel, to do the final scene of his video blog. It was sixteen hours and two minutes since he'd set off (which made it an average of 6.2 kilometres per hour that day). He let out a huge, 'Yes, I did it!' and signed off with, 'That's one for you, Simmo – rest in peace, mate.' He wrote: 'I don't believe in an afterlife but I know he would be stoked if he knew.'

You would have thought Andrew might have a day off to recover, for the first time on the Nullarbor stretch, and look around at what many regard as the best stop on the highway. But no; not Cad. There was no stopping now.

DAYS 154–157, 29 MAY–1 JUNE 2011 MADURA TO PAST CAIGUNA (172KM)

After fourteen hours' sleep, Cad woke up in the same position he had been in when he entered his sleeping bag. He was devastated that the video clip he had been planning all the previous day to be shown at Simmo's fundraiser wasn't going to happen because he had no phone reception. After a quick breakfast and a shave of his bushy beard, he was back onto the bitumen on a sunny day with the temperature in the mid-twenties. He knocked out 30 kilometres before retiring to a parking bay, but there was little sleep because of the mice trying to infiltrate his food all night, even after he brought all his food (now secure in plastic containers) inside the tent.

Next day the alarm went off at 5am but it took Cad a while to get on the road. 'I had totally lost my mojo and my left knee was the worst it had been since I could remember. The flies were driving me crazy from the get-go and I had to wear my fly net all day. It was blowing a gusty north-westerner and the road turned hilly and windy ... I kept stopping and having breaks. I'd just sit there staring into space, yawning with a blank mind, staring like a zombie.' He gave up at 4.30pm after 35 kilometres.

A woman named Joy pulled her campervan over and had a chat with Cad the next day, telling him that Mike Pauly had advised her to look out for a young bloke who was trying to catch him, which Andrew found hilarious: he had been sending messages with travellers to tell Mike he was coming for him. 'She was concerned about him, she said he was doing it tough. I'm not surprised – I'm doing it tough and he's seventy-one. She said he was doing 40 kilometres a day and has been getting blurred vision, so she made him promise to see a doctor in Norseman and he is in a lot of pain from arthritis. He is trying to get home to Fremantle to meet the mayor on 26 June but Joy thinks he'll kill himself, in the state he is in.'

Andrew made it from Madura to the Caiguna roadhouse, 150 kilometres, in three and a half days. But two kilometres before the roadhouse he experienced something like a scene from a horror movie when he had to walk through a thick blanket of locusts. 'There were thousands of them, thick and fast, whipping into Redge and me and covering the road in a blanket. They all went jumping wildly into the air like a sea parting as I walked through. It didn't last long, then it turned into just hundreds and hundreds, with the odd one bouncing off my head.'

After picking up his food parcel he looked at the sign ahead that said '90 mile straight, Australia's longest straight road' and set off for the 180 kilometres to the next roadhouse, knowing he would have to rely on travellers to supplement his water supply (he filled up his two 1.5-litre bottles from the bathroom tap).

At 7pm he was exhausted and left the road to find a camp spot in the dark when, as he skull-dragged Redge through the dirt, the main axle bolt snapped and the weight dropped to the ground. Fortunately, he had bought spare bolts in Augusta and was able to fix it, although a large bird or bat kept swooping on him in the dark.

He ended his diary with this, showing how physically tough the Nullarbor had been: 'I had two massive blisters on the sole of my heel on my right foot buried under a layer of calloused skin. I got back out and grabbed and lanced it, hurt like hell and a stream of red puss came oozing out and I followed up the pain with a good splash of surgical peroxide. It brought a tear to my eye and it throbbed for the next hour. Diary and light off at ten. What a day – oh, and I couldn't walk with my head torch on because there is some other bug in plague proportions.'

DAY 158, 2 JUNE 2011 STOPPED WEST OF CAIGUNA (5KM)

Cad hit the wall, and that was no wonder. He had not had a day off since leaving Ceduna, which meant he had walked 850 kilometres in sixteen days, most of it into a torturous headwind. He'd been smashed by flies, gone through locust plagues, his left knee was in pain before he started each day but he pushed himself through for one reason only: he wanted to reach Norseman and end this challenging, desolate leg as quickly as possible.

He walked just two kilometres into a wind that had become a due westerly and then pulled to the side of the highway, sitting there bouncing rocks off the tyres of his pram. He shook himself into going on but managed just three more kilometres before he saw one of the Telstra huts that had been spaced every 50 kilometres or so along the highway. They were about six by three metres and provided a windbreak that he could not pass up. He pulled out his chair and sat, staring and thinking. He made the unusual decision of pitching his tent and inflating his mattress so he could have a day nap. He stripped down to his underpants on the windward side of the hut and dozed off, only to wake thirty minutes later in a lather of sweat and was violently sick. His choices were to lie in the tent, which was too hot in the sun but out of the wind, or outside with his flannelette shirt and long pants on, with other clothes over his hands to guard them from the relentless flies; he took the latter option.

He was starving but couldn't bring himself to eat the same bland foodstuffs he'd been having for the past two weeks. Then he remembered he had an unopened jar of Vegemite (but no bread), and he ate one and a half packets of crackers with Vegemite; it felt like a luxury because it was a taste he hadn't experienced since Adelaide. For the rest of the day he lay in his tent (by then the sun was under cloud) listening to music, watching every blog for the first 80 days of his walk until he was sick of his own voice and depressed by how much older he looked in less than three months.

'I think I'm going too hard,' he wrote. 'I feel like I am burning the candle at both ends and look like I'm going to run out of wick if I keep this up.' He studied his map and calculated it was 1400 kilometres from Norseman to Perth via Esperance and Albany. He had planned to get a tattoo in Perth, party with his good mate Kane Foley, leave on 25 July and head north, trying to reach Darwin by about 6 November so he could fly to Fiji to attend his cousin Luke's wedding. 'But that means smashing it non-stop and I don't think I have it in me.' He decided he'd just walk as far as he could until the big wet in the Top End began and sit it out in Darwin. 'But that means I wouldn't get home until the end of next year and I don't want it to take that long – all this thinking is hurting my head.'

As dark approached it was joined by light rain, so he cooked and retreated to his little tent, realising he had enough fuel to cook one more meal and enough water for one and a half days. With that thought, he fell asleep about 7pm.

DAYS 159–161, 2–5 JUNE 2011 CAIGUNA TO BALLADONIA (153KM)

When you are exhausted, in pain and numbed by the solitude of endless pacing across a treeless plain on a dead-straight road, what to others would be the smallest of incidents can widely shift your mood. Andrew was evidence of this today.

First, an older couple pulled over and satisfied Cad's pet hate of taking a photograph of him without asking. Soon after came his second pet hate – someone starting a conversation thinking he was Mike Pauly. 'Did you get your phone fixed?' a woman asked.

'What do you mean?'

'I heard you on Macca saying you had a problem with your phone.'

(Incidentally, I had contacted the program to see if they were interested in an interview with Andrew but received no reply.)

'That would be Mike – he's seventy-one years old and walking across Australia for arthritis. I'm thirty years old and walking all the way around Australia for cancer.' Later in the day another couple mistook him for Mike.

He fumed as he walked on, only to have his mood simmered by Norm and Julie, towing a caravan, who politely asked for a photo with him, made a donation and offered him some beef stew on toast and a cup of tea, which Cad struggled to hold because his fingers were numb from walking in the biting wind and rain. He wrote: 'Norm was Sri Lankan born but more Ozzie than most. He had a contagious laugh and had my frown turned upside down. He could see I was cold so gave me a flanno shift to put on instead of my wet shirt. Julie made me stew on toast then more toast and another cuppa. It stopped raining and I could feel my hands again so I made a move. It was hard work putting my wet clothes back on and wet shoes and socks and getting out of their nice little caravan. I took a pic of them before I left, and they will never know how much they made my day.'

The next day he had another experience that lifted his spirits – a giggly Japanese woman. The interaction went like this:

'You walking where?'

'Around Oz.'

(Squeal and laugh.) 'How long you walk?'

'One hundred and sixty days.'

(Squeal.) 'Where you start?'

'Sydney.'

(Squeal.) 'Where you finish?'

'Sydney.'

(Squeal.) 'Can I take picture?'

'No worries.'

(Squeal.) 'I give you Japanese candy.' She then pointed Cad to the banged-up front left of her car. 'Kangaroo.' (Laugh.) Then she pointed to the right side. 'Two kangaroos.'

Cad was left pissing himself laughing after she drove off. Andrew encountered his own foe soon after, a large hawk that twice swooped within two metres of him and hovered above before flying away.

DAYS 162–167, 6–10 JUNE 2011 (DAY 167 DAY OFF) BALLADONIA TO NORSEMAN (192KM), THEN A REST DAY

Andrew reached Fraser Range Station on Day 163, the day after had his first full rest day in more than three weeks. He was walking in driving rain, his numb fingers cupped around his testicles for kilometres, such was the pain from chafing. He tried to apply his trusty 3B cream but his fingers were too frozen and powerless to open the lid, which stunned him, so he almost gave up. Finally it opened but he couldn't squeeze out the cream.

'I finally got it open but it was nearly empty so it needed a squeeze,' he wrote. 'I could go through the motion of squeezing but didn't have enough strength to pull it off – I lost it and dropped to my knees.

This was single-handedly the worst moment of the trip. Physically and mentally exhausted, I felt a tidal wave of emotion flood over me. I thought I was about to start bawling my eyes out. I scrunched my face up, and fuck knows why or how but I started laughing out aloud in hysterics like a mad man – I wanted to cry, I had the scrunched up face but there I was laughing – I scared myself. I thought I truly was losing it. I stood on the tube and there was a big line of 3B across the road. I rolled my pants down and wiped it off the road and onto my nuts, still laughing.

'I headed down the road, and what seemed like 5 kilometres later I saw the sign "Fraser Range 1 kilometre" pointing down a dirt track. Another fucking kilometre! I screamed into the howling wind and ran for what seemed like ten minutes. My throat was burning from all the yelling, every step was like I had lead shoes on. I was getting bogged and kept screaming the whole time. I kept going to cry but was laughing instead like a delusional crazy mental health patient. I stopped to kick a tree until my foot hurt. I just wanted to lie down and die.'

Then he saw another sign that said it was still 800 metres to the station. 'I didn't have any energy for anger, just a silly whimpering laugh. It was like I had smashed my funny bone.'

He arrived at the station mid-afternoon; it was still raining heavily. After a prolonged shower to get his body temperature up (even though the water was lukewarm at best), a seat by the fire in the camp kitchen and a bowl of soup, he slept like a baby, deciding that if it was still raining the next day he was not going anywhere. It rained and he didn't.

Most of the next day he lounged around his cabin reflecting, thinking how he had gone 'from hero to zero' in a couple of days. 'It seems like yesterday I was writing how much of a good soldier I would be but yesterday I was a useless bag of shit.' He decided there would be no more rushing; if he missed Perth and catching up with his mate Toady, who was visiting Kane, well, that was bad luck; maybe he would have to miss Luke and Kristal's wedding in Fiji too, and perhaps he might sit out the wet season in Bali or Thailand, where it would be cheaper to live than Darwin and he could get more tattooing done cheaper too.

He walked the 101 kilometres to Norseman over the next two days. About 25 kilometres from the town, he had reception for the first time in seventeen days and his phone went berserk with voice and text messages from people worried about him. 'I sat there rolling my eyes in disbelief. I'd put a photo of my Nullarbor plan on Facebook at Ceduna saying twenty-eight days [to Norseman], so fair enough if it was thirty days or something.'

About 5 kilometres out of town, three girls who lived on Lord Howe Island stopped to donate money. They asked where he was walking to, and he said straight to the Norseman pub. One said she'd buy him a beer – thus Cad's video blog comment about a date with a hot redhead. He'd also promised himself a pizza and a decent cabin rather than a campsite. Five beers later he had to skip the pizza and rush to the caravan park before the office closed.

A shower, a few rum and Cokes, a night socialising with the three girls and their mate, and Cad had settled back into civilisation. It was like all the trauma of the previous twenty-five days hadn't happened.

7

NO WINTER WONDERLAND

The scenery along the Great Australian Bight on the southern West Australian coastline is spectacular in places – if you stop long enough to take it all in. I wish Andrew had. But typically, he was there at the absolute wrong time of the year, the depth of winter.

He only had himself to blame, of course, and during this stretch he actually wrote in his diary that maybe he should have walked anticlockwise. This would have put him in Queensland during the last month of summer, but he would have at least encountered much more favourable conditions across the Nullarbor and through Western Australia, the most telling being that the headwinds he had to battle would have been at his back!

Cad was warned by travellers on the Nullarbor that he'd picked the wrong time to go to Esperance then hug the coastline to Albany, where I planned to meet him for a night and day while having a break from some work in Perth. They were right; it was as tough a period on the road as any, with the biting wind, constant rain, low temperatures, heavy fog some mornings, and hill after hill.

He had little respite from the rain for the four and a half weeks it took him to walk from Norseman to Perth, including a detour to Margaret River and another to Busselton. This stretch certainly was a mix of the tough business of walking around the country, and the pleasure of catching up with friends new and old, which he did in earnest in Albany, Denmark, Margaret River, Busselton and Perth. This put him further behind his original schedule but provided what in many ways were productive interruptions to the taxing existence his feet and mind were forced to endure on the bitumen.

DAYS 168–174, 12–18 JUNE 2011 NORSEMAN TO ESPERANCE (183KM), THEN TWO REST DAYS

After a day off in Norseman, Cad was back on the highway heading due south to Esperance, on my recommendation as it boasts some of the most beautiful coastline and beaches Chris and I came across during our trip around Australia in 2006. He hadn't been walking long when he came across a twenty-seven-year-old Chinese man named Richard Xutan, accompanied by a rather eccentric seventy-one-year-old American, 'Hutch' (F.A. Hutchinson), who had been cycling for six years and had met Richard in China four years earlier. They'd been riding together ever since, even taking on the Himalayas. They briefly shared stories and took snaps of each other and then went in opposite directions to continue their different, yet equally extraordinary, journeys.

Adam Mobbs, a mate whose family ran a coffee shop in Queensland, contacted Andrew the same day asking if he had any promotional posters he could use so he could take donations at the shop. This was the prompt for Cad to buy twenty plastic donation boxes to be installed at various locations. He asked me to organise posters to accompany them, which I did through a mate at *Big League* magazine, Craig Lough-lin-Smith. Within weeks Cad had collection boxes in New South Wales, Queensland and Western Australia through various contacts. He paid the costs himself.

On the day he wanted to walk 52 kilometres to reach Esperance before dark, Cad was greeted with a 40-kilometre-an-hour headwind after hardly sleeping all night due to the combination of his tent vibrating crazily in the wind and the full moon that was like a torchlight pointing at his eyes. He was having his morning 'smoko' break when a dear old girl called Trudy pulled over and gave Andrew a large umbrella. He was already carting a shotgun someone had given him, as a souvenir not a weapon to defend himself I hope (he'd decided to send it to his mate Kane Foley in Perth when he got to Esperance), and thought, 'Great; more surplus items I'll never need.' Not fifteen minutes later it started raining and he pulled over, pointed Redge into the gusts, put the brolly on his lap, resting on the handlebars, then opened up a packet of biscuits and thought, 'How good is this? Why didn't I think of this earlier?'

He did make it to Esperance that day, despite the trying conditions, but not before dark. He called for a pick-up pizza twenty minutes out of town and crashed in a dormitory at the local hostel, where his food parcel was waiting behind the counter. After eating, he had his first shower in six days. His roommate came in later and proceeded to tell Cad his life story. 'I was so over it I got up and turned the light out mid-sentence – he sucked the light right out of me. I then woke up to Gary snoring like a chainsaw. I sat up and listened to my iPod full pecker, but every time a song would finish I'd hear the chainsaw.'

Andrew shone his mobile phone's light on his roomie, who would stir before starting his snoring again. 'Finally he dropped it from a chainsaw level to a raspy wheeze, and I reckon I got to sleep about two or three o'clock.'

Those who have heard Cad snore (yes, at chainsaw levels at times) will see the humour in this. Nevertheless, he booked his own room for the next night.

DAYS 175–186, 19–30 JUNE 2011 ESPERANCE TO ALBANY (496KM)

Cad had a couple of days' rest in Esperance with little sightseeing (which was such an opportunity lost), however he was featured in the local newspaper and caught up with 'Crawf' (presumably his last name was Crawford) and Sue, a couple he'd met on the Nullarbor, and introduced a passing Taiwanese motorbike rider to his first taste of bourbon and Coke with poor results (for the other guy – we can only imagine how convincingly Andrew would have led him astray). Back into the grind he was instantly met with a howling westerly as usual, the weather report estimating winds of 35 to 40 kilometres per hour for three days straight! Not only did that make walking against the force tiring, camping in such a howler was not easy. 'Got woken up at the crack of dawn because the tent was shaking like anything – the massive gums on the other side of the dirt track were making an awful racket with the leaves rustling, it was deafening. Had to fight the tent like a wild animal to pack it up.'

Walking up hills was easier than reaching the crest, when the wind would push him backwards. Add the intermittent rain and he could muster only an average of 29 kilometres a day over the three days. Plus, his mates the mozzies were back in force of an evening; Cad claimed they 'were not interested in foreplay' when he stopped at his campsite, so quick were they to attack his face, arms and legs.

Just to ensure he was having the best of nights, a tent pole snapped and no matter how hard he tried to wire or tape it together it remained limp in the wind, popping a hole in the tent in the process. To make matters worse, he couldn't get his pegs in the hard ground so, with rain stopping and starting and the wind picking up mid-evening, only his body weight kept his tent from blowing away, something that he was to repeat several times before finally buying a new tent in Albany.

Next day Cad came across a young Japanese man cycling from Perth around Australia and back to Perth. In a scene resembling a pantomime, Cad tried to relay to him, by pictures and sign language, that Norseman had the last supermarket for 1200 kilometres and that the Nullarbor roadhouses did not like providing water. They worked out they would pass each other again in the Northern Territory. It's incredible how many of these sorts of scenes Andrew experienced.

When Andrew camped just past Munglinup he had yet another experience of drunken, abusive young men carrying on all night and slamming car doors just metres from his tent. When he was leaving the next morning two of them were passed out in a car, and a third 'was poking at a big stump caked with dirt, smouldering away; I think he was more startled than me. I gave him the death stare and ignored whatever he said.'

After hours of failing to gain any real momentum, Cad came across a dead kangaroo and tried to prepare for a video blog that he always had in the back of his mind: dressing the dead roo with a hat and shirt and propping him up to have a chat, but the roo was too big to move into position. Yeah, I know – warped, but it would have been funny! (He did enact the scene months later – with Josh Simpson, who by then had joined him.)

It took Andrew a week to walk the 281 kilometres from Esperance to Fitzgerald, an average of 40 kilometres a day despite the unforgiving headwind and the hills. He lifted that to over 43 kilometres from Fitzgerald to Albany.

I'd called to advise him that my mother was in hospital and having tests, which the family feared could be cancer. He called her while she was in Gosford Hospital and chirped, 'Don't cark it on me before I get home, Gran,' which Mum thought was hilarious (Andrew was the only one who could make her laugh with such insensitive comments) and told everyone about it for weeks. Andrew recorded: 'She said, "Oh, Andrew, that's a long time away" in a very unconfident tone.' He was close to his gran and was obviously worried, but after I'd texted him to say it was just a cyst, he recorded: 'I had thought it was the Big C, she's 80-something. I really hope she's still kicking around when I get home.' Fate is terribly cruel; she's the one still kicking now and turned ninety in December 2014.

The next day I saw Andrew for the first time in months. I'd driven from Perth on a day off from the national schoolboys under-15 rugby league championships where I'd been working. I diverted to the road that went east towards Esperance on my way into town and came across him, walking in the rain and wind at a fair pace about 8 kilometres out of town. I screamed out to startle him: 'Hey, mate, are you Cad, the bloke walking around Australia?' The reply was a cheeky smile and 'the bird'.

It took ages for him to get into town (he huddled out of the rain for a while in a bus shelter), and I went to meet him at the top of the main street, by which time he'd cracked a six-pack of beer. I could not believe the pace at which he was walking as we headed to the motel – I had trouble keeping up, and I wasn't pushing a pram weighed down with gear.

It's strange when I think of it now; while I was in awe of what he'd been doing and knew how different his life had been for the previous six months, we talked like it was just a social catch-up, as if he'd been on a few weeks' holiday. Now that I've read his diaries, I see that I never understood how different his life had been until that moment we set eyes on each other. We had a meal together at an Italian restaurant, a few beers and a good chat; he was pissed and talkative, which I liked, actually. We then headed off to a pub on the bay, where I left him at probably 10pm to enjoy some younger company while I went to bed. Esperance was like being back in England: cold, wet and windy, with the many old buildings down near the port.

That was the last meal we ever had together by ourselves, and my last good block of time spent with just Andrew. Next day, after we went shopping for a new tent (he got a good half-price bargain for $660, most of the money provided by his gran and mate Chad), he did interviews for two newspapers and washed his clothes at a laundromat. I headed off late in the afternoon, back to Perth.

About an hour and a half into my drive, it hit me that I didn't even get a photograph of us together, and I had a compelling urge to go back and get a snap taken, like some form of guilt had hit me. So I called and told Cad I was turning around – which was greeted with his understandable disbelief. I hit town about 6.30pm, from memory, and we had a feed and a couple of beers at the pub and got someone to take the shot. I went back to the motel and grabbed a few hours' sleep, setting the alarm for 1am for the four-and-a-half-hour drive back to Perth. Cad still hadn't made it back to the motel when I left.

That photograph is even more special to me now. My sister Alison snapped one of us poolside in Fiji four months later, which is the only photo taken of just the two of us after that. You can imagine how I felt when I read his diary notes about it: 'The old man rang and said he was going to come back to get a pic of us because he had forgotten to get one. He had just driven for two to three hours – fucking keen! I was thinking, "Why the hell?" but I guess it will be a good one to stick on the wall if I get pancaked by a road train.' In relation to the previous night, his diary also had the following insight: 'I remember waking up to the old man snoring like anything, but he said I'd been going at it all night – like father, like son!'

Andrew had the next two days off in cold, windy, wet Albany, socialising handsomely, as was his way. He admitted he 'felt like shit' when it was time to resume his daily exercise routine.

DAYS 190–206, 4–20 JULY 2011 ALBANY TO PERTH (580KM), THEN TWO WEEKS IN PERTH

It was with great reluctance that Cad went back into the cold, wet wilderness to head north-west to Perth after three days and nights relaxing, rejoicing and drinking plenty in Albany. He walked the 37.5 kilometres to Youngs Siding that day, in typically terrible weather, then on to Denmark. But he struggled to get going the next day, and stopping for 'smoko' he wondered what the hell he was doing in such bitter weather. So he broke his golden rule and doubled back to catch up with an English girl he had met, a bit of a free spirit like him; she had travelled many parts of Europe and was on a working holiday in Australia. But he knew he was only delaying the inevitable and woke himself next morning from his brief period of dispirit to push forward towards Margaret River where he'd have his next 'lay day'.

Some long, tough days came on this stretch but he enjoyed the scenery through the forests of huge kauri trees near Walpole, just over 400 kilometres from Perth. It rained every day for a week, became foggy at night and he had to sleep in gloves, socks, long pants, thermal vest and flannelette shirt – all inside his sleeping bag. But he found the new tent luxurious in size – 'you could kick a footy around in this!'

A further struggle came when he accidentally snapped his earphones so he couldn't listen to music while he walked, causing him to think more deeply about his life as he stepped it out. 'I already know my life has changed forever,' he wrote, and he tortured his mind over his future – whether to settle down; whether to keep the Toyota Hilux ute that he'd left to be modified into a show car but was guzzling too much of his money while off the road; whether to 'rip hard'; thinking about what Simmo would do if he was alive. In the end he decided he was going to enjoy himself more on the rest of the walk, and in particular party hard in Perth.

Just south of Manjimup a guy called Martin Smith pulled over and donated $100, telling Cad he'd organise a better sign to go on the pram and that he'd like to walk a day with him and maybe organise more fundraising. Martin owned Orbit Drilling, providing services to the mining industry. Martin did walk with Cad for a few kilometres north of Perth. (I was stunned the next year, when he greeted me at Cad's hospital bedside in Chiang Mai.)

Andrew had asked me to send him some going-out clothes for Perth but he found the St Vincent de Paul store at Manjimup to be a fashion treasure-trove, leaving with a V-neck sweater and a jumper for $3, to be accessorised with a hat and scarf for $7 at the next town – he was now styled to go out in Perth, he reckoned! While he was taking in the scenery that afternoon, a two-centimetre diameter stone was spat from a car tyre straight at his face, hitting him on the bridge of the nose and 'dropping me like a sack of potatoes'. It drew blood but amazingly didn't split his face open. 'An inch to the left or right and I would have copped it in the eye, and two inches down and it would have been missing teeth, it was travelling way too fast to react.'

Cad was going to walk late into the night to Donnybrook when he came across a local called Reen at Balingup, who enticed him in with a pot of hot soup and a few beers, a hot shower and a bed for the night. Reen and his partner, Danielle, had been renovating the old picture theatre in Balingup for years, making it a comfortable home, and Reen had Andrew in stitches telling him tales about how the place used to be a hippie town in the 1970s and 80s. Working as an electrician, he would go to residential jobs and be greeted by people in the nude or only in knickers, with boobs on display, or dressed in sugar sacks.

Cad took a turn off the main route to Perth, the South Western Highway, heading instead towards Margaret River, putting in one 72-kilometre fourteen-hour day (Balingup to Ludlow), which did little for his dodgy left knee. He was in two minds whether put himself through the grief of having to walk into Margaret River, adding an extra 91 kilometres, just to have a couple of days' break and get on the grog, but the cavalier part of his brain won the argument. On the way in, another mate from the Central Coast who had moved to Western Australia, 'Hogsie', pulled up in his truck after sighting Andrew randomly and asked him to catch up in Busselton that evening. Cad ended up staying the night and was dropped back in the morning to where he'd finished walking. It was just another example of how many people from the east coast had crossed the nation to work for good money in booming Western Australia.

The next day, hungover, Cad walked the 28.5 kilometres into Margaret River, where a new pair of sponsored Nike shoes awaited him at the post office, replacing those he'd walked over 2500 kilometres in. Unbelievably, while walking through town, he heard someone yell, 'Hey, Cad!' It was another mate he had not seen for a long while, 'Wickham', whom he'd met while he and Jaime were touring Europe in a campervan; the four of them (including Wickham's partner, Kate) had travelled together for weeks. Kate was from Margaret River and was visiting her father, who still lived in town, so they drove Andrew around for the afternoon to see the coastline and wineries before watching the sun set over the ocean at Gracetown. It was great that he was finally allowing himself some sightseeing.

Cad did not compile any diary notes from that day in Margaret River until well after he'd left Perth, however he did record his daily kilometres. He took three days to walk the 142 kilometres from Boyanup, where he had left the highway for his Margaret River detour, to arrive in Warnbro, just south of Rockingham, on 19 July, which was the scheduled day for him to catch up with his mate Kane Foley, who was living in Perth beachside suburb of Scarborough while working and studying marine biology.

The only video blog Cad made during this fortnight was at Karrinyup Primary School, where Cad honoured his commitment to speak at the school of Sam Pitcher, from the family he'd met on the Nullarbor. He was very nervous about it but he really enjoyed the experience. On the blog (Day 215) he explains that myelodysplasia is a rare type of cancer that took his mate's life, and he was raising money on his walk to help find a cure. He put up his tent in front of the pupils, drew a laugh when he said he walked twelve days without having a shower, and answered many questions like 'what do you eat', 'where do you sleep', 'do your legs get sore' and 'how do you go to the toilet'. His response of digging a hole in the bush drew the biggest laugh of the day.

Kane and Simmo's brother Josh Simpson, who had headed to Perth to look for work and to make the almighty gesture of walking for weeks with Andrew, told me they had a ball with Cad during that period, and it was as hard for Kane to see Cad go as it was for him to say goodbye and resume his very different life. Other mates from the Central Coast who were around there at the time (most working) included 'Porky' (Ben Forster), Garlo (Scott Garlick), 'Toady' (Nathan Harrison) and Billy Holloway. There were plenty of photos on Andrew's computer to bear witness that he had a ball and partied hard for most of his two weeks in Perth – harder than anyone else – before he reluctantly confronted highway life again.

8

SIMMO JOINS THE PARTY

The first 'celebrity walker' – as Andrew tagged any family or friends who accompanied him during his Oz On Foot venture – joined him thirteen days north of Perth. And it was not just anyone from back home but Josh Simpson, older brother of Chris, to whom Andrew had dedicated the walk, and who had been his partner in spirit for the many tough months since the previous Christmas.

Josh joined Cad for twenty days, walking for thirteen full days and 409 kilometres during that period before enjoying four days at Monkey Mia. Cad dropped his daily kilometres to ease Josh in, doing an average of 25 kilometres a day for Josh's first five days to Geraldton before picking it up to 35 kilometres for his last eight days – a very good effort for Josh, who may have been young and fit but wasn't conditioned to that repetitive strain on his legs.

It was not only an emotional pilgrimage for Josh but also a massive change in existence for Andrew, who, in between letting his hair down with other 'crew' as he passed through the cities and larger towns, had a set routine that had become compulsive, and had become highly strung after seven months of solitude and body wear and tear. They struck a strong bond and good friendship from almost three weeks of this shared experience, and it gave Cad a massive boost to have someone by his side he could confide in, have fun with and who could experience his highs and lows. For Josh to cross the country and join Cad's trek was an extreme show of support, and another intrinsic event that left Andrew bequeathing such a legacy on so many people as well as strengthening an indelible link between the Simpsons and Cadigans.

While Josh was Oz On Foot's first 'celebrity walker', they came across a real celebrity during his second day on the job with Cad, who wouldn't even have realised this if Josh hadn't been there.

They were about 110 kilometres short of Geraldton and had decided to 'pump it' to get to the hamlet of Springfield for the evening. As Andrew explained in his diary, a tall, middle-aged Aboriginal man wearing glasses hopped out of a four-wheel drive vehicle. Cad greeted him with, 'How ya going, mate?'

'Where have you come from?' the man asked. 'You raising money?'

'Yeah,' Cad replied, and told him he'd raised over $25,000 for the Cancer Council since leaving Sydney. A $50 note appeared. 'Do you want a receipt to claim it as a tax deduction?' Andrew asked.

'Na, mate, don't worry.'

'What's your name?' Andrew asked.

'Ernie.'

Cad had no idea that the man who stopped was the well-known television presenter and actor Ernie Dingo. In his defence, this would have been the last place he'd expect to come across anyone famous, but Josh couldn't believe Cad hadn't recognised one of Australia's most recognisable figures. Neither could Cad, once the penny had dropped.

'Josh, who was standing behind me, said, "Don't you know who it is? It's Ernie Dingo." "Oh, fucking hell," slipped right out of my mouth. Ernie asked Josh where he was from and he said Sydney, and Josh asked him where he was from and he said he lived up the road and was always from around here. He said hooroo and I shook his hand and said, "Nice to meet you," and so did Josh, and he drove off. I said to Josh: "I'm such a fuckwit, I can't believe I didn't recognise Ernie Dingo." Oh well, it was the first famous person I've met.'

Josh wasn't Cad's only walking companion north of Perth; a couple of other 'Coasties' joined them briefly too. The landscape, weather and environment from Perth to Broome, over 2200 kilometres that took Andrew three months to travel, was such a contrast to what he had experienced in the month and a half from the end of the Nullarbor to Western Australia's capital.

There were no diary entries from Margaret River to a week after Andrew left Perth, so I'll resume the story from there.

DAYS 219–225, 2–8 AUGUST 2011 WARNBRO TO WEDGE ROCK (215KM)

Cad caught the train back to Warnbro, where he'd aborted his walk before his planned few days in Perth that turned into almost two weeks. It took him two days to walk back to Kane's place at Scarborough, and he headed from there to Nowergup, on the northern fringe of Perth's expanding limits. There he had a day off before taking a further three days to cover the 121 kilometres to Wedge Rock. Andrew resumed his diaries from the day he headed towards Cervantes, famous for its remarkable rock formations, the Pinnacles.

DAYS 226–227, 9–10 AUGUST 2011 WEDGE ROCK TO JURIEN BAY (73KM)

After passing large sand dunes before the Cervantes turn-off, Cad called me to ask if I thought a visit to the Pinnacles was definitely worth the detour off Indian Ocean Drive near the end of a 50-kilometre day. It was, I relayed in the strongest terms, so he headed in and recorded that he was duly impressed with the unusual jagged limestone formations sprouting out of the sandy earth just a few hundred metres from the residential expansion in the town. He described the Pinnacles as 'a big sandhill full of pointy rocks'.

Next day the biggest issue he had to confront was that he felt he had lost too much muscle tone and had become 'more flat-chested than a twelve-year-old girl'. So he decided to make sit-ups and push-ups a daily morning, lunchtime and evening ritual, and to increase his protein intake. When he reached Jurien Bay and did a shop he scanned what was written on everything he considered buying and loaded up on fruit and a bag of pistachio nuts, and sculled a litre of milk. He did 250 sit-ups and 100 push-ups next morning and was up to 500 repetition exercises in a session by the following week. He used fifteen-litre water bottles as weights and would do curls with large rocks and whatever else he could find as temporary gym equipment.

Another routine that also returned to his daily grind was fighting the mosquitos as the landscape changed to saltbush. Next day he heard from Josh and discussed last-minute preparations; he was looking forward to the company. He wrote: 'I never really knew Josh before Simmo died and only met him for the first time at the wake. But I think we'll be mates forever. He is a good bloke.'

So vain had he become about his appearance that Andrew called several beauticians in Geraldton, trying to find someone who would do laser hair-removal treatment. 'What a punce – bahahaha – walking around Oz and getting laser hair removal on the way!'

DAYS 228–230, 11–13 AUGUST 2011 JURIEN BAY TO NORTH OF LEEMAN (71KM)

Looking for a suitable campsite, Cad went off to the west two kilometres north of Leeman and found a little settlement of fishing shacks and holiday huts, all uninhabited, scattered around sand dunes just off the beach. He found it quite strange in the dark. 'It was mega eerie. I thought tonight might be the night I see my first ghost, and I was prepared for it. I was saying to myself ,"Don't freak if you see one..."'

He found a grassy patch to pitch his tent but had little reception so walked to the top of a hill where it was good and sat replying to emails and Facebook messages. One was from Jacinta Ridge at the Leukaemia Foundation, who he had contacted about being his nominated charity as he was not happy with the lack of contact or support he was getting from the Cancer Council of New South Wales. So, as he sat on a cement slab overlooking the Indian Ocean in the solitude of his own company – there were no ghost sightings that night – he began what became a wonderful relationship with the foundation for which he would raise over $40,000 in the next year.

The next night he spoke to another mate from the Central Coast, Ben 'Porky' Forster, who was driving Josh from Perth to join him. They were all going to do some fishing and camp overnight together before Ben headed back to Perth. Knowing he would be unlikely to have phone reception when they were to arrive that evening, Cad had to devise a way to notify them where he would be. So he told 'Porky' that about 32 kilometres north of the service station at Leeman he'd leave a sign of some sort on the side of the road, pointing down a track to the beach, where he'd have a fire burning.

Cad had a spring in his step when he started the day, his mood only getting better when a tour coach pulled over. A 'hot French chick' hopped out and presented him with a packet of biscuits, while an English backpacker gave him a six-pack of cold beer. However, his mood blackened soon after, and the day was an example of how vulnerable Cad's character had become after such a long time by himself, when he received a text from Josh saying they would not be coming up to meet him until the next morning. Cad's mood sank – he was so looking forward to company that night. So there was only one thing for it: he drank five beers in just over an hour, noticed the sky had turned grey, walked only as far as the next dirt track that headed off to the coastline, and put up his tent just as it started to rain.

DAYS 231–235, 14–18 AUGUST 2011 NORTH OF LEEMAN TO GERALDTON (126KM)

Porky and Josh left Perth very early the next morning and had gone past the designated meeting point by the time Andrew made it there, but they doubled back and found him. The sight of mates from home, who he'd spent time in Perth with, made him instantly ecstatic, and the provision of bacon, sausages, tomatoes, eggs and onion for the best fry-up Cad had had on the trip soon eradicated any hard feelings that were pent up. After failing to find a suitable fishing spot because of all the weed in the water, Porky headed back to Perth (a three-hour drive), and Cad and Josh began their three-week duopoly on the road; 231 days into Andrew's sojourn, a period during which Simmo had been in Cad's thoughts daily, his brother was now in his company daily in the most compelling get-to-know-you environment either of them would experience.

Cad was conscious that he was now 'match fit' after close to 200 days of walking, but it had taken him eight days from the start before he could muster 30 kilometres a day regularly, so he gave Josh an 'easy' fifteen-kilometre day first-up. Simmo Snr was keen to be up to the task and not slow Cad down, but Andrew could tell he was buggered at the end of the day.

Josh had an interesting first-day experience of life in these remote parts when they went off the highway down a dirt track looking for some water near some fishing shacks. When they yelled out to see if anyone was about, they were greeted rather dubiously by Barry, 'a hermit', who said he was the caretaker of the cray-fishing shacks. 'I quizzed him about who owns these shacks and whether they were owned at all – it was hard to get a straight answer from Barry – he was eccentric to say the least. He had been there sixteen years by himself and lived off tank water and had a couple of little crappy solar panels for lights. I'm not sure exactly what being a crayfisherman-shack caretaker entails – does he go and do maintenance on the rest of the shacks? I just think he's a hermit. I wonder when was the last time he'd spoken to anyone?'

They found a camp spot next to a swampy area, lit a fire, then shared Cad's new tent. Josh took seconds to fall asleep, and in another great irony Cad said he couldn't doze off because of Josh's foghorn-level snoring. It would have been a stereo recital later in the night, although it took hours for Cad to get to sleep as his head was spinning with thoughts about the usual perplexity of his life.

Josh graduated to a 27-kilometre day in the rain next day; midmorning they'd left Indian Ocean Drive for the Brand Highway, where they crossed the path of a middle-aged Queanbeyan man who was riding a pushbike from Darwin through Western Australia back to Canberra. Andrew described him as an 'odd character' who, he found, drank a 'goon' of port every couple of days to break the boredom; they sat and had a midday slurp each.

The next person they met was Ernie Dingo, and so followed Cad's embarrassing moment; I won't say it was the most embarrassing moment during the walk, because it sounds like there were many of those when he was partying too hard. Josh's second night included pouring rain and road trains roaring past less than ten metres away – welcome to life on the highway.

First stop when the boys reached Dongara was a doctor's surgery, because Andrew's 'nuts' were giving him hell again with a rash from the sweating; he was prescribed more cream but also some sleeping tablets, as he told the doctor he been suffering insomnia.

They stayed at a backpackers' hostel that night and mixed with a group of shearers and wool classers, who let the boys borrow some pushbikes to do their shopping and get around Dongara and the adjoining Port Denison. A competitive sprint race home duly developed that left them both panting for breath!

The next night was spent in the company of Bill Holloway, another mate from the Coast, and his mate Mitch; they had driven from Perth for a weekend in Geraldton as part of their rigger's course. They ate together (and drank plenty) at a campsite just short of Greenough, and Billy did the video blog in front of the blazing fire.

Next day Billy joined the boys a few kilometres from Geraldton and did a 'celebrity walk' with them in his thongs. Cad did have the laser hair removal treatment on his chest, stomach and shoulders at 'Gero' for $350, which either showed how much he hated body hair or how vain he was. He was going to get his ear re-pierced but thought the tattooist looked 'a bit dodgy' – and he would surely know! Two nights partying with Bill and Josh and others followed, which had its impact on Josh; when he and Bill were wrestling back at the room Josh managed to injure his knee.

DAYS 238–245, 21–28 AUGUST 2011 GERALDTON TO OVERLANDER ROADHOUSE (283KM)

On the way out of Geraldton on the Sunday morning, Cad and Josh came across the 'Twin River Guard', who, their website says, are 'local re-enactors who recreate, experiencing and living history, predominantly focusing on the European historical era from the beginning of the Viking Migration Period to the end of the medieval period'. Or, as Andrew described them, 'a few crew dressed up in Robin Hood shit in a little park, banging swords together'. He asked to put on a medieval helmet and armour, grabbed 'an axe on a big stick' for a photo and filmed one of the locals saying, 'Hi, we are the Twin River Guard and you're watching Oz On Foot.'

After a 28-kilometre walk north of Geraldton, both boys were suffering from crook knees and had to tap into the anti-inflammatory tables Andrew had been prescribed. They recovered well enough, or went through the pain barrier well enough at least, to record a 37.4kilometre day.

Redge was the heaviest it had been when they left Geraldton and was tough to push, especially uphill; they thought of ditching some water as it added the most weight, but decided against it as the weather was warming up and there was no civilisation for more than 200 kilometres between Binnu and the Overlander roadhouse, just short of the turn-off to Denham and Monkey Mia. They made it to Binnu in the pitch black.

Next day, the boys had stopped at a water tank literally in the middle of nowhere when an old bushie with a weathered hat and long grey beard called John joined them, and they shared one of his 'rollies'. He offered to recite one of his original poems, called 'I'm a Country Man', which they filmed. It went like this:

I'm just a country man; they reckon I've got brains
'cos I can tell the difference between when it's dry and when it rains
City people think they're smart, they watch those TV screens
To find out when it's gunna rain, it's the silliest thing I've seen

They also like eating food and spending money at a shop
I just grow it in the soil, when's this silliness going to stop
But they're really not all that stupid, because all money comes from land
But it goes to all those big buildings that those city folks demand
Yes, I'm a country man; I can tell you when it rains
'Cos me hair gets all wet and it stimulates me brain.

As John recited the last two lines, he withdrew his hat and poured half the contents of his water bottle over his head, to the boys' great amusement, then hopped in his car and waved goodbye without uttering another word, which saw Cad and Josh crack up with laughter.

The same day Cad filmed his long-desired blog with 'Skippy' the kangaroo. He and Josh propped up a roadside dead roo and did the skit where Cad tells poor old Skip it's dangerous around these roads of a night with the road trains and he should get a light. Then he offers him a beer and says, 'This'll fix you up; my shout,' and Skippy downs a stubby and then burps.

They had originally planned to get to Monkey Mia for three to four days' break on a Monday but decided they were going to 'leg it' and be there for the weekend, which in the end meant they covered 203 kilometres in five days, including one 50-kilometre effort.

As they were setting up camp down a dirt track they saw a flashlight heading their way and knew they were going to have company; they nervously waited and were not overjoyed to see a man cautiously walk in with a loaded double-barrel shotgun over his shoulder. Ben proved to be friendly and they ended up relocating to his camp spot (he slept in a swag), which had the benefit of a raging fire and ample beer supply. Ben's wife had just had a baby in her hometown of Busselton and he was driving back by himself to Port Dampier, where they now lived.

With donations particularly lean for a few days, Josh came up with the idea of walking with their shirts off and drawing on their backs with the permanent marker Cad had stored away; Josh had a big dollar sign on his back and Andrew's tanned back had 'walking for cancer' artistically carved on it. It didn't prove a very successful advertising medium.

Next day they crept into wildflower territory, with the foliage so thick it looked like 'a big colourful white and yellow carpet' accompanied by thousands of little brown lizards sunbaking on the side of the road that would run into the bush as they passed.

Andrew was enjoying Josh's company enormously and it showed in the video blogs he posted. To have someone to relate to and break the monotony of his endless unaccompanied hours was one thing, but the fact that it was Simmo's brother, who he struck such an instant rapport with during his time in Perth, was something much more.

Yet he also felt uneasy and agitated at times, knowing that the root of it was that having continual company on the road had interrupted what had become an almost compulsive daily routine of which he had been the sole master, and he couldn't come to grips with why he struggled with that so much. He felt regretful that he would have appeared narky to Josh at times. He wrote: 'I have been a cranky whinger for the past two weeks but I guess I just notice I am because I've got someone to whinge to. I guess I have been on the road for so long I've become stuck in my ways and tiny little insignificant things like not washing up properly or sand in my tent or not packing the pram or tent properly just drive me insane and niggle at me, and Josh doesn't and never will understand. I know I should have got over it while he is with me but that's all I've got out here, my shitty little routine and ways. It's definitely a massive regret as I sit here and write this – I mean, after Josh made a mammoth effort to fly over and walk with me, and I'm grateful for that – but it has made me realise that this is something I need to do on my own from now on.'

The fact was that Josh, who was well aware of Cad's OCD-bent, used to play little tricks just to set him off. He only admitted it the day before he departed, much to their amusement!

Josh called for a 50-kilometre stint on Day 244 so he could have the notch on his belt before he headed home; Cad was not keen but relented. They achieved the goal about 8pm and, not wanting to walk another step, had to bush-bash off the highway to find a suitable campsite, only to give up and sleep in a clearing the middle of the rampant wildflowers. They found a dead tree trunk that was perfect for a fire but Cad had an 'accident' while lighting it and badly burned his hand. With his first-aid kit in disarray because of poor maintenance over the previous two months, he came up with a perfect piece of improvisation: he put some moisturising cream in a condom and tightened it over his three wounded fingers for relief.

They had just over 25 kilometres to make it to the Overlander roadhouse, from where they hoped to be able to get a bus or hitch a ride into Denham or the 10 kilometres further to Monkey Mia, the beautiful ocean World Heritage area where dolphins come to the beach and interact with the tourists. When they passed the sign indicating 5 kilometres to Overlander, Andrew said to Josh, 'Let's jog it home,' but Josh replied with one word: 'Nah.' About 500 metres later Cad jogged past his mate, luring him with a 'C'mon, don't be a wimp'.

Next thing they were into a fast jog, heading for a water tower that had been getting bigger all day and had become their nominated finish line. Cad recorded: 'I copped a wicked cramp in my left calf and stopped to stretch, Josh kept jogging. I stretched quickly and kept on going. Josh had started legging it! I knew he was trying to leave me for dead. I thought, "Fuck that!" and started legging it after him as fast as I could. My chest was on fire. It took ages to catch him, then I casually jogged up beside him. I could see the look of amazement in his eyes. He said, "Good effort." We hit the roadhouse in a sweaty mess. What a scene, there were crew everywhere then they see the two of us, no shirts on, coming out of nowhere.'

They had barely caught their breath when a male and a female cyclist rode in from the north. Cad was amazed to find it was Aitor, the Spanish rider he'd met on the Great Ocean Road six months earlier. After a warm embrace, Aitor informed Cad that he'd changed his earlier plan to fly from Melbourne to Auckland and cycle through New Zealand. He had instead ridden from Adelaide through the centre of Australia to Darwin and was now riding anti-clockwise to Perth, having linked up with a young Italian woman on the way. He'd now been on the road for two and a half years.

Cad and Josh found there were no more buses to Denham until the next day so they stood in front of the roadhouse begging motorists to fit them and Redge into their vehicles; for four hours they had no luck. They took the wheels off Redge to make it look more compact and stayed in the hitchhiking position until just after sunset, by which time they had a sign on paper which said 'Denham please', with a smiley face underneath. Cad claimed the artwork would create a change of luck and two hot female backpackers would soon pull over.

Within five minutes their prayers were answered; a campervan slowed down, Andrew screamed, 'We're on!' and almost jumped in front of the headlights with his hands under his chin, begging for compassion, while he held the sign with his elbows. With that two German backpackers (male, unfortunately) stopped and the boys had a lift to their designated destination, Monkey Mia.

DAYS 246–249, 29 AUGUST–1 SEPTEMBER 2011 TIME OFF IN MONKEY MIA

Two days before they arrived at Monkey Mia, a woman who introduced herself as Maria pulled up and suggested they should detour there. When they told her that was already the plan she suggested they ask for her on arrival and she'd help them out. It turns out Maria was the manager and she upgraded them from the dormitory to a beachside room, had ice-cold beers and pizza waiting for them, and during the next four days they were treated by the staff like celebrities, which they overwhelmingly appreciated. It was one of the best periods of Cad's walk, just being able to relax with Josh and the crew he met at the resort and having a lot of laughs together. They were taken out fishing, saw the dolphins close up, partied and just wound down for four days.

Josh headed back to Sydney the next day – back to 'normal' life on the Central Coast – while Cad returned to his abnormal life of solitude. It would have been hard for both of them, moving in their completely different directions. It wasn't lost on either of them how different their lives were going to be for the next year, and they kept in regular contact.

While Cad felt comfortable to be the sole master of command again, it only took days to hit him how lonely life was to become, and how much Josh's company, commitment and naturally genuine character had boosted his spirit.

'Walking for those few weeks up the coast of WA was one of the best and most rewarding things I have ever done in my life,' Josh later told me. 'I wanted to get out there and give him some company on the road. I mean, how could I not? He was walking around the country in memory of my younger brother. Cad always had his mission in his head, but to decide at the wake to dedicate a solo walk around the country raising money for myelodysplasia was something so unbelievable and special to me and the family. I was so stoked to get the chance to see what it was like out there as I wanted to see what it was all about in his environment.

'Walking some mornings was definitely tough especially the "5 kilometres devon", which we named the first

5 kilometres of the morning when everything is aching, especially your feet, but after limping and powering through the first 5 kilometres you were right and broke the first pain barrier of the day. It was easy for me; sure, it bloody hurt and at times and I didn't really feel like walking, but I had Cad by my side to get me keen and for only a short time I was there I kept him keen. Some days we would walk along talking for hours and realise we had just clicked out over 20 kilometres. Others days we would have the headphones in and just smash out kilometres, but every day we spent a good while talking about everything and anything, and the most random left-field things sometimes; we got to know each other very well.

'For him to complete a solo walk around Australia is just an unbelievable and psycho super human effort, something none of us will ever truly understand. To get up day after day and just keep trudging along and getting it done and staying true to his word is mind-blowing, something he deserves so much credit for. Cad is a very special human.'

When I look back at Cad's video blogs and see the laughter and contented look on his face on-camera during that period, it was obvious how much fun his walk had become. It is something I am so glad he and Josh shared, and it was clear to me, when he was reunited with Josh on the last day of the walk in Sydney, what a special bond they had. I'd like to think that has also created an ongoing bond between

Josh and me. On top of getting on so well anyway, each of us knows we have a more intimate insight into Cad's life on the road than anyone else, with Josh experiencing it with him for so long and me having read his diaries.

9

BROOME OR BUST

This was the stretch where the mental roller-coaster really hit Andrew. As far as I can ascertain, it was the period in which he went to a doctor who diagnosed him as suffering depression and prescribed antidepressant medication. This would surprise those he met, partied and relaxed with during these few weeks. But the insomnia set in again, and he went from highs to lows and back again – up when around people, and down when by himself. Obviously the isolation hit him hard after spending time with so many people over the previous couple of months. Plus he was tired, very tired.

After Josh headed back to the east coast of the continent, Cad was back to his daily routine and his own company. He recorded that he felt comfortable to return to what had become a compulsively orderly routine. But he lost companionship. I feel that after being surrounded by mates in Perth, then Josh and briefly also Billy, then being hosted so well in Monkey Mia, the loneliness hit him hard.

He decided his commitment was to get to Darwin for Christmas. Denham and Darwin were more than 3500 kilometres apart, and were also separated by the onset of summer. So he set himself the mission of hightailing it to Broome, where he'd decided to take time out to fly to his cousin's wedding in Fiji. That was two months away, and on his return he'd have a month and a half to sweat it out and get to Darwin by Christmas – sweating certainly being the appropriate word for the spirit- and strength-sapping trek to the Top End to come.

Shortly after Cad had embarked on the walk from Sydney, his schedule was to be in Darwin in early November, from where he would fly to Fiji. Now he would be leaving from Broome for the wedding, and would have to endure probably the longest flying route in the country – Broome to Perth, then Perth to Sydney.

It was 2 September 2011 when he realised the partying with mates of old was over and he was back on his own. He'd already been walking for nine months, yet so vast is the west coast of Australia that he had over 1900 kilometres to go to reach Broome, the intriguing holiday destination on the continent's north-west corner. Despite logging eighteen 50-plus-kilometre days, it took him two months to get there, primarily due to two-to-four-day rests at brilliant locations like Coral Bay and Exmouth on the Ningaloo coral reef, and several mining towns where he had mates taking advantage of the opportunities provided by the resources boom of the time.

DAYS 250–258, 2–10 SEPTEMBER 2011 OVERLANDER ROADHOUSE TO CARNARVON (202KM), THEN FOUR REST DAYS

After scoring a lift from Denham back to the Overlander roadhouse to recommence his journey, Cad had a phone conference with staff from the Leukaemia Foundation and was introduced to Nina Field, who was allocated as his case manager. They would develop a close relationship via the many phone calls from Nina checking on Andrew's progress over the following months, and Andrew was delighted to meet her personally when he crossed the finish line in Sydney. He was taken aback by the interest and involvement from the foundation, and during that first conversation he requested that all monies raised go to myelodysplasia research.

As I read his diaries, it was obvious to me that his moods fluctuated wildly, but on this first day back into his singular existence he was momentarily on a high. He sat outside the Overlander roadhouse eating a Chiko Roll and sipping on a can of Coca-Cola; he looked to the seemingly endless road to the north and recorded a strange rush of exhilaration: 'I had cold shivers shooting up my spine, it was weird and hard to explain, it wasn't so much a thought in my head but a feeling – like "how good is this", I'm out here having a ball, not working, spending my money – I really, really couldn't give a stuff about money or a career or a house, although my mind changes like my undies. Right there, right then I couldn't have been happier.' I suspect it was as much that he'd realised how glorious those few weeks with Josh and others had been, and the instant rapport he had with the Leukaemia Foundation.

So buoyant was he that when a road train carrying livestock whizzed past, spraying cow poo over his shirtless body, and he was unable to clean himself because he had run out of wipes, he just shrugged his shoulders and carried on.

But the dilemmas continued. The next day, while trying to straighten an axle on Redge, three spokes on the wheel snapped or bent out of shape. The wheel locked up, so he dragged the pram off the road and set about doing a temporary repair job. It was almost 200 kilometres to the next town, Carnarvon, and he had no phone reception. Fortunately, a family pulled over about 200 metres away to adjust the load on their roof racks, so Andrew sprinted over and gave the father an Oz On Foot business card with my phone number on the back, asking him to call me and ask if I could get a replacement wheel sent to Carnarvon. Fortunately, Morris Stanley, the company that distributes Chariot parts in Australia, provided the parts free, as they did again later in the trip, as they became great supporters of Oz On Foot. In the meantime, the wheel wobbled along but kept locking up as a spoke kept slipping out of position.

Comic relief came the next day, relieving the boredom of his only conversations being with the herds of goats that heavily populated the area. It took the form of a sixty-seven-year-old who was travelling by himself in a motorhome, towing a motor scooter. He stopped to offer Cad a banana and have a chat, and the conversation quickly turned to how many women he'd had sex with on his journey – none older, he declared, than his 'African Queen', who was forty-two. 'He reckons he has got fiancées everywhere ... he ran off to get his camera and showed me pics of a Sudanese fiancée, who I think is in Cairns, and another twenty-something-year-old in Alice Springs and another in Darwin.' The man explained how the motor scooter was a chick magnet and he didn't believe in foreplay: he was straight to the action, because at his age he could have a heart attack in five minutes. 'He was full of himself but hilarious to listen to,' Cad concluded.

Andrew came across yet another outback cyclist, this time a sixty-five-year-old British man who had been on the road for two and a half years. He was flying home from Perth to start life on the pension. Sex didn't enter this conversation!

By now Cad had a howling tailwind, which gave him the reverse problem faced while on the Nullarbor, where he had to push the pram, head and body crouched, into the headwind. Now, when he had a downhill slope, he had to sometimes put the brake on to stop Redge running away.

Cad ended up staying four nights in Carnarvon with two women, Kris and Jackie, who had been referred to him by one of his new friends in Monkey Mia, and was back on the (borrowed) tools briefly when he offered to build them a compost bin and do some repairs in the kitchen. His final night was spent at a hostel. He had his wallet pick-pocketed by a group of local teenagers while, after a few beers, he was in the heart of what he thought was an inspirational conversation about doing something with their lives. Fortunately a passing tourist had seen what happened and he had his wallet returned.

DAYS 259–266, 11–18 SEPTEMBER 2011 CARNARVON TO CORAL BAY (233KM), THEN FOUR REST DAYS

After deciding to stay an extra day in Carnarvon to attend the local horse races, Cad kicked on and had way too much to drink that night, which saw him limp out of town with his head between his tail, embarrassed by his drunken behaviour at the end of the night at the hostel, where he'd made a racket. He truly was depressed – in fact, he was driven to tears – another example of the highs and lows he was experiencing.

On Day 258, as he was loping slowly out of town, a truck pulled over: it was Danny, a friend from the Central Coast who was working in town and whom Cad had not seen or heard from in years. He pulled himself together and took up the invitation to stay a night with Danny and his wife in Carnarvon, delaying his departure another day. He recorded that it was a blessing that Danny had come along: he would have spiralled further if he'd been restricted to another lonely day along the highway, musing over his bad behaviour.

This period of his walk was a metaphor for his life. He would seem to be on a high, the life of the party, the one everyone wanted to be around or even emulate, but privately would often feel down because he drove himself too hard, tried to cram too much in, tried to touch the sky, although he never seemed to stop reaching or searching. When he wore himself out and felt the pressure he'd party hard to escape.

Those who watched his Day 260 video blog, which ended with the Green Day song 'Boulevard of Broken Dreams' playing as he is seen walking away from the camera over a wooden bridge, would not have known what it was truly in reference to. Now you do.

Andrew had decided not to wallow in grief, however. It took him four days to walk the 226 kilometres to just outside Coral Bay (days of 50, 60, 65 and 51 kilometres), walking until between 8pm and 10pm each night.

On the way in to Coral Bay, on the morning of 15 September 2011 (Day 263), came a chance brief meeting with some Belgian travellers, which typifies the surprise sight so many tourists were confronted with when, seemingly in the middle of nowhere, they came across this lone man and a pram. A further surprise for Rik Gruwez, from the beautiful town of Brugge, was that a photo he snapped as Cad walked away after that meeting of minutes would become the cover of this book (he'd emailed it to Cad, and I was able to find, through the Oz On Foot Facebook page post, its originator).

Let me use the travel notes of Rik and his wife, Corry, who came across Cad during their two months in Australia (that took in Perth to Broome and the Gibbs River Road in the Kimberleys), to describe what they encountered: 'The day ended with quite a surprise when we saw at the horizon an unfamiliar shape. It did not hop like a kangaroo, did not run like an emu and did not sway like a drugged possum. In a fashion similar to "Is it a bird? Is it a plane?" we kept guessing as we came closer (you can see a very long way ahead on these roads). It turned out to be a man pushing a pram with a solar panel mounted on top of it. Cad, as he is known, is walking around Australia – yes, ON FOOT – for charity, donating the proceeds to cancer research. We had a chat with him, donated some Aussie dollars and took a photo. Then we both went on our way. Although we were both heading for the same destination, we would be there in six minutes, whereas Cad would need two hours. Respect!'

At Coral Bay Cad struck a friendship with 'Captain Sensible' and 'Barbie' (the nickname of a man) while playing pool at the hostel where he stayed, and what followed were three days of socialising in his usual inimitable way, snorkelling over the coral just metres from the beach on a reef that is in every way just as spectacular as the more renowned Great Barrier Reef, and caught up on rest.

DAYS 267–274, 19–26 SEPTEMBER 2011 CORAL BAY TO EXMOUTH (152.5KM), INCLUDING FIVE REST DAYS

Andrew had two big days on the road after he left Coral Bay; it was as if he felt, having had a few days enjoying himself with too much alcohol and too many late nights, that he had to take it out on himself by pushing hard. He walked 49.5 kilometres then 64 kilometres to get to Learmonth Airport, the RAAF base about 40 kilometres shy of Exmouth, which was further north along the Ningaloo Reef but off the main route to Broome, the North West Coastal Highway.

His insomnia was back and he woke at 1am and struggled to get any sleep after that, yet set the goal of completing a 60-kilometre day. He had lunch at the 22-kilometre mark but was so exhausted he rolled his mattress and had a day snooze in the shade. Twice people stopped and woke him up to ask if he was alright. 'I couldn't keep my eyes open, I made myself get up and it took forever to come to. I was smashing rehydration tabs in a drink and sipping on it. I smashed a full pot of Weet-Bix, then finally made myself get into it. I really had to do 60 kilometres today to make town tomorrow. I told myself I was going to be there so I had to.'

Despite his left knee paining badly again and blisters appearing on his feet, he walked until 1am and kept pushing on towards a huge glow in the distance, which he assumed was the Learmonth RAAF base, and camped between the road and the high barbed-wire perimeter fence of the base.

The next day, at about 13 kilometres from Exmouth, for no apparent reason Cad decided to start jogging; the jog increased to a three-quarter-pace run, which lasted about three kilometres until he felt like his chest was burning. From there, he walked uphill and jogged downhill and on the flat until he reached the outskirts of Exmouth in a sweaty mess.

'I was hurting but pushed on,' he wrote. 'I legged it all the way then I was about to collapse but saw an "info centre 500 metres" sign and thought, "That will do." I started getting faint-headed and was nearly passing out. I collapsed in a sack of shit across the road on some grass under some trees. I got the biggest rush of pins and needles in my legs and arms. I had to work hard to crawl over to Redge and get some rehydration tablets in a cup with water. It took ages to get my breath and come good. I couldn't get my shirt off because it was stuck to me.' He soon found out the temperature was 32 degrees, even though it was only late September.

He hung out with some great people, was able to snorkel on the reef and just felt at home. A big Exmouth attraction is the chance to dive with the whales and that was certainly on Cad's to-do list, but he had to settle for snorkelling as he didn't get around to organising a dive.

He'd arranged to meet up with Brett (whom, I assume, he'd met en route) and stayed with him, Jacinta, Matt and Merv for the first night. They took him for a drive to the reef and they swam with turtles all around and humpback whales breaching just a few hundred metres away. Next day was snorkelling at Turquoise Bay after going just outside the reef in a small boat, and he saw two reef sharks, a turtle and an eagle ray. He also tried riding a surfboard for the first time and was stoked to manage to stand up. He also went spearfishing for the first time and nabbed a good-sized coral trout. While in Exmouth his new friends helped him create a new sign on the back of a for-sale sign, which was then glued to the front hood of the pram and remained there for the rest of the trip: 'OZONFOOT.COM – WALKING FOR CANCER AND MDS.'

After four great days he packed two food parcels to be dropped at the roadhouses on the 540-kilometre leg between Exmouth and Karratha – Nanutarra (276 kilometres before Karratha) and Fortescue roadhouse (96 kilometres short of Karratha). Merv was able to drop one parcel to Fortescue roadhouse but Cad had to find a courier for the second, so he went to the information centre and stationed himself there for two hours hoping to find a tourist heading north – to no avail. He called the courier companies in town but had no luck there. Then, as he sat there pondering his next move, a tyre on Redge went pop. He tried three patches but it was still leaking, so he called the hardware store and a woman who worked there was kind enough to drop a new tube off on her way to the bank, as she knew Andrew was stranded without 'wheels'.

Once mobile, he went to the Big 4 tourist park but a woman in the office wouldn't let him wander through and ask people to take his food parcel, which certainly got his back up: '"But we get people wandering around annoying the guests all the time," she told me. "Oh, so you often get people who walk around Australia looking for someone to take food so they don't die?" Stupid bitch!' Eventually, he went to the post office and sent the food parcel in the mail, but by that stage most of the day was gone and so he walked only five kilometres, clearing the outskirts of town.

At that moment Cad made a vow, deciding to turn over a new leaf: no alcohol, no cigarettes and no swearing until Broome! The prompt seems to have come from hearing someone swear more than he did during a barbeque with his new mates in Exmouth. 'No swearing! Geez, it will be hard, I've got over a decade of job-site potty mouth to wash out – easier said than done. There was a guy at the beach party who swore more than me, and although I know the swearing sounds bad, especially in front of the chicks, it made me realise just how much of a bogan it makes you sound like. No more swearing in my diary either, or in texts, emails or anything – and I need a new phrase for "God knows" ... maybe "Santa knows"?'

A couple of days later he gave himself more incentive by deciding to start a 'swear jar' and donate $1 to the Leukaemia Foundation every time he used foul language. Cad may have been a bloke who was renowned for living up to what he promised he'd do, but this was one challenge that was going to be too great!

DAYS 275–286, 27 SEPTEMBER–8 OCTOBER 2011 EXMOUTH TO NEAR KARRATHA (530KM)

Incredibly, only a few hours into the next day's walk, another other tyre blew, but at least Andrew was able to patch this one up. Later in the day he'd just passed the Learmonth RAAF base when some of his new mates from Exmouth – Billy, Gavin, Ash, Nathan, Jacqueline and John – pulled over with a barbeque on the roof rack of a vehicle. Cad couldn't believe the effort they went to, driving 35 kilometres out of town to give him company and a good barbie dinner. Gav operated a microlight aeroplane business called Birds Eye View that offered scenic flights (and lessons) in the extra-light aircraft over the Ningaloo Reef and national park, and had even flown one of the tiny planes across Australia, refuelling many times along the way.

The gang left about 9.30pm; they never knew how chuffed Cad was that they'd come out to farewell him in style in the bush, although perhaps it was just another indication of how quickly he could gel with people. 'It was the first time I'd had a send-off like that. I felt really welcome in Exmouth and felt like I could fit in. It's joined Melbourne in the top two places I'd like to live post-walk.'

The next night he made it to Giralia Station, an outback homestay, with a mass of ants, locusts and the occasional dead snake on the roadside becoming his new companions; the snakes unnerved him, considering he had to often go into the countryside for a 'bush turd'.

Almost as much went into the swear jar ($12 on the first day under the new censor rule) as he took in donations – from one phone call and talking out loud to himself! By now the temperatures were regularly in the mid-thirties, and the vegetation mainly dry rocky outcrops and spinifex, with Mount Alexander to his right. There was another $26 in the swear jar by the time he made it to Nanutarra roadhouse with less than a litre of water left; this led Cad to adopt a daily cap of $25!

Soon after leaving the next day, he sat on his chair and found himself staring into the mountains in the distance thinking about 'the real world and what everyone is doing back home'. His isolation really hit, and it was obvious his feelings had become magnified after experiencing so many enjoyable times with Kane, Josh, Billy and so many others since Perth. He diarised that evening, trying to explain how detached his life had become from normal life:

'It doesn't matter what people are doing, I'm in my little outback bubble and anything that is happening anywhere else on the planet is totally and utterly irrelevant to me. I can't remember the last time I read a paper or watched the news. Who knows what's going on – who cares, if it's big enough people will ask if I've heard about it no doubt. I thought about everything I'd sacrificed to be here, the hard work and hard road travelled to get the house finished and sold to be here right here right now. And I looked around and all I can think of is what I'm missing out on by sitting here. What am I doing out here alone? It's ludicrous. Shit is about to start getting heavy [presumably he was referring to the heat and trying conditions further north], I'm really not prepared. Can I do this for another year?'

It typified the erratic mental state that really affected him on this long leg: days earlier he was on top of the world after a great time in Exmouth; before that he enjoyed himself in Coral Bay after vowing not to party hard again after his drunken embarrassment of Carnarvon; he was down after Josh left him at Denham yet relieved he was back to being responsible to himself only. It had been a continual rollercoaster since probably the start of the Nullarbor.

What he wrote in his diary that night shows the depth of his depression: 'I'd give away every step, every memory, every godforsaken anything to do with this walk to have my life back. The only thing keeping me going at the moment is Simmo and the promise I made at his wake to Matty and Jamie, and as much as I hate to admit it, I don't get my life back until I walk home and honour that promise and honour Simmo. I've got nothing to look forward to on a day-to-day basis – making the next roadhouse to get a cold drink, make the next town so I can spend my days off washing clothes and shopping and doing shit I don't want to be doing and getting drunk. I'd rather look forward to getting reception and calling my girlfriend [a reference to his split with Jaime].'

He wrote about not looking forward to speaking to family or friends, and dreading replying to phone messages and emails and Facebook messages and not understanding why. He wondered why 'the lonelier I get, the more I want to push everyone away'. He even considered removing his Facebook and Hotmail accounts and changing his phone number so he could cut himself off until he arrived in Sydney, which shows how random and irrational his thoughts could become.

He continued:

I'm sick of sleeping in a tent
I'm sick of sleeping on a shit air mattress
I'm sick of sleeping with a blow-up pillow
I'm sick of walking
I'm sick of wearing a hat
I'm sick of wearing shoes unless I'm in bed
I'm sick of pitching and packing my tent every day
I'm sick of living out of a pram
I'm sick of pushing it around
I'm sick of eating out of a pot
I'm sick of eating the same thing every day
I'm sick of drinking warm water
I'm sick of the sun
I'm sick of the wind
I'm sick of insects – ants in particular
I'm sick of feeling tired
I'm sick of looking tired
I'm sick of being sore
I'm sick of stretching
I'm sick of protein shakes and supplements
I'm sick of waking up every hour

I'm sick of cars beeping at me
I'm sick of putting on a happy persona when I speak to people
I'm sick of feeling depressed
I'm sick of crying
I'm sick of being alone
I'm sick of working out so I don't look like I'm anorexic
I'm sick of posting blogs and photos
I'm sick of doing 'thanks to' [on his website]
I'm sick of beating myself up over every stupid thing I've ever done or said
I'm sick of smelling like BO
I'm sick of waking up sweltering in a hot tent
I'm sick of traffic
I'm sick of listening to trucks all day
I'm sick of writing in this diary
I'm sick of having chafing
I'm sick of having blisters
I'm sick of Oz On Foot
I'm sick of life

This was one of the saddest entries I read in Cad's diary, for two obvious reasons: firstly, for how detached I felt from him at that vulnerable time of his life, after seeing him only three months earlier and thinking he was fine; and secondly, because of how little of his previous life that he yearned for he was to experience after completing the walk. But in addition to the obvious, thirdly, I felt guilty when I realised that on the day he wrote that I was enjoying myself in a corporate box at the NRL Grand Final at Sydney's Olympic Stadium, oblivious to my son's dilemma and depression.

Typically, he slowly regained his 'mojo' over the next few days and he recorded how he enjoyed receiving donations and food from several people he met on the road, including a 'big cuddly guy called BJ' who gave him $5 to spend on himself. After reaching Fortescue roadhouse, Rob, who was working as a train driver for the mines, shouted Andrew dinner and a few drinks. The next day Andrew met Shane, who was returning to Jurien Bay after having spent months taking part in a blockade to stop Woodside Petroleum's proposed gas plant 60 kilometres north of Broome. Andrew found the issue fascinating and stuck 'Protect the Kimberley' and 'Save the Kimberley Whale Coast' stickers onto Redge.

Soon after, Sheree, Tania and Shane doubled back with a pack of energy food and drinks and offered to pay for a night's accommodation for Cad at the Eramurra mining village (Civic Pacific mine site) where they worked, 12 kilometres further north. He enjoyed the use of the gym, showers and the buffet dinner in the mess hall, all part of his first look at mine accommodation. He was fascinated to see the social segregation of the workers – Asians at one table, the Irish at another, Polynesians and Maori group, 'the tattooed crew' and the 'old stick-in-the-mud-looking crew' seated separately.

He laughed when a couple of the older miners asked, 'What's all this balloons-on-the-table shit about?' – only to be told it was a fundraiser for 'some guy walking around Australia for cancer'. Then they noticed a photo of Andrew with his pram on a poster on all the tables and the penny dropped: 'Oh, is that you?'

Later in the night, Cad was asked to speak about his trip and gave the background about reading *Giant Steps* and Simmo's death and his journey so far ... and dropped the 'f word' at least once that he could recall! The generosity of that night was wonderful, with him receiving several large donations and one of the lads accepting a dare to eat a whole jar of hot mustard for $700 ($100 from each of seven workmates). More than $1300 was raised, on top of $1000 on the road over a week.

His spirits had quickly, if temporarily, been restored.

DAYS 287–294, 9–16 OCTOBER 2011 REST DAYS, THEN KARRATHA TO ROEBOURNE (51KM)

At the end of the next day, after logging 57.6 kilometres, Cad's mate Steve Browne from the Central Coast picked him up just 10 kilometres short of Karratha, where Steve and his wife, Jessica, were living and working. And so began eight action-packed days of fishing (two days out on a boat, landing some good-sized fish and seeing some whales), partying, relaxing and enjoying the company of good friends and their friends. In between, Andrew returned to walk the 10 kilometres into the booming mining port of Karratha, and did a 41-kilometre walk further along the route to Roebourne before heading back for another four nights with the Brownes.

It would turn out to be his last extended 'time out' experience with friends on the road during his whole Oz On Foot expedition, and he was only just over halfway through. He certainly made the most of it, and left Karratha in a much better mental and physical state than when he'd arrived. It was either while there or shortly before that he consulted a doctor about his mental state, which saw him spasmodically unable to control emotion and crying without apparent reason, and he was diagnosed as suffering depression and was prescribed medication. From what I can gather, he took the antidepressants for a short while but, after speaking with close mates (especially Matt Delaney) and having second thoughts, he decided to send the pills home in a box marked 'do not open'. I didn't stop to think what might have been contained in the box when it arrived, but I know the story now. This was the period when he really questioned himself about continuing, and he relayed that to his mates. But, fuelled by the generosity of the Pilbara people, where his donations peaked, and by the determination or stubbornness that came from within him to refuse to surrender, he kept going.

Like at other times during the walk when he felt low, his antidote was to have fun, to party and to enjoy to the maximum the time he had with people around him, knowing his existence would change as soon as he set foot on the bitumen again. Karratha was another case. He almost landed a massive manta ray of over 250 kilograms but it was just too big to get on Steve's boat, but Cad was proud of the good sized cobia he pulled in. However, his other 'conquest' left a bit to be desired, according to the Brownes: a $50 pair of 'happy pants', which Cad was most taken by, but others were not, on account of the crotch being located closer to his knees than his groin. When he had to lift Redge from a ute after doing the Roebourne leg, the pants caught on the vehicle's tray, which saw him tumble to the earth and just avoid injury, to the accompanying squeals of laughter from those present.

Cad had already conducted a backyard ceremony of burning the shorts he'd been walking in for months, an event that didn't go according to plan. A squirt of petrol didn't quite light the pants, so he was a little more zealous with the quantity ... which saw a backyard bonfire erupt, to the startled reaction of the Brownes, who spent weeks trying to get the grass to grow again. 'One of the funniest things, of many funny things, I'd seen from Cad,' confessed Steve.

The Brownes and Tara and Jason took Cad to the KI International pub for Thursday night's 'mic night', where anyone could get on the microphone and sing a song or tell a joke or story. Cad was egged on to make to talk after being introduced by a staff member, and hours later walked out with almost $4000 raised for the Leukaemia Foundation!

Cad blogged of his Karratha stay: 'Rolled into town last Sat'dy night, Browney picked me up, was only supposed to be here two days; eight days later ... strewth! Had to leave the old detox and swear jar at Mairee Pool on the way in and picked them up yesterday at Roebourne; bloody kidding yourself thinking of taking either of them into Karratha. Had a ball, mate ... Thanks to Steve and Jess for putting me up, and Jase and Tara for everything. Anyway, leaving the Pilbara, living the dream, but eight days there has left me with a massive eighteen-day slog to get to Broome for my cousin Luke's wedding.'

DAYS 295–310, 17 OCTOBER–1 NOVEMBER 2011 ROEBOURNE TO ROEBUCK PLAINS ROADHOUSE (766KM)

After three successive 50-plus-kilometre days, Cad made it to his next bit of civilisation at South Hedland and was quickly befriended by a big Kiwi, Tom, who was the publican at the Hotel Fini in Port Hedland. Big Tom organised a fundraising night at the pub, which involved Cad again making a speech, something he had become comfortable doing. Yet he was very uncomfortable (just like his old man) when Tom called him up to sing karaoke. The good news was that Tom spared him total embarrassment by doing a duo with him; the bad news was that it was the Proclaimers' song '500 Miles'. The fact that $1425 was raised softened his displeasure. 'Tom is a legend, I won't forget him in a hurry,' Cad wrote.

The Pilbara was certainly the most productive region for donations, and Cad was accepting hundreds each day from those who stopped along the way, on top of the lucrative fundraising evenings at Eramurra, Karratha and Port Hedland; obviously, a front-page story and photograph in the *Pilbara News* and a television interview had lifted awareness of who he was and what he was doing. Contrasting that was the fact he felt dreadful, with a bad cough and chest cold, but that didn't stop him walking a minimum of 40 kilometres a day for twelve of the next thirteen days while the thermometer nudged 40 degrees.

In fact, he took only sixteen days, not the planned eighteen, to get from Roebourne to Broome, thanks to an average of 48 kilometres a day on the logbook and one day off (at the Sandfire roadhouse), making it his most intense period since the Nullarbor. (Mind you, he'd had twenty-one of the previous forty-eight days off since reaching Monkey Mia with Josh.) The blisters on his feet were as bad as they had ever been, and the chafing was back in earnest.

He was physically and mentally shot in the last days before Broome, however the thought of relaxing in

Fiji with familiar faces was ample incentive not to slow down. For days he could see storms to the north, and when he finally encountered rain for the first time in about three months he actually rejoiced, standing in the middle of the highway, shirt and shoes discarded, with arms outstretched with his head to the sky, screaming, 'Yes. Yes! It's not hot and there are no flies ... Yessssss!'

Andrew decided he'd walk only to the Roebuck Plains roadhouse, which was at the junction of the road to Broome and the Great Northern Highway where it took a right-hand turn towards the Northern Territory. He was done. He'd pushed himself enough. He couldn't be bothered continuing by foot to Broome and would cover that 'dog-leg' on his return.

DAYS 311–314, 2–5 NOVEMBER 2011 REST IN BROOME

Next day Cad was able to get a lift into Broome where he stayed four nights in a backpackers' hostel, hired a motor scooter and visited the protesters' blockade at the gas plant. He had a long-overdue haircut, some genuine rest (but also two visits to the gymnasium and a private consultation with a personal trainer about diet and stretching) and some late-night socialising around town with fellow backpackers. He also caught up with his first boss when he was an apprentice carpenter, Phil Browne (father of Steve in

Karratha) and his wife, Linda, and son Sean ('Shug'), who were living in Broome.

He had a good break and was ready for the long journey to Fiji and to be in the midst of family and friends.

Did he rest and recuperate? Not on your life.

DAYS 315–322, 6–13 NOVEMBER 2011 BROOME TO FIJI AND RETURN

One part of Andrew was so glad he went to Fiji for Luke and Kristal's wedding, to be there for what was a special occasion in a great location, and have a rare catch-up with family. However, another part of him regretted that he'd made a break from his isolated existence, because it made it so much harder to return to walking.

I'm certainly glad he made the effort, because it's the family's memory of the last time as a larger group we were with Andrew and was such a special experience for all who were there – even though he was obviously a troubled soul when he arrived.

The sojourn from Broome to the Naviti Resort took twenty-two and a half hours from door to door, including eleven and a half hours of flying time (he had five hours in between flights in Perth, and two and a half hours in Sydney). He was in Fiji for six days, before returning to Broome the day after the wedding, which was held on the eleventh day of the eleventh month in 2011.

He arrived in Fiji late in the evening and, incredibly, went straight to the gym when he made it to the Naviti Resort. Next morning he jogged to the Warwick resort and back, a distance of nearly 13 kilometres, a feat he repeated a couple more times before easing down after four alcohol-free days (my guess is that he was back on the antidepressants) and relaxing, even partying a couple of times – too hard, as usual, with cousins and many of the 100 people who had flown in for the wedding. You could tell by looking at him that he benefited from the break, even though it had been such an ordeal to come from so far away.

He caught up with extended family and some friends. He particularly enjoyed seeing his niece and nephew Kayla and Max, whom he'd seen little of, as he was living in England during Kayla's first eighteen months and Max was only ten months old when he'd started his walk (he was twenty-one months old in Fiji).

It was tougher than any of us realised for him to return to the road. When Cad left the day after the wedding, there were plenty of the family there to say goodbye with handshakes and hugs, but probably not a full sense of how different our paths would be after he was driven away on the coach to the airport.

Cad was not one to show emotion or reveal his inner thoughts readily, so I was surprised, and sad, to find this in his diary: 'I was pretty gutted I didn't get to say goodbye to Kayla, Nicole and Glenn. I saw Max for the last time at brekkie and saw Nicole at brekkie as well but didn't say goodbye, I thought she'd be up [at the reception area as he departed; unfortunately, the kids were asleep in the room and she'd looked for Andrew earlier]. I said goodbye to Mum and Dad and got on the coach. They stood on the top of the stairs waving. I don't think they could see me through the glass. The bus pulled away and I had tears dripping off my chin – fucking hell, what a mess. I wasn't blubbering or making a sound, just had the waterworks going. It's official right there and then, I'm over it. I didn't want to go back to Broome and start walking.' Then he started stressing about having to do a shop and organise people to drop food parcels at roadhouses for him, and about the heat and humidity he would soon encounter.

After an overnight stop in Sydney with his good mate Todd Bailey, Andrew left for Perth the following evening, hopping on a connecting flight to Broome. He was back in one of the harshest yet most beautiful corners of the world.

And back to cruel reality.

10

THE KILLER KIMBERLEY

When Andrew returned from Fiji he should have been refreshed. He wasn't, despite the obvious benefit of a week's break from the monotonous and relentless existence since Josh had left him sixty-six days and 1934 kilometres before Broome.

Mentally, to have seen family and friends and to have withdrawn from the torturous daily routine of walking in the heat, humidity and plagues of flies was good for him. But physically, he couldn't bring himself to slow down. His jogs between the Naviti and Warwick resorts, where Katherine, whom he'd befriended in the bus from the airport, was staying with her family, gym sessions and a couple of late nights socialising on top of the arduous travel schedule that covered 19,000 kilometres by six planes and two buses hardly provided the respite his body needed.

After his return to the far north-west of the country, he stayed two days in Broome to prepare himself for the toughest part of his walk, the Kimberley Ranges – 1013 kilometres across the breadth of Western Australia from just east of Broome, which is 19 degrees south of the equator, through to Kununurra at 15.77 degrees south – during November and December, the hottest two months of the year.

It was the start of the 'big wet', the cyclone season. The coolest temperature roadside would have been 36 degrees Celsius. Records showed the average maximum daily temperature at the weather recording stations in the region were was 40.7 at Fitzroy Crossing (airport) in November 2011, and 39.8 at Warmun in December. You could safely raise that by four or five degrees along the edge of the highway, with the heat bouncing off the bitumen like a furnace. It was madness.

The temperature and humidity increased the further north he travelled. The Bureau of Meteorology recorded average mean temperatures of 34 to 40.4 degrees Celsius for all but one day (down to 30.5) in the region during the time Andrew was there (plus high humidity). And they were mean temperatures; the maximum daily heat levels would have been somewhat more. Many people stopped to tell him their car thermometers recorded 45-degree heat outside their air-conditioning.

Add to the climactic conditions the isolation, and Cad knew it was the leg that would make him or break him – or at least crush his spirit and suck all the life out of his body. To be frank, it was a crazy thing to do; he was putting his life in danger.

Somehow he found the focus and physical capability to walk over 1000 kilometres in twenty-seven days before having two days off in Kununurra. He averaged 45.5 kilometres each full day he walked (there were twenty-two of them) in the searing heat. Simply unbelievable!

This was without doubt the most poignant part of his trek in that it tested his body and mind more than any other leg, causing him to dig deep to see what was inside him in circumstances he had never before encountered in his thirty years. In several interviews he did during and after the trek, he said the Kimberley was the toughest leg; I can still vividly see him relay that quite nonchalantly to David Koch on national television on the *Sunrise* program the day after he'd reached the finish line.

Yet it was only when I read his diary notes that I fully comprehended what he went through. We'll pick up the journey from outside Broome, just over ten and a half months since he took off from Sydney the day after Boxing Day 2010.

DAY 323, 14 NOVEMBER 2011 ROEBUCK ROADHOUSE TO EAST (26KM)

The day I am about to describe, almost totally in Andrew's words, best captures the most hellish personal challenge he was about to endure, yet somehow overcome. It shows the enormity of the physical and mental pressure he had inflicted on himself by a combination of not preparing his trip well enough, leaving at the wrong time of year and going in the wrong direction, and the delays – a crook leg in Tasmania, socialising for weeks in Melbourne and Perth, and on the leg from Perth to Broome, plus attending two weddings because he would not break commitments. The greatest impact of that – the harsh weather at the start of the wet season in Australia's Top End – were about to haunt him.

It started on a Tuesday when Sean Browne gave him a lift to the Roebuck roadhouse, 30 kilometres north-east of Broome. They enlisted a local Aboriginal man to help unload Redge from the ute, and the guy told Andrew the location of an unmarked waterhole about 90 kilometres east of Fitzroy Crossing and 270 kilometres from Roebuck. But before diving in for a refreshing swim, the man warned Cad that he had to find a rock, put it under his armpit, rub it on his arm then throw it in the water, otherwise he might be bitten by a snake. It was one of the many traditional Aboriginal beliefs that he would learn about. Cad then found a passing plumber to take his food parcel through to Fitzroy Crossing.

He was given a fairly confronting indication of what lay ahead when he walked over to talk to a cyclist, who, riding in from the other direction, had hurriedly walked into the roadhouse store.

'I had a good chat with old mate [the cyclist] about all the things to come and it sounded dire. He told me about bulls and water buffalo on the roads and storms and bullshit heat and humidity. He was from Darwin and he said it's so much worse near Kununurra. He had been flogging himself from four in the morning for two weeks, riding up to 200 and something kilometres a day to get south and out of the heat. He said he was just getting smashed and there were hills coming. He said it was so stale with no wind and he was drinking twelve-plus litres of water a day ... we exchanged info about gear, as you do. He said he needed a pop-up tent because the ground is so hard he had no chance getting pegs in.

'He headed to Broome and I sat there eating and sculling water and procrastinating for another couple of hours until about 11 or 11.30. I had forgotten to get new wheels and, upon further investigation, found mine were fucked. I rang the bike shop [in Broome] and am getting them to order some and send them through to Halls [Creek] – it might be two weeks, 'cos they have to get them shipped in from Melbourne ... what a hassle.

'Five kilometres up the road and I was instantly wet from head to toe, it was the worst day since Lavers Hill [in South Australia]. I was already dripping with sweat sitting in the shade at the roadhouse, it was ridiculous. I stopped a million times trying to fix the front wheel and arms. It was heavy and had been lifted in and out of Shug's ute and now the steering is stuffed. I was hating it, every step was an effort. I walked for what seemed like an eternity and freaked out when I turned around and could still see the roadhouse sign.

'A storm brewed up within an hour ... the red dirt on the side of the road had turned to slush and made it a boggy nightmare every time a car came and I had to get off the road. A lady pulled over with a wet car to warn me there's bad weather ahead.

'The landscape was distinctly different. It was a lot greener and more trees and not as scrubby, more termite mounds were appearing. There were cicadas filling the air with their noise, competing with the distant rumbling of thunder that never seems to stop. No sooner had the last storm passed that another was brewing to the north-east. Again a bit of rain, but this time I called its bluff and didn't get changed.

'I kept forgetting to drink water and would find myself stumbling along until I felt sick or exhausted from dehydration and heat exhaustion. The "sip a song" had gone right out the window. I was giving myself the shits and kept yelling out loud, "C'mon, sip a song" [his plan to have a sip of water at the end of each song on his iPod]. I had to take an hour for lunch under a tree to rehydrate. I left feeling better but just did it again an hour later; I need to get back on my A-game. I sat there at lunch with the sweat literally pouring out my chest, neck and forehead. I stopped bothering to wipe it away because it would constantly flood out again, and that's sitting in the shade.

'I started to seriously doubt for the first time of my capabilities of being able to make Darwin let alone continue in this shit. I finally see what everyone was on about and I know it's only just begun. It's not that I didn't believe them; it's just that until you experience it for yourself you can't even imagine how bad it is. I bumbled along until I finally got some reprieve about 5pm, when the temp dropped and breeze appeared as the third storm brewed.

'I was fucked. I had bad chafing – I'd felt it all day but hadn't bothered to do anything about it. I stopped under a tree and checked it out – it was bad and the skin was broken which means the 3B [cream] is no good. I cleaned it up and sat there naked trying to air it out. The conditions were only just favourable to do some walking and I really needed to do some kilometres or I wouldn't make the next roadhouse and would run out of food and water. But I had made the decision to stop and sort my chaffing or it would be the end of me. I cleaned it up and covered it with Savlon, I'd tried every which cream but old Lofty was right, Savlon was the best – I should have listened to old fisherman in the first place above anyone else.'

The state of both the weather and his body became an almost daily ordeal for the next forty-one days. But he kept on keeping on the highway and his mission not to give in.

As the wind began to howl he hurriedly found a rock and smashed in his tent pegs to set up camp. He realised he'd forgotten to pack cans of fruit and vegetables so he had rice and tuna. He then discovered he'd forgotten to put in his towel and half of his underpants, presumably leaving them on the clothes line at the backpackers' hostel in Broome. Then he ran out of Savlon cream.

He didn't require sleeping pills to drop off, so exhausted was he, but woke at least five times and each time sculled more water, utterly dehydrated. And this was just the first day of what was the toughest period of his walk!

DAY 324, 16 NOVEMBER 2011 TOWARDS WILLARE BRIDGE (50KM)

Cad's alarm went off at 4am; he wanted to beat the heat for a few hours. But after doing a workout and getting organised, it was almost 7am by the time he hit the road. He was dripping with sweat just minutes into walking, before a headwind, which he usually dreaded, gave him some relief. He telephoned the bike shop at Broome and was stoked that his wheels had been sent and the cost was only $95 for three, although he was affronted that the guy at the bike shop thought he was the Stormtrooper. 'Shit I hate that guy,' Cad recorded, in reference to the persistent mistaken identity occurrences he'd had to endure. He was referring to Jacob French, a twenty-one-year-old who at that time was walking the 5000 kilometres across Australia from Perth to Sydney dressed as a stormtrooper character from the *Star Wars* movies while raising money for the Starlight Children's Foundation (he completed his trek in nine months).

A diary entry gave an insight into how Cad was toying with cutting corners but just couldn't bring himself to cheat. 'I spoke to Steve [Parkin] and Dela [Matt Delaney] while at the servo and was whingeing how I was over it and I think I'll just walk the shortest way straight home. But then this morning I was thinking, "This is about Simmo and the Leukaemia Foundation as well now." I don't know what to do. I just need to keep off the piss and keep on the move and hurry up.'

A woman called Kim in a 4WD pulled over and invited Andrew to dinner that evening at their home further along the highway. He thought he was walking into another storm but it turned south and cooled the afternoon down – to 37 degrees! He was just about to give up on finding Kim's place when he saw it at the 50-kilometre mark for the day. Kim's husband, Rob, had the contract for roadworks with Derby Council and the house was their base during the months they worked in the region. Cad was overjoyed at the prospect of a shower and a dinner of lamb shanks, vegetables and mash (with Rob, Kim, their daughter and some workers), and having Rob fix the bracket on his wheel the next morning before writing a cheque for $300 to the Leukaemia Foundation.

DAY 325, 17 NOVEMBER 2011 TO WILLARE BRIDGE ROADHOUSE (55KM)

Cad woke at 4.40am and was on the road an hour later after breakfast. He wrote: 'I stopped 3 kilometres up the road and literally wrung my shirt out. I sat under a tree in disbelief. I would wipe the sweat from my forehead, chest and stomach and count to twenty-two seconds before it was flooding again. I stopped bothering to wipe sweat from my eyes; the time it took to take my fly net and sunnies off outweighed the time it would take to fill back up. I just kept trying to blink it out. All day the sun was nailing me but there was no use trying to use sunscreen because it would just sweat off. I had to put my orange hat on and close the flaps around my chin but it made it ten times worse. I saw my first boab tree in the bush, three of them next to each other. Nothing to get excited about because after those three there were hundreds.'

By 2pm, Andrew was exhausted: 'I stopped about two to give up and sat under a tree. I was fucked and could hardly keep my eyes open. I didn't even have the energy to shoo the flies away. I made myself keep going and finally the storms that had been brewing on all four horizons moved close enough to block the sun. It was so good! ... I finally made it to the 40-kilometre mark at five o'clock and could have my shirt off because the sun was buried behind a mass of black cloud ... I had to tie my shirt around my neck to keep the flies off my back, it was gross.'

The hazards of walking solo along the narrow highway, where a pedestrian would be the last thing truck drivers would expect to confront, became evident just on dark when Cad hit a series of five one-lane bridges over rivers and creeks; at the last one he had to wait for a road train to pass before gingerly scurrying over the bridge. He made it to Willare River roadhouse about 6pm and there asked a young Irish woman named Jeanette (who he recorded as being 'hot') if his food parcel had arrived; she told him she was getting worried about when he would appear and that she was going to send a car out to find him if he hadn't by tonight. Jeanette gave him the camp spot for free. Cad reckoned he'd found another piece of heaven in that the camping area had lush green grass and ample shade (and a pool), a far cry from the bare dirt he'd become used to. 'Had the world's longest shower and crashed at nine.'

DAY 326, 17 NOVEMBER 2011 REST DAY, WILLARE BRIDGE ROADHOUSE

After waking at 4am and rushing to the toilet, his system feeling like it was rebelling against what it had been put through, Andrew went back to sleep until seven before waking and 'feeling like I had been hit in the head by a sledgehammer ... I'd drunk fourteen litres of water yesterday, the most in my life, then two more last night, but was still pissing yellow this morning [suggesting he was dehydrated].' He decided he desperately needed a day off.

Mid-morning, 'PK', an associate of Phil Browne's who owned an electrical business in the region and had been told to look out for Andrew, pulled in from the highway for a break sat next to him for a chat and revealed he had lost his son at age nineteen just fifteen days earlier; he'd drowned after jumping in the water at Dubbo when his dog fell from a boat. Andrew was obviously deeply affected by the news and relayed in his diary the story of PK's son and how PK needed to get back into work to take his mind off the tragedy.

Soon after, I received a call from Andrew that I still vividly remember. He spilled out how down he was and so over the walk, and I almost begged him to give up and come home after he reached Darwin. That in itself was an amazing achievement, and he'd also raised a good amount in honour of Simmo so no one would think any less of him, especially considering he had initially committed to walking only to Perth. It was his wellbeing that was most important, and if he was hating it that much, why torture himself? But he said he wouldn't cut the walk short. After we hung up, I seriously considered dropping everything, flying to Broome, hitching out to meet him and walking to Darwin with him, but then considered how I'd only slow him down and would not be able to physically handle the heat and distance involved.

Only when I read his diary notes after his death did I fully understand what he was going through. He wrote of our conversation: 'Spoke to the old boy on my sat phone about shit I need and he got me a fan, so hopefully it will help me sleep. I told him I'm fucked up, he said to just come home and no one will think any less of me. He just doesn't get it – I'll think less of me. I'm locked in now. I'm not going home until I walk home, me and Simmo all the way.'

My concern was that he'd be too determined for his own good.

DAYS 327–330, 18–21 NOVEMBER 2011 EAST OF WILLARE (177KM)

The diary entries of that day provide another insight into Andrew's attitude towards people of so many different walks of life that he met. Three people had warned him about the Aboriginals in Fitzroy Crossing and Halls Creek, and that he should be wary carrying his cash donations. 'Personally, I think the chances of a blackfella, or anyone else for that matter, pulling up to rob me doesn't even warrant the thought involved. After five carloads of Aboriginals pulled up today to see if I needed water and to donate, it makes me think less of the matter again. It's funny how the three people that told me to be careful are all east coast crew, spoon-fed the same crap and brought up with the same mentality as me. I don't doubt for a second that crime is rife in the towns, and the fact you can't get full-strength takeaway [beer] anywhere from Derby to Kununurra says there is an underlying problem with alcohol, but I think I've more concern for my own safety in the cities when it comes to being mugged.'

He decided in the end that only individuals could be judged, and it was folly to generalise: there was good and bad in all sectors of society, and so that was how he would treat people of all races and nationalities during his travels.

Armed with a tea towel that he used to wipe his forehead every two minutes, Cad enjoyed the cloudy day. When he saw an oversized load accompanied by a lead and rear vehicle and police escort go by, 'as always' he was looking for his mate 'Dinkum' from Broome. Lo and behold, he was in the vehicle behind the truck. 'We had a quick chat and he slung me $50 and asked me how Fiji was.'

His other visitors during the day weren't so welcomed – a flock of crows who circled him constantly all day. 'It started with a couple and the gang steadily picked up numbers throughout the day. It was unnerving watching their shadows continually sweeping across in front of me. "Not today, boys," I kept saying when I looked up. They would come down lower with a bit of attitude when I stopped for a break, to see if I'd dropped dead I'd guess.'

He also encountered the first of the wild bulls he'd been warned about. 'It was making a deep roaring noise like a lion but in just short bursts. I could hear it but couldn't see it. I switched off my music and shit myself ... it followed me for kilometres making that noise. Thankfully, it was behind a fence. I got a glimpse of it once as it trotted along but only its hind – I was screaming "yah!" as loud as I could but didn't deter it – it was weird. I don't know why it followed me.'

It began raining heavily next day and Cad's knees were playing up badly by late afternoon. 'My left knee has always been fucked but my right jumped on the bandwagon today and they both started pinching real hard late arvo and making me miss a step and have to kind of skip to recover, they were just buckling under me. Looks like I'm up for some more X-rays and physio in Darwin.'

His knees were soon forgotten when dark came and he'd camped for the night just a few metres off the road in a sandy water run-off channel. Insects took over his attention. It was a hazard he again had to get used to.

'When I camped I got flogged by mozzies as I stretched, they nailed me through my shirt as it pressed taunt against my skin. I took my shoes off because my feet were killing me but got pumped through my socks. I covered myself in Aerogard but it did little to help – welcome back, mozzies! The bugs were unreal – it was impossible to use my head torch, instead I had to put my torch ten metres away and tried to cook in the shadows. My pot still filled with bugs – who knows how many I ate. I've been eating hundreds of ants every morning after they set up camp in my packet of oats, they all float when I put the milk in and I can usually lose a few dozen but I'm over it and just eat them now. Between the bulls, the bugs and the mozzies and the flies still up past their bedtime, they sucked the remaining life out of me. I retreated to my tent a broken man ... I woke up several times with shitloads of bites on my hands ... I think I am getting bitten through the fly as I sprawl against it.'

After rejoicing at waking only five times and being able to go back to sleep rather than lie awake for hours, Cad was awake at 4am and away at 7am after completing his diary entries, but with a case of chronic diarrhoea.

John from Fitzroy Crossing pulled up in a four-wheel drive and gave Cad three mangoes and, when asked if there were any waterholes ahead, gave great detail about one 30 kilometres to the east and that Cad couldn't miss it, but he suggested it was better to use water from the tank under the windmill. Andrew scoured for hours as he walked but couldn't find any windmill. He pitched his tent on a cement slab next to a picnic table as other campers looked on unimpressed.

Cad recorded that he passed the 9000-kilometre milestone the next day (I logged it as four days later), but otherwise it was just another long, tough day that began with his first steps at 5.30am after he realised ants had broken into every unsealed packet of food and he had to turf his nuts and fruit. He kept the equally invaded oats as he couldn't replace them until he reached Fitzroy Crossing, about 88 kilometres away; he had nothing else for breakfast.

If there was any day when his body may have collapsed and succumbed to heatstroke and he may even have died, this was it. He stopped under the shade of a boab tree after just two hours on the road.

'I was so tired it was impossible to keep my eyes open. I straight passed out sitting up. I was probably out for an hour and woke up feeling worse. I made myself drink a cup of rehydration powder then passed out again with my head on my solar panel. Was out again for a while then I had another cup. I had a sore neck so I grabbed my tarp out and just collapsed on the rocks and shit, no pillow, no mattress. I remember being really uncomfortable but didn't have the strength to get up. I was out for probably another halfa [hour] again and I woke up in a pile of sweat and started vomiting. I felt like I was zonked out on downers. I drank some more rehydration tablets and powder until there was none left.

'I was so out of it I was trying to put the wrong lid back on the wrong bottle and tried about half a dozen times until I realised what I was doing. I sat there staring into space for at least an hour and then I snapped out of it all of a sudden – mentally not physically.'

He became very hungry and ate much of the next day's rations. Fortunately, he had the benefit of a tailwind and incredibly knocked out 44 kilometres through sheer determination. That evening Andrew fathomed that he should be averaging a day off every four to survive.

DAYS 331–332, 22–23 NOVEMBER 2011 TO FITZROY CROSSING (44KM), THEN A REST DAY

Fortunately, the word had spread far and wide throughout the region that Andrew was pacing the Great Northern Highway alone. There were many people who took it upon themselves to ensure he had voluntary support, some obviously concerned about a misguided young bloke out in the wilderness by himself in ridiculously oppressive heat.

One of PK's workers, a guy from Nelson Bay in New South Wales, dropped off some water, a tub of ice and a bottle of Powerade, enlarging Andrew's water supply to eight litres, but that was still not nearly enough to last him two days. A woman pulled up in a 4WD while he was having lunch and said John had given her a message to pass on: drop into the Shell roadhouse at Fitzroy Crossing and grab some nibbles, then go to the lodge for dinner, bed and shower. Andrew scratched his head to think of who this John was.

When he had phone reception shortly after, there was an email saying another random traveller – Linda, who had earlier pulled over to donate money – had also arranged a night's accommodation at the BP roadhouse.

He later joined PK and his workers for dinner on the other side of the highway at the Shell service station. One of the workers, called 'Irish', put the mysterious John on the phone and Cad still didn't know who it was until he mentioned mangoes – it was the farmer he passed two days earlier. He also discovered John had a cattle property of about a million acres nearby.

Andrew asked PK to bank his donations collected since Broome – $1565, which was amazing, considering how little traffic was on the road. He spent the day relaxing, did a $195 shop to last him a week, and talked to electricians Yarny and Milo, who were sharing the donga next to his. Most of the day was spent getting much-needed rest.

DAY 333–339, 24–30 NOVEMBER 2011 FITZROY CROSSING TO HALLS CREEK (288KM)

After Cad left Fitzroy Crossing, not one person stopped to talk to him the whole day. The temperature was a 'cool' 37 degrees Celsius, with lower humidity than he'd encountered, flat roads and grassy cattle country. He was able to sleep without sweating and in fact was cold during the night for the first time in months.

Cad was on the road by 7am, walking into a headwind that persisted all day, the scenery endless grassy plains but no more boab trees in sight. The soaring hot wind burnt his eyes and made them water constantly, forcing him to walk with his head down. Later in the day he came across some ranges with sheer red cliffs dotted with caves, which impressed him.

Kevin and Digger ('a couple of characters who asked if I'd met "John the fossil"') stopped and offered Cad a beer and, upon refusal, a sip of Sambuca liqueur. Digger, a helicopter pilot, was working on local cattle stations. They mentioned a waterhole about 30 kilometres ahead, and this was one Cad could find, surrounded by a clump of trees; he lifted Redge over a barbed-wire fence to get closer. 'It wasn't what I had expected. I had pictured crystal waters in a sort of stone walled gorge but it was more of a black swampy set-up half-full of reeds. But there was plenty of room to swim around. There were probably three-metre-high rock walls to two sides and just reedy banks to the others. The boys said it was deep, but after hearing PK's tragic story I wasn't diving into black water, so I climbed down and belly-flopped into it. It was nice and cold and refreshing.'

Clint, a guy in his thirties from Melbourne who was working as a welfare officer in Aboriginal communities, had also driven in to use the waterhole, and he chatted with Cad for a while, leaving him about $60 worth of donations in gold coins. Clint said the water was much murkier than usual, and a small waterfall often flowed through the rocks. Andrew asked him about the stone under the arm advice he'd received and Clint explained it was to protect him from a serpent dragging him under, not a snakebite. While he may not have been convinced by their traditional beliefs, Cad had really endeared himself to the Indigenous majority in these parts. He wrote: 'The blackfellas crack me up, they all slow right down and go around me and beep, and I see hands come out of every window to wave. I always give them a huge wave, they make me laugh. I wave to the farmers and the crew in the four-wheel-drive utes and they just ignore me, which shits me to tears when I make an effort.'

After a second skinny-dip, Cad pitched his tent next to the waterhole, filled his water bottles and was asleep by 9pm.

Next day he was taken by the sight of the Ngumban Cliffs, which he encountered early in the day. 'The road weaved through the Ngumban Cliffs which were quite impressive. They were rich red ranges covered in boulders and spinifex with sheer cliffs poking out of the tops of its steep banks, it was same as the Pilbara.'

The hot dry headwind really sapped his energy and he pulled up early, setting up camp at the entrance of a road to an Aboriginal community and sleeping like a baby for once. When he woke, Cad realised he'd drunk thirteen litres of water the previous day, leaving him just five litres, so he didn't wash up or wash his teeth, conserving what supplies he had. He was on the road by 7am, again into a dry headwind. Fortunately, Graham and Jeff, who had just painted the Halls Creek roadhouse and were returning to Broome, stopped and gave him a litre and a half of water (and a $50 donation), and soon after another car stopped and he landed a further half a litre and $45 in donations.

He'd walked 45 kilometres by 2.30pm and had tried to conserve water by sipping little amounts regularly. At 4.30pm he reached a rest area with just half a litre of water in his stocks and desperate to find a water tank; Cad thought he'd have to flag down cars for the first time to survive, with Halls Creek 108 kilometres away.

He left the pram on the road and walked down the dirt track to the rest area, finding a car parked there belonging to two women. He went back to fetch Redge and went in and found some more inhabitants, so he did the rounds scabbing water – one bottle from 'an old hermit', four 'goon bags' from a young couple who'd just pulled in, and eight litres from an elderly couple. It was now safe to camp for the night and walk for another day.

In order to not have to rely solely on the generosity of passing motorists, he contacted the roadhouse just past Halls Creek where he'd had supplies dropped off to see if they could arrange for some water and food to be relayed to him by any travellers heading west. The woman at the roadhouse, either ignorant to how dire his situation was just unsympathetic, was hardly co-operative. After establishing his food and water supplies were there, Cad explained what he was up to and asked if someone could be organised to transport a portion and leave it at the entrance to the rest area.

'I'm getting low on food and water and I really need it [one of his bags of supplies]. "Yeah, well, all we can do is ask the truckies and they will drop it off at Halls Creek for you," she replied. "No, it's no good to me at Halls, I need it out here." Then the rude bitch starts getting narky at me down the phone. I said: "You don't understand, I have no support crew, I'm walking from Fitzroy to Halls, I need to get it here." "Well, there's nothing I can do about that, I can only ask the truckies and they won't stop for you." "Well, that's just it. I don't think truckies are the answer; you need to ask anyone but truckies. Is Matthew [who Cad had arranged his supplies to be sent to] there?" "No, he starts at twelve tomorrow." I gave up after ten minutes of painful conversation. I can't believe I kept my cool and kept telling her I appreciate it and thanks and please. I just wanted to scream down the phone at her.'

As soon as Andrew reached the highway early next morning, he saw a big cardboard box and three large containers of water on the side of the road – the woman at the roadhouse had come good after all. After emptying the water into his bottles, he'd suddenly gone from one extreme to the other – he had forty-five litres, plus plenty of food.

He was extremely fortunate that the goods had been delivered as six hours later he'd walked 30 kilometres and not one car had stopped, meaning dehydration would have been a very serious issue. He was in bed at 7.30pm and didn't wake until 5.30am – ten hours straight sleep, probably an overnight record since before Perth.

As Andrew reached Halls Creek, he came across five policemen having a break outside the bakery and stopped to say hello. He was amused to find that the copper had put the radar on him and clocked him walking at 5 kilometres an hour. He went to the post office to pick up new tyres and the battery-operated fan I'd sent up, headed to the caravan park and had his first shower for seven days. Smelling like roses, he did his washing, had dinner, answered a heap of emails and text messages and completed his diaries. Fortunately, Sheena, a traveller he met overnight, agreed to take a food parcel and meet him at a rest area 100 kilometres ahead in three days.

So much for a day off on average every four days. Cad had had one 'lay day' in thirteen, but the afternoon in Halls Creek, after he'd had to cover only 12 kilometres to reach town that morning, was certainly a welcome break.

DAYS 340–342, 1–3 DECEMBER 2011 HALLS CREEK TO ARGYLE MINE (132KM)

When he went to get his clothes off the clothes lines, Cad found a $20 pair of Nike socks had been stolen – the pitfalls of caravan park clothes drying, unfortunately. He had further frustration in not being able to get the iPod I'd sent up to work, but after calling me to see if there were any instructions and consulting the iTunes website with no joy, he worked out that he had to drag two fingers over the screen instead of one.

As he walked through town, Cad again tried to endear himself to the locals, which he assumed was not usual behaviour for tourists. 'I said hello to a few old

Indigenous, and judging by their surprised reactions, I'm going to assume that the white minority here don't bother saying hi much. I caught a couple of old ducks by surprise when I stopped and said hi, there were big smiles and "Oh, hello there". Yesterday I spoke to at least a dozen blackfellas about my trip and stuff, and they love it and come over and see what I'm up to. One old boy with an Akubra hat and a white beard pulled his four-wheel drive over and crossed the road to say hello, shake my hand and say, "You have a good walk," while his wife waved from the passenger seat. That's not the case with the whites here – they just walk past with a bemused smirk on their faces. I always say hello when they're staring at me but my greetings are rarely reciprocated.'

When Andrew starting walking at 10am the temperature was already 38 degrees. Thunder started at 2pm, black clouds rolled in and Cad observed he wasn't going to miss this storm. A strong wind blew up from behind and he had to strap down the solar panel to stop it blowing away. He observed: 'The wind was getting so strong I could hardly walk in it. With no real warning it went from spitting to pissing down and I put my booties on and was just in board shorts. But the wind changed to the west and was whipping the rain in so hard sideways it felt like hail, it really stung. It got a bit crazy so I had to point Redge into it and huddle behind it. I was freezing and shivering and I couldn't believe how much the temp dropped.

A car slowed as it passed then stopped and reversed. She wound down her window and said in a concerned voice, "Are you alright?" "Yeah, I'm walking around Oz." "That's the worst storm I have ever driven in in my life," she said. I thought, "You should try walking in it." I told her I was okay and battled on.

'I put a shirt on so the rain didn't hurt so much but I had to retire behind some trees and resume my huddling position. I squatted and sat there with my knees cramping and shivering. I stared into the trees across the road thrashing around in the violent winds and thought to myself, "What are you doing here, you don't want to be here, just go home!" The sun poked its head out about 5 to 5.30pm – it was the first time I had wished for sun in a while. I dried off and got changed and then it started raining lightly again. It rained until I was asleep.'

Next day was the first day of summer and he walked until after dark but pitched his tent and was asleep, exhausted, by 8pm. Cad was up at 4.30am without having to use an alarm clock and on the road at 7am, into a headwind as usual, and was so exhausted he reckons he only had 'half a go' and was 'gutted' that he'd only walked 35 kilometres by 3pm. He felt he'd stacked too much food so ate a mango, two kiwifruit, an orange and five bananas and tried sunflower kernels (for the first time in his life, no doubt). While walking, he finished the audio book *The Search for Al Queda.* Cad had an enormous appetite for world affairs, history and politics, and said, 'I learned a lot about a lot, from Saudi finding oil to the India–Pakistan conflict over Kashmir, and a lot about Middle Eastern history dating back to the Crusades.' Then he returned to his Spanish lessons for the last couple of hours.

Andrew was also stalked by three wild horses for a while, which really unnerved him, then some sort of bird of prey taunted him for ages. Imagine being out in the wilderness by yourself in stifling heat battling psychological demons as well as the weather, totally exhausted from so long on the road and then being confronted by these wild beasts. '[The bird] flew ahead and landed in the middle of the road and sat on the lines until I got close and then it would take off and hover in the wind and then fly ahead and wait for me to catch up. It did it at least seven or eight times. It was weird – maybe it had babies in a nest and was luring me away, although I haven't seen or heard any baby birds and I doubt it's that time with the wet approaching.'

He'd hoped to log 55 kilometres in the day, but as dark clouds rolled in and it started to spit with rain, he hastily retreated to a small dirt patch twenty metres off the highway and made it his home for the night. 'I knew dirt meant ants but I didn't care ... I spoke to the big pile of black ants congregating around their nest. "Okay, guys, I'm only here for one night. I won't piss you off if you don't piss me off. Have we got a deal?" I find myself talking to the flies a lot these days as well, instead of stressing out I tend to take a calmer approach and say, "C'mon, mate, leave me alone, just get on my back with your mates otherwise I'm going to have to squash you."' The lecture didn't work on the flying ants, which infiltrated his food; he had to pick at least forty out of his dinner.

During the night, Andrew woke in a heap of sweat to a gale-force wind, so got up to push his pegs in deeper with a rock and piled rocks on top to make them more secure; he also dug a channel for the oncoming rain.

At least he saw what he described as the best light show of his life. 'One straight big bolt had about six arms coming off it half way down and shooting back into the clouds. I woke up at 1am to World War III – the thunder was deafening, it rattled my bones. The wind was pushing the side of the tent in so far I thought the poles were going to break, water was pissing in the ceiling because the fly-sheet and tent was being pressed together. I woke up to water dripping on my head. I quickly rounded everything together and stuffed what I could into wet bags.' He was up at dawn to examine the puddles of water inside the tent but packed up everything wet and muddy and battled on.

He passed the Ord River, the first waterway he'd seen flowing since the west coast of Western Australia. It was early in the wet season and he'd encountered no great rain, so most of the rivers or creeks he'd previously passed were well below full whereas the Ord feeds from the damned Lake Argyle, so is always flowing. The Kimberley region comes alive in so many ways in the wet season (November to March) when 90 per cent of its annual rainfall comes (over 750 millimetres in the four months) but for Andrew this meant he was likely to encounter ferocious thunderstorms but little passing traffic as tourists are far more common in the dry season. The people in an old bus who he had arranged to carry his water pulled up, but his supply was fine and he told them take it to the next roadhouse at Turkey Creek. He walked until midday when he stopped for lunch, only to be confronted by an unexpected visitor.

'I sat down and got some food out when I heard a bull making noises. I've got to know this noise well, they are always carrying on at night when I'm in my tent, I don't think they like the speakers as they usually shut up when I turn the music off to sleep. I had my back to them and yelled out, "Yeah, yeah, tough guy, give it a rest," then turned around and there were about thirty cows and two bulls walking towards me, not in a bunch but spread out in a line. I turned my music off and turned around to face them. They stopped about forty metres away and formed into a bunch and all stared at me.' Andrew flapped his arms and yelled but that only encouraged the two bulls to smash their horns together as if they were about to attack him. He quickly packed up and walked to the other side of the road looking for a tree, but the landscape was bare so the advice he'd received to climb up a tree was rendered useless. 'My mind was racing for a plan B but nothing. I didn't look at him [the black bull] except out the corner of my eye and when I passed I used my [rear-vision] mirror to keep an eye on him. My heart was racing, I'm not looking forward to the water buffalos.'

Soon after he saw three brown horses with white blazes, which seemed identical to ones he saw late in the day two days earlier, and he thought surely they could not have travelled the 70 kilometres, or maybe they did. They charged towards him, stopping about twenty metres away, and as Cad reached for his camera to get a shot a car towing a caravan came past and scared them away.

His day of walking ended after he trekked through some magnificent red mountains and gorges – the best scenery of the trip so far, he reckoned – while enjoying an audio book on WikiLeaks. A young bloke called Andrew arrived to give him a pre-arranged lift to the Argyle diamond mine camp to stay the night. (Cad did not record when or how this was arranged; I imagine while he was at Halls Creek.) He was treated like a celebrity, which he thought was amusing, and stuck to his commitment not to have a drink but mingled with the miners, who raised $920 for the Leukaemia Foundation.

DAYS 343–348, 4–9 DECEMBER 2011 REST DAY AT ARGYLE DIAMOND MINE, THEN TO KUNUNURRA (231KM)

After gorging himself on food for two nights and a day ('I have no self-control in joints like this'), Cad was given a lift back to where he'd finished walking and resumed his Oz On Foot mission. He'd done the 30 kilometres to Turkey Creek by lunchtime.

I'd suggested he do a helicopter ride from Turkey Creek over the Bungle Bungle Range, which I had done five years earlier, and I'd shout him as a Christmas gift, but typically Cad wouldn't slow down long enough for such a treat. It was a pity as it is an absolutely breathtaking experience. He also knocked back a free night in a donga with dinner there too and instead picked up his food dropped off at Turkey Creek by yet another traveller by request and pressed on to make an impression on the 190-odd kilometres to the next town, Kununurra. He lasted for another ten kilometres until dark came.

A 60-kilometre day by foot in these conditions the next day was a phenomenal effort. He hadn't been on the road long when the driver of a road train pulled over and offered him a Powerade and a $20 donation. He said his name was Robbo and Andrew described him as 'your average-looking truck driver – big guy, tattoos and a beard. He was a good bloke, he was driving a four-bucket road train taking iron ore from the mine I passed yesterday arvo to Wyndham port. They do two loads a day for a week, then a week of nights, then a week off. He said he grew up at South West Rocks [on the New South Wales North Coast], where he did his electrical apprenticeship and now lives at Wyndham.' When Cad reached the next roadhouse, the manager gave him $20 with a note that read: 'for the walking guy – from Robbo'. She said it was to buy food and drinks.

After a seventy-five-minute break he plugged on until 9pm, when some locals stopped to chat and asked him if he'd seen any snakes or ghosts, to which Andrew asked, 'Are there ghosts around?' 'Yeah, blackfella ghosts,' came the reply. They informed him there was a rest area 20 kilometres ahead, so he decided to go for broke to reach it so he had a decent campsite. Along the way, another group of Aboriginals pulled up to let him know the rest area wasn't far but to be careful of water buffalos and snakes, and that there were cane toads all over the road nearer to Kununurra. All the while lightning and thunder was raging around him. The woman asked if he'd seen a scrub bull yet (he hadn't) and warned him they would chase him, and if one did he should run up a tree.

Ghosts, water buffalo, bulls, mosquitos, ants, cane toads, wind, rain, lightning, thunder, loneliness, fatigue, soreness ... and Cad couldn't sleep because the moonlight was like a torch shining on his face. There was nowhere to hide, no one to call, no companion to help him. Just one man, his pram, his rations, his tent and his incredible determination.

Cad ran into Robbo again the next day, and they got to talking about sundry subjects when Robbo told him how he moved to Wyndham about a year earlier after he'd been back east around the time his son retired from football; his son used to captain the Sydney Roosters and retired after the 2004 Grand Final. Cad commented: 'Now, for most of my mates they would have known who it was straight away, but I could have been in the hot seat on *Who Wants To Be A Millionaire?* going for the million dollars and still not have a clue; I would have to have phoned a friend. "Who's your son?" "Brad Fittler." "Oh, okay. How's he doing?" "He's doing it tough, actually." I thought he was serious for a minute, and then he said, "He just bought a joint for $3 million."' Robert Fittler had left his wife when she was pregnant with Brad, and was not reunited with his son until Brad was nineteen, but they have since kept in regular contact.

The vegetation turned more tropical with lots of palms, and Cad realised what the lady who warned him about cane toads meant; they were flattened all over the road. A couple of farmers who had been ploughing a field to plant sandalwood trees gave him drinks and donations, then Robbo came past on his way to Wyndham just before the junction of the Great Northern and Victoria highways. They had one more chat before going in different directions and never crossing each other's path again.

The heat was so bad that Andrew had to vacate his tent by 6am next morning. He was in a foul mood when he hit the road but a traveller called Anton pulled over and snapped him out of his misery by offering cold water, juices and fruit in a little cooler bag, packed with ice, throwing in a new wide-rim straw hat he'd just bought and a $30 donation. Cad reported his sweating had hit a 'category 4' before he'd walked ten metres but he came up with the idea of clamping his fan to the pram handles and the breeze blew straight to his neck. 'Absolutely gold! It definitely got me through the day.'

Just out of Kununurra he came across a narrow bridge with a 'no pedestrians' sign but Cad hurried across anyway, only to force a truck to stop suddenly to avoid hitting oncoming traffic – a dangerous moment. He held up his hands as if to say 'sorry'. Not real safe either was the fact he was carting $2800 in donations, which he immediately offloaded at a bank.

The previous day a guy called Brendan pulled over in his car to give Andrew a cold drink and offered him accommodation for the night in Kununurra at a company-supplied cabin. He was going to take up the offer but after a night of drinks and laughs with some carpenters working on contract in town, including some Irish lads, he bunked with them in a caravan park cabin; being entertained by the Irish had become one of his favourite pastimes. 'I didn't stop laughing – "good crack", as they put it.'

DAYS 349–350, 10–11 DECEMBER 2011 REST DAYS, KUNUNURRA

Typical of the generosity of those who admired Andrew's mission, the manager of the BP service station (Scott), which also had a mini-mart, insisted Andrew did not pay for his supplies (food and a tarpaulin that he badly needed) and told Cad he had slipped a donation in his bag. There was $100! The two days' rest was much needed but consisted of catching up on his blogs and diary, returning emails and messages, washing, shopping and a few hours of purely doing nothing.

DAYS 351–352, 12–13 DECEMBER 2011 MAKING THE NORTHERN TERRITORY BORDER (84KM)

The only highlight of Cad's traipsing down the highway in 40-plusdegree heat was when a four-wheel drive pulled over with a couple of blokes who had come across him earlier near Fitzroy Crossing. One geed the other up to sing Andrew a song. 'He could sing like an angel and play [guitar]. I sat there eating my tuna while he jammed out a song while leaning against the truck, it made for quite good smoko entertainment.'

Next day he woke early having lost an hour after crossing the border between Western Australia and the Nothern Territory. The constant heat for weeks had really fatigued him now, and at about 11am he rested under the shade of a tree. 'I spotted a big tree and stopped to eat but was falling asleep so I lay down to doze and woke an hour later in the sun saturated with sweat. I hardly had enough energy to get up and plonked myself back down in the shade. I got another hour's [sleep] then sat there drinking a workout drink trying to wake up. It was 1.30 and I'd done stuff-all.'

It looked like heavy rain ahead and a couple pulled over and gave Cad a disposable raincoat, insisting he also take ten cans of chunky soup and gave him a further $50 donation. The wind and rain came soon after and when Cad tried to put the raincoat on in the gale it was shredded to pieces, but after thirty minutes of torrential rain it slowed to a drizzle. The temperature had cooled which gave him good walking conditions right through to dark (about 7pm) when he pitched his tent on a dirt track, with a disaffected bull snorting at him just metres away.

Having abandoned his plan to make it to Darwin in the eleven days remaining before Christmas, he'd decided he would walk only as far as Katherine in 2011. Next step would be to get to Darwin by bus, then head to Thailand for two months to rest his body and mind and to try to put some meat back on his badly withered body, which by this stage weighed a paltry 55 kilograms.

This part of his walk, the soul-sucking Kimberley, shows two things. One, just how serious the consequences his poor timing and lack of initial planning could be; and two, that just how far the power of the mind could take a person, to a level they never thought possible. Cad had conditioned his body to withstand conditions that most of us could not envisage enduring.

11

COUNTING DOWN TO CHRISTMAS

Christmas was around the corner. It was 13 December, his grannie's eighty-seventh birthday, when Cad had walked into the Northern Territory on Day 352. He was, however, in no mood for celebrations. Sadly, at this time, two weeks short of a year on his one-man, one-pram Oz On Foot expedition, what had begun as an adventure into the unexpected had become a massive burden.

Mentally, he was in a very bad place. He recorded some of this in his diaries but opened up more to his closest mates, who had become extremely worried about him, and briefly to me. I admit I didn't want him to keep walking into 2012. I was already in awe of what he had achieved and he wasn't far from his $50,000 fundraising target; walking from Sydney to Perth was a big enough effort, in my books. He was drained, demotivated, physically worn-out and emotionally very vulnerable, and it became obvious that he was going to have to take closer to two years out of his life rather than one to complete his task. I told him straight that if the cost was too much and it had become such a misery, just walk away – now.

When he crossed the border from Western Australia, he was also very close to crossing the line when it came to his mental and physical health. He was hanging out for Christmas for one reason only: he could hang up his well-worn walking shoes. He had been toying with whether to sit out the wet season in Darwin, where it would be almost unbearably hot and humid but at least he could have a month or more away from endless walking, or whether to head to Thailand, where food and board would be much cheaper and he could do some sightseeing and enjoy another culture. Asia won out.

But he had to get through another eleven days in the Territory's outback first, and overcome a countdown to a Christmas that was unlike anything he'd experienced before. It was very different from the previous year's, which had seen our family gather at Cad's recently renovated house at North Avoca.

DAY 353, 14 DECEMBER 2011 EAST OF THE BORDER (40KM)

The day began with Cad waking up before sunrise, having to air all his wet belongings after catching up with his diary and chasing the first cane toad to invade his tent ... only to find the ants had gone wild right through everything again. Two blokes he'd met a couple of days earlier were supposed to drop off eight litres of water but he missed them.

The scenery changed dramatically with rocky ranges appearing all around the low-lying plains, which were rich and grassy and dotted with huge thick-trunked boabs. Andrew was ecstatic to come across a rest area that had two water tanks. He lodged himself under the tap and had a wash, shampooed his hair, cleaned his clothes and was sitting there naked to drip-dry when a four-wheel drive pulled up (he hurriedly draped a towel around his waist). The driver, a tall South African, locked his car as he went to the toilet and then approached Andrew with his own 1.5-litre bottle of cold water. Without asking if he'd like a drink or offering a donation, the man questioned why on earth Cad would be walking in these parts during the harsh summer.

As Cad continued on, he saw six storm fronts around him with lightning illuminating the sky, so knew he was in for rain. The mozzies moved in first, right on queue at dusk, followed by scores of other insects. Cad's words best describe what he confronted from then:

'I was at my wits' end and was screaming fuck this and fuck that and give me a break as I tried to cook and pitch my tent. I don't think I was far off turning into a blubbery mess at one stage, it really is getting too much. "Just leave me alone," I screamed as the mozzies continually nailed me through my saturated clothing, which was sticking to my skin. I couldn't pack up and get in my tent quick enough, but not before getting a stick and digging a three-inch-wide, three-inch-deep trench on an angle across the front of my tent. I really didn't need to wake to water under my mattress. Instead I woke at 10.30pm to a sandstorm whipping my skin and blinding me. After I woke it filled my tent and there was nothing I could do. I could hear thunder and I strapped my solar panel down. The wind was ferocious, I wrapped myself in my sheet and laid there copping it. Sand stuck to my wet lips and then I fell asleep somehow ... what a day!

DAYS 354–356, 15–17 DECEMBER 2011 TOWARDS TIMBER CREEK (103KM), THEN A REST DAY

Perhaps Andrew's diary notes best explain what he awoke to, and how he reacted. He was obviously near the end of his tether.

'Woke up to a sand-filled disaster at five o'clock. I couldn't keep my eyes open. I turned my alarm clock off and woke back up at seven, sweating. I turned my trusty fan back on, wrote in my diary and slowly stuffed around packing up and getting ready. I'm over it, well and truly. I'm aching all over, it's like my body has just given up for the year and mentally I'm not far behind.

'No ants, I reckon because I coated my tyres with Aerogard before I went to bed. It took forever to get the sand off everything. It's up my nose, in my hair and ears and handfuls in the corner of my tent. In hindsight it was a stupid idea camping in a massive sand patch knowing there was a storm and wind coming. I didn't get on the road until nine, every step is a punish, my legs are like jelly and I'm shuffling along like an aged pensioner...

'I walked for hours until I gave up and sat in the sun on the side of the road to eat. I'm starting to lose it and found myself screaming aaar-ghh and other nonsense into the stale hot air. I broke down and found myself laughing hysterically into the air. It felt like I was crying, I don't know if that has happened since the Nullarbor. I poured hot water on my head but it offered little relief, there wasn't so much as the tiniest breeze. Sweat was pouring out of me like a garden hose. I shuffled on until about two and finally found a dry bit of bush to the side. I sat under a shitty little tree, which offered very little in the shade department. I slipped my silver sheet of insulation into the branches and huddled under the tiny patch of shade it created. It was an effort to force food in.'

A bit further on Cad saw a small running stream off the road and clambered down a rocky embankment with a pot, all excited, and poured water over his head, only to find it worse than a warm bath. He finally found a large bush that provided ample shade and sat there for an hour. He vowed not to leave until the sun had set. In front of him was a massive storm front shedding torrential rain and he begged it to come his way, only for it to pass across the sky in front of him.

About 5pm the sun slipped behind clouds and he continued, with thirteen kilometres to go to a rest area. The landscape changed to fenced cattle properties, with boab and gum trees. He made the rest area in the fading light, only to be greeted by Aboriginals from a nearby settlement drinking and yahooing around the picnic table until 12.45am, and resuming again at 3.30am after a car had pulled up.

Next day Andrew decided to have a go at making it 48 kilometres to the next rest area. A couple of hours in he came across a flowing creek and decided the opportunity to have an Oz On Foot wash was too big to pass up. But after stripping down to his undies, grabbing his soak and diving in, he couldn't get out quick enough: the water, again, was like a hot bath.

That evening he saw a fire at the other end of a rest area and invited himself to join a Belgian couple, who were shocked to see someone walk out of the darkness, with no sound of an entering vehicle. Despite the heaviest rain he'd experienced on the trip falling at about 4am, Cad slept like a baby.

Cad woke to find ants in everything, as usual. He only had to walk for two hours to Timber Creek, where he booked a donga for the night (for $60) and enjoyed air conditioning and his own fridge and television.

DAYS 357–358, 18–19 DECEMBER 2011 TIMBER CREEK TO VICTORIA RIVER ROADHOUSE (93KM)

It was interesting to read in Andrew's diary how bad the cane toads were at Timber Creek. When Chris and I came through this way to Darwin in May 2006, the Territorians were very concerned about the infiltration of the toads from Queensland from the east and how they might infect the landscape. Well, it seems their worst fears have been realised – there were hundreds littering the highway.

Cad thought it must have been the fact that he'd had most of a day off after doing 217 kilometres in a week and that the temperature was cooler (the Bureau of Meteorology recorded 33.3 degrees mean temperature) but he found walking a 48-kilometre day in ten hours with just two brief breaks at the 15-kilometre and 30-kilometre marks as 'easy'. His headspace must have been much better, perhaps because he could see that the end of the year's pain was only days away.

It wasn't the case the previous day, judging by the video blog he recorded in the morning: 'I saw a rope yesterday and I was eyeing it off, I was ready to tie a bloody noose in the end of it and lynch it over a tree. It sucks out here, man; the last five days have been probably the hardest five days of my life. Just me and the bugs, and the flies and the mozzies and the cane toads, and the swamp and the humidity. It's a shit, really there is no other way to explain it, capital S-H-I-T ... I'm over it. I'll get to Katherine; Darwin is just not happening this year, so I'm going to get to Katherine, and the first thing I'm going to do is get a ham and pineapple pizza and a bottle of vodka and that's me done, mate. Pulling the plug for the year. See you in Katherine.'

As he approached Victoria River, he was captivated by the scenery of the mountain range above. When he arrived at the settlement – little more than the roadhouse and associated buildings – he was greeted by the owners, Roy and Teresa, saying, 'Ah, you're the walker; we've been waiting for you.'

There were a couple of surprises waiting too: a bag full of lollies, fruit/chocolate bars and dried fruit from John from Fitzroy Crossing, with a note saying it was for 'the walker, from the mango guy from Fitzroy'; and also a free night's accommodation paid for by a truckie called Peter he'd met west of Timber Creek. The boys he'd had a couple of fun nights with at Kununurra had dropped off Cad's supplies, telling Roy they'd 'corrupted' him in Kununurra. There were two attractive French women working at the roadhouse, about whom Andrew commented: 'I was trying not to blatantly perve; it's been a while since I've seen anything worth looking at.'

DAYS 359–360, 20–21 DECEMBER 2011 TO KATHERINE AND BACK FOR AN UNSCHEDULED 'DAY OFF', THEN FINALLY LEAVING VICTORIA RIVER (17KM)

I vividly remember talking to Andrew this day. He had a tyre so badly punctured that he couldn't fix it and had to hitch a ride with a truck driver the 195 kilometres to Katherine, pick up a new one and get back to resume his walk. It meant he'd lose a day, the repercussion being that he'd have to push hard to even make Katherine for Christmas Day and instead would be walking in the heat along the outback highway while most of the country, and certainly his family, were into their Christmas fare. He was so stressed by the setback when I spoke to him that I (stupidly) suggested he take the pram with him and not double back, as he would be the only one who knew he'd missed that leg of the trip. He would in no way consider that; it was cheating.

The day began with the two hot French chicks interviewing him on video as he pumped up his tyres – on the pram, not his ego! They still had the cameras rolling as he started to walk over the bridge when, poof, the tyre blew out. He fetched his well-used spare, only to find it had patches glued on the same area of the tyre, so obviously there was something puncturing them on the wheel, but he couldn't find what. With the help of Teresa and Roy, Cad tried six times to fix the two tubes, and said goodbye twice more as he departed, only for the tyre to blow out each time, even with heavy-duty tractor-tyre patches which another property worker, Troy, had given him. He had no choice but to get a lift to Katherine to get new tubes, then return; a truck driver named Peter was happy to take him to Katherine on his way to Darwin.

With the tubes donated by the Katherine toy store, Andrew had to walk three kilometres back to a roadhouse with his valuables in one 'wet bag', his tent and bike tubes in another and his mattress and sheet in a third, hoping to hitch a lift back. With no success by 9pm, he gave up and accepted an offer from Alex, a helicopter pilot he'd met at Victoria River earlier in the day, of a bed for the night at the dongas near the airfield.

The next day Andrew hitched a ride west with Darcy, a truck driver who'd told him the evening before that he could give Andrew a lift if he could not get transport overnight. Trouble was that Cad didn't hear, or had forgotten, that Darcy was going only as far as the junction of the Buntine Highway, about halfway back to Victoria River. Here Cad was, dressed in T-shirt, board shorts and thongs, with no water, having to bail out and sweat it out for another lift on the Victoria Highway with the temperature approaching 40 degrees. He wrapped the bed sheet over him and sat there for two hours, several motorists ignoring his pleas for help before getting a ride with a young couple from Adelaide. They dropped him back at Victoria River, and after eating for the first time in seventeen hours, Cad quickly packed Redge and was off early in the afternoon.

During this ordeal, however, Andrew had his second brush with fame without knowing it. While he was frantically trying to patch up his punctures the previous day, a local whose surname Cad only picked up as 'Jones' came into the roadhouse with Alex and an old fella with dementia called Clancy. They were laughing about how Clancy, who had only left the area once in thirty years (he went to Darwin but tired of the hustle and bustle within hours and caught a bus straight back), had decided he wanted to get away from the place that day (but never did). Anyway, while chatting to Alex in Katherine overnight, Cad learned that 'Jonesy' was actually the multimillionaire Milton Jones, owner of the Coolibah Station and North West Choppers, Australia's largest scenic helicopter operator and air-mustering service, whose life was the subject of the Channel Ten documentary series *Keeping Up with the Joneses* in 2010–11.

Cad wrote that he would never have picked Jones for a successful and wealthy Australian whose life would be portrayed on TV. 'He just seemed like your average old farmer to me.' He later saw a roadside sign promoting the business with 'as seen on television'. But his brush with relative fame left him annoyed as much as impressed. 'When I thought about it, I thought, "What a tight-arse!" He didn't even donate after sitting there asking me about my trip.'

DAYS 361–362, 22–23 DECEMBER 2011 TOWARDS KATHERINE (96KM)

Cad had an anxious moment when he saw two Indigenous men walking on the other side of the road in his direction then cross the highway and come straight towards him; he feared he was about to be mugged. Then he saw they had jerry cans, and three women were walking a fair way behind them in the middle of the road. They had run out of petrol.

They walked past with blank looks on their faces, which was extraordinary, considering the spectacle of a lone white man pushing a pram in these parts. Andrew noticed they only had a Coke can between them; he had passed no running streams that day and it was at least 40 kilometres to Victoria River roadhouse. So he doubled back to offer them some of his restricted water supplies. He could smell alcohol on the men and they seemed drunk, which didn't help communication, but Cad persisted as he wanted to save the women, who appeared innocent victims of the men's miscalculation or irresponsibility.

'You want some water?' Cad asked.

The first man turned back. 'Water, yeah,' he replied.

'You know you've got 40 kilometres to walk? Maybe you should try to hitch.'

'No one stop,' he answered.

Andrew gave them a full 1.5-litre bottle of water that he could barely do without and watched the men scull half the bottle down. 'I'd give you more but need it myself, mate.'

'Where you walk to?' one asked.

'Back to Sydney.'

'Alright, good luck, boss,' the man said, enquiring no further.

As Andrew walked off, he saw the three women catch up and the men share the remaining water. One of the girls yelled out, 'Where you come from?'

'Sydney.'

'Where you go?'

'Sydney.'

'Ahh ... good luck!'

Andrew passed a stranded old blue ute 6 or 7 kilometres further east, a teenage boy standing next to it trying to hitch a ride, jerry can in hand, with another sitting on the road. 'We run out of petrol,' he said.

'Yeah, I know, I just saw your friends up the road. You got any water?'

'No.'

So Andrew gave him half a bottle of his water, then as he walked past he saw two old people inside, making it eight travelling in this old ute. Andrew looked in his rear-view mirror as he kept walking and saw the boy go to the car window but not offer any water to the old folk. 'My conscience got me and I yelled out to come and get some more [water]. I filled up his bottle and told him to share it. I watched him walk back but he still wasn't sharing, the little prick.'

Andrew was still three days short of Katherine and would need to come across a stream to replenish his water supply, so even I was surprised he did such a humane thing and ensured that the misguided family, who surely – by virtue of having three jerry cans – must have expected some passing motorists to top up their inadequate fuel supply, had some fluids. These little things en route showed a side of him so many of us would not possess; I would have kept walking.

He made it to a rest area at the Buntine Highway junction and camped for the night, but a group of locals pulled up next to him and made enough noise, including a constantly barking dog, to render sleeping almost impossible.

After a 53-kilometre day, Andrew admitted he could no longer back up with a second tough day walking, especially with his knee paining from his first steps which saw him needing to pump painkillers into his system. 'I feel okay after a day or two off and feel like I'm up for smashing it again, but I just can't back it up anymore. It's a world apart from my Nullarbor run or my smash up to Broome.'

He had several people stop for a chat during a day when Cad was not up for talking. One was yet another of the many who, after bailing him up and learning what his charity walk was about, talked about how they had thought for a while about doing some sort of marathon walk, run or ride, yet had not. 'If I had a dollar for every old dreamer that had been playing with the idea of doing a walk or ride, I'd be rich. They have all been probably taking about it for years'. It wasn't a sign of his intolerance but just an insight into how Andrew ticked a little differently – if you say it, especially to others, why don't you do it?

Twice during the day the old blue ute that had run out of petrol the previous day drove past, all passengers waving at Andrew. He was comforted to know that they all survived.

DAY 363, CHRISTMAS EVE, 24 DECEMBER 2011 TOWARDS KATHERINE (48KM)

Cad had spent the past few days throwing unneeded food and clothes that had become rancid into bins at rest areas, lightening the load as he was struggling so much; he knew he'd have to buy new clothes in Darwin. He kept his water supplies low too to drop weight, replenishing from water tanks at the rest areas that were every 30 to 50 kilometres.

A lovely moment came when an old couple who he'd met at Victoria River passed on their way back to Katherine and stopped to give him a small plum pudding and Christmas fruitcake, the woman giving him a warm hug despite Cad being hot and sweaty. He really was grateful for her spending a moment to transfer some Christmas spirit.

However, his spirits didn't stay high for long when he thought about how he would be spending Christmas Day walking at least until early afternoon. He recorded an extended video blog (in two takes) that he was not able to post until Boxing Day in Darwin but which best sum up his demeanour as he confronted that he was going to experience a lonely Christmas; the task he had set himself a year earlier, to complete the trek in twelve months, was naïve thinking. Anyone who watches this can sense his larrikin character but underneath he was struggling, and extremely so.

'Day 363. It's Christmas Eve, late arvie. Still have about 50 to 55 kays to get into Katherine – hopefully I'll get there tomorrow afternoon at a reasonable hour. It wasn't exactly how I wanted to be spending my Christmas but I'd only be sitting around on my own, pulling my "pud", so I may as well be walking. I just dropped in to tell everyone I'm having an extended break. I'm going to hole up and wait out the wet season and I'll resume the walk on the first of March. I feel really guilty about having a big break, for some reason. I know a lot of you probably think I'm taking the piss but I just don't care, to be honest. I just don't care at all about this walk anymore, I'm that over it. I totally underestimated it, I called fifteen months at the start and there is no way on God's earth – I don't believe in God, no way on Santa's earth – we'll fit into this time of year.'

The second recording began: 'I do care about honouring my promise to walk home for Simmo, which I'll do whether it kills me or not, and I'm still keen-as to raise some money for the Leukaemia Foundation so I'm into it again next year. I don't know why I feel I have to justify myself but some of you probably think I'm having a good holiday out here, but there is nothing that even resembles a holiday about getting up before the sun, packing up your tent, walking for twelve hours, putting your tent back up, sleeping on the ground, eating shit out of a can. I mean, ah, groundhog day, twelve hours a day, I'm lucky if I have a day off a week. And if I do get a day off, and I've only had five in the last six weeks, I'm cooking, cleaning, admin, maintenance, all the garbage I don't want to be doing. So I've lost my mojo somewhere along the way. Hopefully I'll have a smile on my face when I come back on the first [of March]. Merry Christmas, Happy New Year, hooroo.'

DAY 364, CHRISTMAS DAY, 25 DECEMBER 2011 TO KATHERINE (34KM), THEN COACH TO DARWIN

What a way to spend Christmas Day. Cad felt lonely, and he was, except for the flies that were driving him mad and causing him to scream at them 'like a psychopath'. Only two cars passed in the first two hours.

He had had no phone coverage for days and family were trying to contact him all morning to send their season's greetings and hopefully chirp him up, as we knew how tough it must have been out there. Chris and I were in Brisbane at Nicole and Glenn's (they'd moved there just under a year earlier from the Central Coast), having Christmas away from our greater family for a rare time. When Andrew found reception there was a flood of voice messages and he was going through them when I finally got onto him. He sounded exhausted and very down when he answered.

Here is how he recorded his Christmas: 'I was listening to my voicemails when dad called. I spoke to him and Mum and Nicole and I felt bad because I was short, I couldn't stop yawning. They asked me if I'd just got up, I said no, I'm exhausted. I think it was unhappy they could detect in my voice, not tired. It made me feel shit. Here I was sitting out here in this shit when I should be on my way to getting drunk with family. Dad said, you know, "Just come back after Thailand, no one will think any less of you." He just doesn't get it. I couldn't give a fuck what people think anymore. This is about me and Simmo and that's it, and the [Leukaemia] Foundation.

'I turned my phone off, I didn't want to talk to anyone else. I thought, "I'll call them tomorrow." An hour or two later I decided to stop being a Christmas scrooge and rang Aunty Al and Gran, she put a smile on my face. I heard Al say, "Andrew's on the phone," and her voice lit up, "Oh, it's Andrew." I rang about a dozen people, friends and family. It was actually good for me and cheered me up and passed the day, I was on the phone for hours, and then I was there [in Katherine].'

I was relieved when I heard that my mother, sister and his cousins had spoken to him later in the day, as I felt so helpless that there was nothing I could do to lift his spirits or ease the burden of what he was putting himself through. As on many other occasions over the previous few months, I was very concerned about his health and how it was affected by the heat and isolation.

He went straight to a camping ground and arranged to have a shower – his first for six days – and headed into the town centre but everything was closed, which left him gutted as he'd dreamed all day about having a barbeque chicken for Christmas. Two roadhouses were open, though, and he plonked himself outside one with a cardboard sign that read 'Darwin for Xmas, walked from Sydney'.

Two hours later he was still there, so he walked inside and booked on a Greyhound coach to Darwin, which was leaving in an hour.

DAYS 365–367, 26–28 DECEMBER 2011 IN DARWIN

He'd contacted a mate from the Central Coast, Adam Manks, who had moved to Darwin and said he'd put Andrew up for a few nights when he got there, and a big Boxing Day barbeque had been planned. Cad at first felt like being by himself in a hostel but changed his mind. His last diary entry for 2011, written while on the bus to Darwin, read like this:

'I just wanted to sit at the hostel by myself until I leave [for Thailand] but it is amazing how much my state of mind has changed in a few hours. It will do me good to hang out with crew. I feel better already knowing I'm away from all the shit for a couple of months. It's like a huge weight has been lifted off my shoulders. Bring on Thailand, I'm hangin'.'

Cad seemed a different person when he posted, three days later, one final video blog for the year on his website, his hair freshly cropped close. 'Day 367, just doing the tourist thing around Darwin today. My mate Manksey has given me a 'bit of a tour of the town, we're in the World War II oil storage tunnels at the moment, doing the tourist thing and enjoying my time off. So I finished the year with 10,400 kays and 45,000 bucks raised for the Cancer Council and Leukeamia Foundation, so thanks to all those who donated and who have been keeping track of my journey and ... I'll see you in the New Year.'

I was relieved – I'd had a couple of phone conversations with him before then – and so glad he was getting away and having a break, although it meant he was further from home and harder to keep in contact with. What would 2012 bring? I had no idea, but I knew Andrew wouldn't come home unless it was on foot. He was talking about that being in September.

Who could have imagined what was to happen? He would finish his trek two months earlier than planned, having pushed himself to a new level – he went from Darwin to Sydney, over 5000 kilometres, in three and a half months. That's half the distance he walked in the whole of 2011.

12

RESTED AND HOMEWARD BOUND

Andrew was a different person when he resumed his walk on 2 March 2012 after just under two months living in Pattaya Beach, Thailand. He was 12 kilograms heavier than when he jumped on the Greyhound coach to Darwin on Christmas Day, and he was also happier, healthier and mentally stronger.

I can't give a lot of detail about Cad's time in Thailand, but I know that in order to gain such weight and to achieve his long-desired larger chiselled frame, he lifted weights daily in the gymnasium, maxed-out on supplements, stuck to a prescribed high-protein diet almost religiously, and undertook a course of the steroids that are readily available in some parts of Thailand. We had several conversations about his use of steroids, me warning him of the dangers and begging him not to indulge in such a practice, and Cad telling me his usage was controlled and only brief (six weeks). Typically, if he was determined to do it, nothing would stop him. And he was so conscious of the muscle tone and weight he had lost, from a combination of no longer working on the tools as a carpenter or home renovating and the bulk he had lost from walking endless hours in the heat. When he returned he was proud of his new-look frame.

He chose Pattaya over Phuket (which he disliked) as he had some contacts there through friends on the Central Coast. He also met a Thai bar girl, Choli, who moved in with him for much of his time there, and he had fun. Contact with her via Skype and phone continued through the rest of his walk. While there, he travelled into Cambodia for three days so he could renew his Thai visa, and he saw many parts of Thailand.

By now Cad had also become a regular coffee drinker for the first time in his life, something which was magnified further for the next three months of walking as he began to rely on excessive daily dosages of caffeine to get him 'up' for the task of keeping going while his body wanted to rest. I could never remember seeing him have a coffee before; one of his goals as soon as he finished the walk, which he achieved, was to wean himself off his reliance on caffeine.

He knew he would still be bombarded with rain and energy-sapping heat and humidity for a short period when he embarked on part two of his trek from Darwin, with just a day and a half to prepare and acclimatise. But all he wanted to do at that point was reach the finish line as quickly as possible, and to honour his commitment to himself, Chris Simpson and the Leukaemia Foundation.

When I calculated the statistics of his mileage while compiling this book, it only confirmed how strong his will was to get home as soon as humanly possible. From when he walked out of Darwin on the homeward leg, he covered 2357.6 kilometres in eighty days of walking, an incredible average of a tick under 60 kilometres a day. He allowed himself just nine days off en route, not including six days on the Central Coast to attend a fundraiser in honour of Chris Simpson and sort out storage of the possessions of his that were housed at our home, which we were selling. It was an astonishing physical triumph.

His vow was still strong in his mind: 'Simmo and me, together, all the way.'

DAY 430, 29 FEBRUARY 2012 GETTING READY IN DARWIN

After leaving for the airport in Thailand at 5.30am on 28 February, Cad arrived in Darwin at 4.30pm the next day following a ten-hour stopover in Singapore. He arrived at Adam Manks' place a couple of hours later to find his gear had gone mouldy and rusty, despite being under cover for the two months. He bought a new mattress, and Adam ran him around to stock up on food and pick up other gear that had been posted to him (including new shoes to walk in – his eighth pair).

A reporter from the *NT News,* Megan Palin (the daughter of my cousin Anne), met Cad for an interview, and the paper ran a story the next day, plus an extensive online interview in which you could see his new body shape.

Over the next couple of days he also did a television and two radio interviews, which raised public awareness of his walk to the highest level of the trip and were the catalyst for on-the-road donations lifting to a very healthy level.

He didn't get to sleep until 1am, making it a marathon period since his last snooze. But lack of sleep had rarely slowed him up before, and it didn't this time.

DAYS 431–434, 1–4 MARCH 2012 DARWIN TO ADELAIDE RIVER (105KM)

As Cad put it, it was Murphy's Law that it would be raining the morning he returned to Oz On Foot life after that February being one of the driest the Top End had had for many years. And by the time he'd cleared the outer suburbs of Darwin and was back on the Stuart Highway, he had severe chafing around his groin, which had broken the skin. The good news was that after hundreds of 'beeps' from drivers going in the same direction, obviously aware of his mission after hearing it on the radio or reading about it in the newspaper, two people pulled over and donated

$100 each (with many others donating smaller amounts).

He had to walk south to cover the route to Katherine, which he had travelled in the reverse direction by coach on Christmas Day 2011; he could manage just over 20 kilometres after an early-afternoon start and was so exhausted that he was asleep by 7pm – and stayed that way for fifteen hours.

His solar panel was not working and he could not work out why, so he had no power for his phone or iPod. A woman called Maureen pulled over to offer him a bed at Acacia Hills, about a third of the way to Adelaide River. By afternoon Cad had been confronted with his first 'scary' tropical storm, with the thunder and lightning so close it shook the ground, and to make matters worse, he had a flat tyre mid-storm. His chafing had drawn blood, which ran down his legs, and his trusty 3B cream brought tears to his eyes as he applied it. Welcome back to life on the road.

Maureen met him at a turn-off and said her neighbours Ian and his Thai wife, Tou, wanted to put him up. He had an enjoyable overnight stay and breakfast with them, talking with Tou about Thai culture and Ian about mango farming and the fascinating story of how he met the well-educated Tou and of their life since, which involved building the farm from nothing twenty years earlier to the very successful Tou's Garden, 35,000 mango trees on 1000 hectares. He found Ian an interesting character; in his twenties he'd worked with the Gadafi regime in Libya (on a government operation to set up wheat farming). He'd also worked in Thailand for many years, marketing the supply of wheat and barley.

Andrew was hobbling badly when he went through the small but pretty settlement of Adelaide River, 113 kilometres south of Darwin midway through his fourth day back on the road, even though he hadn't been able to contend with more than 25 kilometres a day for the previous three days (he did 35 kilometres on the fourth). He was greeted warmly by the locals (less than 250 of them are recorded), taking his donations to $700 in just four days. Peter, the general manager of Territory Iron, told Cad he'd organise a bed for him at Pine Creek, a further 113 kilometres on.

It was raining again as Cad trooped out of Adelaide River and he came across his first crocodile, only metres off the side of the road. 'It must have been huge, it made an almighty splash as it scrambled into a pond in the middle of the long reeds just on the side of the road. It scared me; there were thick head-height reeds looming above me on each side of the road out of the low-level swampy plains. I thought there could be a croc lurking on the side of the road anywhere along here. I shifted over and started walking near the middle [of the highway]. I was glad to reach some hills because I was freaking out that I'd have to try to sleep in the swampy shit ... but on account that I'd seen more than my share of fresh dead snakes I wasn't keen to trudge in and make a clearing.'

He finally found a dirt road leading to a farm and camped there, bursting the blisters on most of his toes before he went to sleep without eating. It was the first time he seriously considered cheating and jumping a few kilometres just to end his agony early. At that stage he was still planning on walking all the way south to Alice Springs then hitching back up north of Tennant Creek to the Barkly Highway junction that headed east to Queensland, just to ensure his walk would be recorded by the *Guinness Book of Records;* he had been told he'd have to walk to Alice and also to Cairns for the feat to be 'official', although it seems illogical to me that going as far as Alice was regarded as part of working 'around' the country. Cad aborted that plan in the next couple of weeks.

DAYS 435–439, 5–9 MARCH 2012 ADELAIDE RIVER TO KATHERINE (189KM)

Not long into the day a Wicked campervan pulled up and a big Dutch guy offered, 'Wow, you're walking!' in a voice of amazement. Next thing Andrew was sitting in the van eating fruitcake and drinking coffee with the pair, exchanging tales. The Dutchman, Edward, gave Cad an army-issue blanket, which came in very handy later. Andrew learned that the tourist was a soldier who said he had experienced four tours of Afghanistan and was taking time out to spend five months driving Australia and New Zealand. After earlier coming across several others who were riding pushbikes around the country, he was in awe of Cad for undertaking the journey by foot alone. 'I thought it was funny but it actually meant a lot to me that a bloke who had done four tours of Afghanistan thought I was hardcore. It made my day.'

Sunburn became Andrew's biggest enemy, as any suncream he applied was soon washed off with sweat. 'It hurts to touch my face or just yawn.' He made it to Hayes Creek roadhouse and immediately ordered a works burger and sausage roll – at the princely cost of $19! As usual, of all the many miners in the bar, most of who just stared at him, an Irishman was the one to break the ice with, 'You that fella walking for cancer?' The lad, nicknamed 'Irish', like every other Irishman Cad met on his journey, donated $30, while the Aussie workers were all inclined to offer him only a free beer. Andrew headed for the public toilets, which provided a hot shower at a cost of $3.

Cad decided to 'smash it' the next day to reach Pine Creek, 55 kilometres away, where a comfortable bed at the pub was waiting courtesy of Peter, but he found it was hard going even after he decided, having been quite nervous about the traffic for days, that if he held his line the road trains and campervans could veer around him rather than him having to step off into the long, wet grass on the roadside.

'Today was up there with the ten hardest days of my life,' he diarised. 'It just seemed to go on and on, and I had no music, which made it worse ... I wasn't ready for such a big day, and if there wasn't a bed waiting I would have called it a day hours ago ... I finally got to the Pine Creek turn-off [in the dark] and nearly cried. I had just assumed it was on the highway but there wasn't even a streetlight. I could see the streetlights of the town through the bush but they seemed a lifetime away.'

Cad limped in, with chafing, blistered feet and a rash from head to toe causing pain. He found Peter in the bar but excused himself so he could shower before joining him. The rash concerned him. 'It was giving me sharp shooting pains all over my skin, mainly on the back of my neck and scalp; it worried me heaps and I was thinking about hitching to Katherine Hospital.' He had no dry clothes, so washed all he had to try to remove the putrid smell and had to wear a wet shirt and shorts back to the bar. Peter introduced him to the workers, and the mining company donated $500.

Next morning, not wanting to wait until the shop at Pine Creek opened at 10am, Andrew assessed his food supplies – six cans of tuna, three cans of peas, three sweet potatoes, ten biscuits, one packet of Fruit Tingles and a fruit cup – and felt he could make do for two days until he arrived in Katherine. Fortunately, these stocks were boosted by two McDonald's muffins sacrificed by a couple of women who stopped to chat, and another who provided two apples, two oranges and two cold drinks – and a lecture about using sunscreen!

After ending his day 7 kilometres short of his target, he set up camp with a huge storm beckoning. When it hit, the wind pulled his tent pegs out and he had to hold the fly so that it did not blow away; water was flowing through the floor of his tent. He managed to do his video blog in the middle of the storm while holding onto a wall of the tent.

When Cad arrived in Katherine early on the third day out of Pine Creek, he did not have a morsel of food left, only a litre of water and no working battery. An old local approached as he walked into town and offered him $15 to buy something to eat, yet it didn't quite cover the cost of a foot-long Subway meal ($17).

He was then in search of someone who could fix the solar panel. The marine shop owner claimed it was the regulator and sent him to the camping store for a new one. From there he was directed to the electrical store, where it was confirmed he needed a regulator; the proprietor, impressed by how far Andrew had walked, offered him one for free. But it still wouldn't work, and he had to go to the motorbike shop to get a new battery for $60, which fixed the problem.

The rest of the day consisted of washing his reeking clothes, depositing $1120 in donations into the Leukaemia Foundation account, spending over $40 on his three takeaway meals for the day and $300 in Woolworths on food for a week – inflation rules in the middle of nowhere!

DAYS 440–442, 10–12 MARCH 2012 KATHERINE TO MATARANKA (117KM)

Imagine this scene: as Cad crested a hill, he saw the outline of a jogger coming at him from the opposite direction through the heat haze bouncing off the bitumen. Then it was gone. Shortly after he saw it again, and then 'two idiots out the middle of nowhere, crossing paths' stopped to talk.

The jogger was a Frenchman named Remi Camus, whom a Belgian cyclist Cad had crossed paths with, Patrick, had told Andrew to watch out for. He was running solo from Melbourne to Darwin, pulling a modified mini-trailer, averaging 45 kilometres a day, and boasted how he had run 113 kilometres one day. He ended up doing the trip in 100 days. 'He was a confident, cocky sort of bloke who had been on the road for ninety-something days ... we compared stories about trucks and flies and mozzies and the like; it was funny that we both knew exactly what each other was on about.'

According to the thermostat on the Frenchman's watch, the temperature was 39 degrees, which gave Cad a better sense of what heat he had walked in and what the Frenchman had also unbelievably endured, running an Olympic marathon daily. He felt the temperature was warmer in the many days before and after however.

Camus had two video cameras to record his trek and planned to release a documentary and write a book about the adventure. It's quite remarkable to consider how many cyclists, mostly European, Cad came across in outback South Australia, Western Australia and the Northern Territory, but to be just the third person to walk around the country and unexpectedly run across the path of just the eleventh person recorded as running from coast to coast or around the country is something to savour. They took photos of each other and went their different ways.

Despite a painful foot, infected from a wasp-bite the previous day, Cad walked until 10.10pm. For the first time, he needed the army blanket the Dutchman Edward had given him, as the night was cool after an extremely hot day. Perhaps he was finally going to encounter some more temperate climate as he headed further south.

DAY 443, 13 MARCH 2012 MATARANKA TO LARRIMAH (65KM)

Larrimah is noted for the Pink Panther Pub, just off the Stuart Highway, and when Cad reached the landmark about 9pm he was relieved, exhausted and overwrought with stress. He'd walked 65 kilometres, a record on his Northern Territory leg, but only because he had no other choice. He described the preceding hours as the worst night of his life: he'd been walking in driving rain with poor vision and nowhere to pitch his tent, leaving him with no alternative but to limp on. At one stage he stopped and screamed into the vastness like a grand orator to a packed amphitheatre, letting all his pent-up frustration and anger out, with not a soul to hear his pleas.

His diary notes from the moment a tyre burst give an indication of his mood: 'I tried to go hard but was getting nowhere fast when my tyre burst again on the inside near the nozzle – same spot! I was having a tantrum, I was over it. "I fucking hate it, I don't want to be here, it's such a chore, it's such an effort, every step is an effort. It's like I'm walking through thick mud."

'I found myself screaming into the air, arms in the sky, "Yeah, great idea, let's walk around Australia," turning to face every direction like I had a surrounding audience. Not long after, I changed the tube and it started to rain. I packed everything away and took my shoes and socks off. I thought it'd pass – I was wrong. I had been optimistic this morning and thought about reaching Larrimah – 65 kilometres – but after walking in the rain for twenty minutes I passed a "20 kilometres rest area" sign and realised I'd only done 45 kilometres. I nearly cried, I tried so fucking hard today. I started looking for somewhere to camp but there was nothing: no clearings, no farm gates, just thick wet grass.

'I power-walked until it got dark. Now what? I decided to keep going, it was absolutely flogging down without a break and I could hardly see a metre in front of me and at times I walked into the grass on the side, it was off its head. I was wading through ankle-deep torrents thinking, "I hope this isn't a creek." I power-walked my arse off, my feet were killing me and my chafing was excruciating.

'A car slowed down and then chucked a U-turn. "Does your sign say walking for cancer?"

'"Yeah, mate."

'"If you can do that, here's $50," the bewildered driver said.

'But tonight was the worst night of my life. No music, no idea of the time or distance to go, I just wanted to die but I had no choice, I had to keep digging and keep digging but there was nothing left. It became dire and I started screaming into the rain again. Please, I begged, give me a break, but my prayers were not answered. It had been pissing down hardcore for nearly three hours.'

The clouds broke enough to get a glimpse of the moon, which gave out a skerrick of light, and then he could finally see the streetlights of Larrimah. He shuffled into the pub just after 9pm to be greeted by

Lyn behind the bar, who met him with, 'Are you the walker?'

'Yeah.'

'Oh, we've been expecting you.'

Cad thought it would be too late to get a meal but was over the moon to learn they'd make an exception for him and make him a bacon, egg and tomato toasted sandwich. It was a feast.

Rob, whom Cad had met when leaving Katherine (and whom he described as 'your typical bushie – weathered face, scraggly goatee, a weathered old Akubra and yellow fingers from his Winnie Blue rollies'), had taken up what seemed his regular residence in the bar and soon had Cad in stitches with his yarns. 'He had a quick wit for someone who spoke so slow.'

When Andrew went to say goodnight and look for somewhere to pitch the tent he was told by the publican Barry that he could use a bed in the room at the end of the bar that was reserved 'for blow-ins', and they'd even throw in a fan for him. For a passing tourist it might have been spartan; for Cad it was luxury, particularly as it kept pouring outside.

When he looked in the mirror for the first time for days, he was shocked at how distressed he looked. But that hour in the Pink Panther Pub typified how, at his lowest ebb, the hospitality and warmth of people around him could lift his spirits off the floor. Those people, like so many others at so many different locations, were a godsend, a powerful tonic before bedtime that provided the mental fuel for him to keep going.

DAYS 444–446, 14–16 MARCH 2012 LARRIMAH TO DUNMARRA, RETURN TO DALY WATERS (138KM)

Due to a good night's sleep, a shower and the benefit of a bed rather than air mattress and tent, Cad felt remarkably fresh when he woke up. He departed armed with Anzac biscuits from Lyn and an offer from Rob and his wife, Bronte, to spend the night in a donga on the property they worked on 37 kilometres further south. It rained most of the day but Cad arrived at his destination by about 4pm for a second night out of his tent and spent the evening chatting with Rob and Bronte outside their caravan.

As he walked away next morning he half-envied their carefree lifestyle in such a peaceful setting but half-pitied the fact they didn't understand how much of life was out there that they were missing out on. Again he had to walk all day in the rain but somehow recorded over 50 kilometres to get to Daly Waters, where he was well looked after by hosts at the Hiway Inn, Cheryl and Peter, who offered him a free room and meal; he was well attended to by many of the drinkers, led by, of course, the Irish!

Peter and Cheryl had an interesting story. They had been on the road for five years in their caravan when they suffered a broken axle on the van and had it towed back to the inn so that it could be repaired. Five years later they were still there, as managers of the pub and loved the place and the life. Cad claimed the meals were as big and good as at any roadhouse or outback pub he visited.

They invited him to stay another night and enjoy St Patrick's Day and the 'World's Greatest Shave' promotion, where people have their heads shaved to raise money for the Leukaemia Foundation. As tempted as Cad certainly was, he decided he wanted to keep going, although Peter said that if he reached Dunmarra and changed his mind, he'd drive down to bring him back for the night.

Cad arrived at Dunmarra just on dark, and after going through a mission trying to discover whether a box of food he'd arranged to have dropped off at the roadhouse was there (it was finally found at the bottom of a fridge under other food), he decided he'd take up Peter's offer and double back to Daly Waters. Peter and Cheryl arrived a while later to drive him back for what ended up being one of the most enjoyable stop-offs of his trek.

DAYS 447–448, 17–18 MARCH 2012 REST DAYS, DALY WATERS

The old Daly Waters pub seven kilometres off the highway is a more famous tourist spot; if you don't arrive by 4pm outside of summer you won't get a campsite next door or a place in one of the two evening meal sittings. However, Andrew was glad he chose the Hiway Inn as his temporary residence.

After struggling to devour the Inn's 'truckie's big breakfast' of a steak, sausages, bacon, egg and spaghetti, Andrew did his washing and administrative chores (diary, blog, responding to messages) then headed into the bar early evening for the Greatest Shave, and was first to have the shears applied to the melon (courtesy of Cheryl) and took to the clippers himself later. His video blog from the night is wonderful. He met workers from all walks of life and a group of young men who had just done a jackaroo course at Newcastle Waters station and were having their first taste of outback employment. There were plenty of drunken characters by the end of the night, with some cockies slipping their pants down as they danced to country and western music.

Next day was spent recovering, with a trip to the old Daly Waters pub. Cad was so grateful for, yet embarrassed by, the generosity of Peter, Cheryl and their staff and friends and left early next morning for a ride back to Dunmarra with a pocket full of donations and a heart full of good memories. When he woke he found a note slipped under his door from a couple he had chatted to the previous two nights with a $100 donation, which indicated the instant rapport Cad was able to strike with people and their genuine admiration for what he was doing. It read: 'Stay strong, brother. Don't let tiredness distract you from such an amazing act. It's not too far til the end. Gav and Stacey.'

DAYS 449–454, 19–24 MARCH 2012 DUNMARRA TO THREE WAYS (333KM)

First night, after being hammered through his drenched shirt by mosquitos and having to walk with his head torch on while desperately looking for somewhere suitable to pitch his tent, Cad found the old highway and turned off to spend his first night without rain for nearly three weeks at Newcastle Waters, nearly 700 kilometres down the highway from Darwin. The 'town' area is to the east of the main highway, and subject to flooding in a big rain, but he never saw the lights of the few houses and one shop en route to the massive Newcastle Waters cattle station, which is located on the historic stock route from Adelaide to Darwin at the junction of the route west into Queensland.

The next day Cad got to talking with a contractor who was responsible for filling water tanks in the rest areas on the Stuart and Barkly highways and he warned

Andrew about the howling south/south-east trade wind that roars down the Barkly, and that he had come across many cyclists who head east into it at the wrong time of year and retreat back to Tennant Creek after surrendering to the unconquerable task of matching the monster in their face.

With that advice, Cad confirmed what he had been considering for weeks: he was going to abandon his plan to walk all the way south to Alice Springs then hitch back to the Barkly Highway junction and walk east. The winds were due to pick up early April, which left him a week-long window, once he started tracking east towards Townsville, before the imposition of pushing Redge into an almost gale-force foe became insurmountable.

Andrew reached Elliot about 4pm ploughed on until nearly 9pm, before finding a dirt track where he could camp, setting up beside Nev and Dellie, who ran barramundi fishing tours in the Top End.

Shade was becoming hard to come by as the landscape had changed over the past two days to mostly low scrub and grass, and by another two days it was red earth and spinifex as far as the eye could see. Andrew believed the temperature was well over 40 degrees next day but he had promised himself to have only brief rests at the 10-kilometre marks up to 40 kilometres. He couldn't last until the fourth scheduled break due to the heat, being confronted by a mass of ants every time he stopped and persistent march flies in their hundreds; he could see their shadows on the road so dense were their swarms. Cad constructed two full pages of notes about his battle with the march flies, indicating what an obsession they had become in what he had called 'Zombie Valley'. He planted himself in the shade of a bush for an hour when a vast area of cloud provided rare shade and the temperature dropped noticeably.

But for the most part there was not a cloud in the sky, and he had to trickle warm water out of his bottles to keep his mouth lubricated in the heat, as road trains whizzed past and few caravans and campervans navigated the Stuart Highway. It had become a lonely, relentless, mind-testing existence when he made it to the Renner Springs roadhouse early afternoon on Day 452, and it was another 135 kilometres to go to the next piece of civilisation (Threeways roadhouse) and his left turn to Queensland. He vowed as he approached to eat only food he had stocked and not concede to the temptations behind the counter and the ridiculous prices he would have to pay, but in the end relented to acquire a pie and paddle pop.

Despite walking into a wind, on Day 453 Cad did his second successive 60-kilometre day, this one in eleven and a half hours, which was thirty minutes better than the day before. Trouble was he had to endure a constant nosebleed, which became a problem for over a week.

After being drained by the heat for so long, Andrew couldn't believe it when he woke up on Day 454 feeling cold, with much of his gear flying across the rest area car park in the cool wind. The howling gale in his face didn't relent all day and he had to walk with his head bowed to stop his hat blowing off, but he couldn't save the solar panel that glided past his nose onto the highway when a road train passed – but still worked when he picked it up off the road!

He passed two cyclists in their seventies, Jim and Mike, both millionaires who were riding from Melbourne to Darwin then to Perth (for the third time). Jim said the pair had ridden together through many countries and continents.

He reached the Threeways roadhouse by 6pm after a tough 48 kilometres into the wind, and was ecstatic to be in air conditioning and pick up his box of supplies that had been sent ahead. He was desperate for a shower, only to be told it cost $6. A truckie sitting at a restaurant table suggested he not bother this time of day because the water wouldn't be warm. 'Mate, I haven't had a shower for six days – that's not going to worry me!' Cad told him.

DAYS 455–456, 25–26 MARCH 2012 REST DAY, TENNANT CREEK, THEN BACK TO THREEWAYS

Cad hitched the 25 kilometres south to Tennant Creek (on the road to Alice Springs,) so he could bank $1200 in donations and do the usual time-off chores of washing, repairs to Redge, cleaning his gear and shopping – $350 for twelve days of food – and also did an interview for the local newspaper. Next afternoon he scored a lift back to Threeways, which is at the junction of the Stuart and Barkly highways, the latter heading east to Queensland, but didn't arrive until 4pm, so he set up camp and spent four hours replying to emails and doing his diary, ready for an early start next day. He said the people running the roadhouse were as inhospitable as any he encountered on the entire trip.

DAYS 457–459, 27–29 MARCH 2012 BARKLY HIGHWAY TO BARKLY HOMESTEAD (186KM)

Andrew had decided to do the 186-kilometre stretch to Barkly Homestead in three days and not the planned four, figuring he'd use the rest areas for overnight camps at 68 kilometres and another 63 kilometres further on. He certainly went out hard with a 70-kilometre day (Google Maps was often inaccurate), his biggest since before Perth eight months earlier. It was a long, lonely day as he walked with his head bowed into the strong wind, something he was to get used to; he only had one car stop all day (four backpackers), and very few went past. It was the quietest traffic day he had encountered.

The elements were at their fiercest the next day: draining headwind, flies out in full force, and when he stopped for the night the mosquitos were relentless and he found himself back in mice-infected territory. Cad thought he would be ingenious and put a few small Easter eggs outside his tent, hoping the mice would be attracted to them and not what was inside. He failed; there were holes through most of his food packets and mice droppings through the pram.

The relentlessness of the journey was definitely getting to him; he was out in vast, flat, barren countryside and still so far from the finish line. He felt trapped by the existence that saw him counting down towards his second birthday on the road (nine days away), a second year without income and daily steps towards his fear that he would spend his approaching years without a partner. 'It's like being in prison but I think prison could be much easier – no flies, no mosquitos, no sun, no wind, same shit food, same shit bed but no walking.'

He struggled late in the third day along the Barkly, and after the 30-kilometre mark had to stop every hour. Tracey, whom he'd met at the Tennant Creek tourist park, stopped and asked him if he wanted to throw Redge in the back of her ute and get a lift to the homestead, but Andrew wouldn't take a shortcut, even with only 5 kilometres to go.

DAYS 460–463, 30 MARCH–2 APRIL 2012 BARKLY HOMESTEAD TO CAMOOWEAL (259KM)

Cad awoke in his tent to the discovery that just about every packet of nuts and all his muesli bars had been invaded by ants; he threw the bars out and painstakingly repacked the nuts into another container.

He hit the wall at the 40-kilometre mark and thought that would do for the day, but then decided that if he walked on he could make Camooweal, the most western Queensland town en route, in four days rather than the planned five.

It was obvious how little things made big impressions, or were big distractions, when walking day in and day out. Cad was fascinated by a snake slithering across the highway, yellow with brown spots, 'beautiful'. He took photos until the snake became aggressive, and as he went to walk on he heard a car coming. He doubled back and stood there waving his arms so the car would divert and avoid the snake, but it didn't slow down or alter course and drove over it, prompting Cad to give the young driver 'the bird'. Cad was devastated. 'I felt terrible, I should have just left it [the snake] alone and it would have been off the road. I went back and it had stopped wriggling.'

Two days later the amount of traffic picked up dramatically, mostly four-wheel drive vehicles towing boats, leaving Cad to think there must have been a barramundi fishing weekend or some similar event organised. He hit grasslands with lovely grazing fields as far as the eye could see, but they attracted the flies in a great mass, and they did not relent for a second.

A grazier stopped soon after and Cad asked him why the flies were so bad; he replied it was to do with the grass the cattle grazed on, called Mitchell grass (thus the region's name as Mitchell Grasslands): wherever there was the grass, there would be flies in the millions. Cad asked how long the grass fields lasted. 'Oh, to [Mount] Isa ... then it's sheep country.' He had to try to eat with his net over his head but it was hopeless and he had to turn his earphones up higher to drown out the buzzing noise of the flies. He walked seven hours without stopping, just to avoid the flies swarming all over him when he stopped.

His reward was to find a rest area that was inhabited by three women, who kept him awake by 'cackling' all night and playing country and western music, then having more music blaring before sunrise as they packed up. 'I think it was Lee Kernaghan; they all sound the same to me.'

Next day he walked out of the Northern Territory to Camooweal. Just thirty-three days after leaving Darwin, he was in Queensland.

13

SIXTH STATE, FIFTEENTH HIGHWAY

Stepping out of the Northern Territory into Queensland after many long, lonely and challenging days due to the constant headwinds, few settlements and little human interaction, Cad hit the tiny Queensland hamlet of Camooweal, 12 kilometres past the Northern Territory– Queensland border. Before this trip he would never have thought a place with a population of 187 would feel like the big smoke, but he was relieved to see the town lights after walking the 440 kilometres of the Barkly Highway in a week – an average of nearly 63 kilometres a day – into a biting headwind that had broken the spirit of many cyclists.

He was physically exhausted, badly in need of a shower and a good meal, but everything, according to a truckie sipping on a cup of tea beside his rig, had closed at 9pm, including the service station. He found the caravan park and, with the light switch on a thirty-second timer, showered in the dark (with his nose bleeding most of the time) before cooking outside when the owner walked up, shining a torch Cad's way and wondering who the intruder was at such a late hour (10pm). When he realised it was Andrew he was less alarmed, telling Cad he was expecting him at some stage as his food parcel had been dropped off.

Next day he was off into the wild again; he'd changed states but not conditions – it was over 40 degrees Celsius.

DAYS 464–467, 3–6 APRIL 2012 CAMOOWEAL TO MOUNT ISA (183KM)

Andrew knocked out 70 kilometres from Camooweal until he called it quits at 11pm after fourteen hours of walking, backing up from doing 69 kilometres the day before. It was no wonder he was being belted by regular nosebleeds, day and night. Next day he came across some workers and mentioned how the flies were driving him mad. 'Old mate' (as Andrew called anyone whose name he didn't recall) gave him a small tub of rosemary and cedarwood cream, which he claimed would keep the flies at bay, but not the native bees (which was apparently what Cad had thought were big march flies). The magic remedy didn't relieve his plight: 'Old mate's cream just made my face sticky – it was like I'd buttered my face with honey, and the flies just hovered around like Great Whites to a shark cage.'

Andrew was surprised to see Gav and Stacey, the couple who had left him a note and $100 under his door at Daly Waters, pull up. He was glad to have a chance to thank them. He rested at 40 kilometres but made himself do at least 50 kilometres for the day, despite his feet causing him grief on the rough bitumen surface. When he had a 500metre stretch of smooth tar he said it was like 'walking on cotton buds'.

It was during this part of Queensland that he came across four bicycle riders – Aaron Turner, Daniel Seehusen, John Clark and Tim Holman – who, with a support vehicle, were en route from London to Melbourne (24,000 kilometres in fourteen months, via Europe and Asia) as part of their Ride2Rescue fundraising trek, raising awareness of international child trafficking. Their first meeting was when a couple of the boys were in their support vehicle on a 'beer run' into Mount Isa about 15 kilometres away to get supplies for their evening meal and came across Cad. He recorded: 'They said they were living in my shadow as all they have heard about is the walker. I said, "I know how you feel – all I hear about is the Stormtrooper!"' On their way back from Isa, the boys had Cad's requested can of Coca-Cola with a double cheeseburger as a bonus, which made him 'ecstatic'.

The next day was Good Friday and Cad only had to walk 9.5 kilometres from his camping spot to reach Mount Isa but little was open in the town. After running into the riders, who pointed him towards an IGA supermarket, Cad went overboard at the first 'real supermarket' he'd seen since Darwin, and soon had a trolley filled with twenty packs of potato chips, ten family-size blocks of chocolate and numerous biscuit packets, before telling himself to 'pull your head in' and put half back.

He caught up with the Ride2Rescue guys again that night to exchange experiences; he was envious that they had $50,000 of sponsorship arranged before they'd left (to cover expenses), plus they had set up an official charity to accept funds and had much of their gear donated. He was also envious of all their support from family and friends too, some of whom had accompanied them on legs of the trip; they were trying to organise hundreds to ride into Melbourne's Federation Square with them to complete the journey. They'd been busy organising for six months before they left on their journey, and in Malaysia the international Rotary club had organised a fun ride, while an ex-pat Australian Rules club helped in Singapore.

By contrast, Andrew was paying all his expenses himself, except for some shoes I was able to get from Nike, from my mate Peter Wynn and from the Parramatta Eels NRL club; some camping gear from Roman; parts to repair his pram from Chariot (Mark Morris from Australian distributor Morris Stanley was very supportive); and repair work on his pram from bike shops as he travelled. But that was his, and my, fault for not putting more effort into preparation, although several large camping retailers did not even bother replying to my sponsorship requests.

Cad wrote: 'I thought a lot about how much money potentially I could have raised ... I used to think I was cut out for this but I was wrong. I don't and didn't have the mental strength for this shit but really the fundraising is one of the only reasons I'm still walking. I owe it to myself to finish now I've come this far. I don't know what to expect of anyone. My family are all proud, and at the end of the day what more can they do. Dad does what he can. But ... all this only makes me appreciate Josh [Simpson] coming to walk with me on the other side of the country, that's something I'll never forget, and it makes me regret the way I was [while Josh was with him] even more than I did then.'

Cad was just on one of his downers sparked by his fatigue and isolation, second-guessing himself and looking back with regret. But when I consider his 'no one cares' thoughts, it almost makes me cry to think he never saw the true picture. Many, many people were in awe of his achievement, and said so. He wasn't cut out for it? That's nonsense too. I know that I, and most people I know, would not be cut out for such a challenge, but Andrew Cadigan? No one can question that he was.

With the thought of unrealised fundraising potential in mind, his brain was ticking overtime with another Cad Grand Plan, and he was soon on the phone to appropriate authorities on the Central Coast and the Leukaemia Foundation, trying to organise a charity walk from The Entrance to Terrigal when he reached the Central Coast near the end of his journey (I knew nothing of this until I read his diary). After making calls to councils, police, ambulance, Rotary clubs and water distributors over the ensuing days, he became frustrated with the red tape and lack of responses from authorities and aborted the effort.

DAYS 468–469, 7–8 APRIL 2012 MOUNT ISA TO CLONCURRY (120KM)

With a slow leak in his tyre caused by stray tacks at the camping area, Cad was into it at 6am and didn't let up for hours in quite heavy traffic. With no road shoulder, road trains were pushing him into long grass on blind corners but still coming close enough to blow the solar panel off the handlebars. The surroundings were spectacular, as he recorded: 'Beautiful scenery, red rocky hills covered in spinifex and dotted with small gums and the road just weaved in and out of them through the gullies.'

He made it to Cloncurry in the dark and walked all the way across town to the caravan park where he looked for the Ride2Rescue boys, finding they had saved him some pasta and chicken ('I was stoked I didn't have to cook'). Cad really hit it off well with these guys, especially Tim.

In mid-2013, after reading about his meeting with the Ride2Rescue crew in Cad's diaries, I contacted John via their website to inform them of his plight; they were truly shocked and devastated to hear he had died. They were also wonderfully forthcoming in their admiration for his achievement, which they'd already relayed via their own internet blogs.

DAY 470, 9 APRIL 2012, ANDREW'S THIRTY-FIRST BIRTHDAY EAST FROM CLONCURRY (45KM)

It was not the birthday Andrew had wished for. His spirits were badly eroded and he could still not see the end in sight. He woke up at six and gave the boys two food parcels to take ahead to Julia Creek. A few kilometres out of town the boys reached him and they gathered for a photo and said their last goodbyes. 'And that was that – another six faces that came and went,' Andrew wrote.

Cad turned his phone off so he didn't have to field birthday wishes and speak to people, turning it on only to check Google Maps and Facebook posts, so he wasn't interrupted and slowed down but also because he was in one of his low moods. Kane Foley called while the phone was switched on but Cad didn't pick up; he texted him back to say thanks for the call but he would speak later. 'I replied to all my Facebook comments,' he wrote in his diary that evening. 'Facebook is easy, I can put on a brave face when I have to, to talk to people and do my blog. But I really didn't feel like talking to anyone. Today is fucked – it's my birthday to remind me I'm another year older, another year out here. But that's not it, my head is still not in a good place and with every big day I keep piling on it makes me feel mentally and physically shitter. Tonight I would have walked over 800 kilometres in two weeks – that's pretty off its head, really. But I'm not stopping until I break or I'm home packing for Thailand.' It appears that at this stage he was already planning to head back to Thailand when he finished the walk, although he kept this to himself and changed his mind several times over the coming months.

He called Kane back; Foley was driving back home to the Central Coast from Perth. 'I shouldn't have bothered; I must have sounded like a whinging sad sack. A few people rang and left messages. I didn't ring them back. I don't know what my problem is. I whinge that no one rings me and I don't want to speak with them when they do.' I know he did speak with his parents, sister and Matt Delaney that night.

After heavy rain, he camped on a dirt patch with the ground so hard he couldn't get the pegs in. His blog was posted in the morning, and if he was feeling down on his birthday he disguised it a little with his laconic recording. 'Another day in the sticks, another birthday, another year older, another year wasted doing this crap. And another highway. Just got on the Flinders and that's the thirteenth one. Started on the Princes, around to Adelaide, up and down Lincoln, back up the Flinders, across the Eyre, down the

Esperance–Coolgardie, around the south coast on the South Coast Highway [in Western Australia], funny enough up onto the South Western to the Brand, up the North Western, up the sweaty Great Northern, down the Stuart, across the boring Barkly, this one will take me across, then back down the Bruce, onto the Pacific and then finally done. That really goes to show how bored I am out here, that I've just memorised all them. See you tomorrow.' He almost got it right; he'd overlooked the Bass and Midlands highways in his birth state, Tasmania.

DAYS 471–476, 10–15 APRIL 2012 CLONCURRY TO HUGHENDEN (364KM)

The weather became much cooler overnight and Cad realised he needed to buy a flannelette shirt and beanie again. The headwind was as persistent as ever at 25 kilometres per hour. He travelled 65 kilometres in twelve hours, electing to economise time by eating standing up, figuring that when he sat down he'd go to his phone, check emails and Facebook and waste ten minutes each time.

At Julia Creek he picked up the food parcels plus a pair of sunglasses I had posted to him, and the relief from the glare was so great 'it felt like I had an operation to remove cataracts or something, I could see clearly again for the first time in weeks. My other sunnies were so scratched it was ridiculous.'

The headwind picked up to 40 kilometres per hour and it was cold in the early hours of the day; 'It was like I'm walking uphill all day.' For weeks Cad had been trailed by hawks but they'd picked up in quantity now, often ten circling him as he walked, but on this day (473) he saw at least a hundred. 'It was like a scene out of Alfred Hitchock's *The Birds.* '

He made the Richmond roadhouse next day at 6pm, where the owner, Judy, ploughed on the hospitality, treating him like a long-lost son and providing a room, T-bone steak and dessert for dinner, and chicken sandwiches for the next day's journey. 'I'll never forget ya,' he told her as he walked off. 'What a nice lady,' he diarised.

He felt he needed a physical booster so ordered some protein powder online but, having to be in Charters Towers before the weekend to pick it up (so he wouldn't have to stay over the weekend), he abandoned his planned day off in Hughenden on the Saturday; this gave him six days to travel the 250 kilometres from town to town. That was going to put extra pressure on him, but it was typical – always rushing when he didn't have to. On the flip side, after talking to Josh Simpson, he decided to head back to the Central Coast in late May for the Sink One For Simmo fundraising weekend, despite the fact that it would be a travel mission, depending on how far down Queensland's east coast he had walked.

The next day, battling into the howling headwind, he made it to Hughenden on nightfall and kept going until he reached a driver-reviver station that was being packed up. The volunteer, a lady called Mim, yelled a greeting: 'You made good time.'

'Yeah, early day, only 50 kilometres today,' Cad replied.

'Want a cuppa?' came next, and it was music to his ears as he pulled in for a chat.

'She was a legend, probably fifty,' he wrote. 'She was the local teacher who came here for nine weeks nine years ago. Nice lady.' And she donated $50. The Hughenden generosity continued when Robyn and Steve, the caravan park owners, gave him a free site, and 'Blue', who was staying in the hotel, shouted him dinner and breakfast.

DAYS 477–481, 16–20 APRIL 2012 HUGHENDEN TO CHARTERS TOWERS (249KM)

In his diary that day Andrew spent some space pondering religion and explained his attitude to it, after being confronted by one of the many devout Christians he came across on the trip, some of whom he resented for trying to force their beliefs down his throat. In particular, he despised the sight of handmade signs nailed to trees, depicting 'God is

Coming' or such messages, which he felt was defacing the natural landscape out in the bush. Often, despite being highly fatigued, he would find the energy to climb up and remove the signs.

Andrew said he was an atheist, despite having attended Catholic schools for seven years, but he had no issue with those who believed in God and was comfortable that they had such faith in their beliefs, although he did not share or understand them. But he resented the 'God-botherers' who tried to inflict their beliefs on him in an overbearing manner, and he'd come across quite a few.

One day he was twice confronted by overzealous Christians and figured out what he felt was a glorious technique to avoid their rantings. He would simply state that he was a devout Christian who had attended Christian schools; he'd agree with their views, claim he had a Bible with him ... and they would let him be.

On Day 479, Cad had not had a day off since Tennant Creek, twenty-three days and almost 1400 kilometres earlier. He came to a lookout and realised he'd climbed 200 metres in altitude in a week since Mount Isa. He was finally on a downhill run to the town of Pent-land with no wind to contend with – relief! He made a rest area at 8.30pm in darkness with no moon to light the sky, and – as so often happened – he was greeted by a traveller who seemed to be expecting him. 'You've done well!' a voice bellowed.

They talked for a while but the man couldn't contemplate how Andrew didn't want a beer after a long day on his feet. Andrew by now could predict the life story of some of the loners before he was told; he figured the bloke was a miner (yes, from Townsville), and divorced and living alone, and a 'pisspot'. By the end of their chat, all these suspicions were confirmed.

The next evening he came across another 'interesting' character who operated a roadhouse. Cad asked if he could fill up three bottles with water from the tank. He was told it was not safe as it was bore water and any water taken from the premises should be boiled before being drunk ('ra ra ra') so they would not get sick and come back and make a claim against him. Andrew filled his bottles up nevertheless (and described the bloke as a 'rude prick').

As Andrew went to leave, the man yelled at him, 'I can give you the cure for cancer and you wouldn't have to waste your time walking around Oz.' Cad rolled his eyes and replied, 'Yeah? And what's that?' 'Got a pen and paper?' the man inquired. The bloke, sitting and leaning on a handrail the whole time, told him the story of how he went to hospital after a cardiac arrest, but when the doctors found he had cancer in both kidneys (and one had burst) and also prostate cancer, he was told there was nothing that could be done to save him. Days later he discovered a magic potion, and miraculously two weeks later the cancer was 90 per cent gone; it had completely disappeared in six months.

Andrew was certainly suspicious of large holes in his tale, the more detail he gave. The miracle formula consisted of 250 millilitres of pure Canadian maple syrup mix with seventeen measuring teaspoons of aluminium-free bicarb soda, boiled together for four minutes. Take three teaspoons a day for three days, then one teaspoon a day forever after. The man, who Andrew learned was named John, revealed that people call him up from all over the world for his miracle recipe and that the reason Canadians have a low cancer rate is because they have maple syrup on their pancakes every morning.

I read about this miracle mixture and found plenty of literature that endorsed it as being very effective. I wonder if Andrew, usually very inquisitive about such matters, also checked it out on the net.

After Cad stopped for the night 33 kilometres out of Charters Towers, he checked his food supply the next morning and found only enough oats for a small bowl, an apple and Brazil nuts, all of which he had for breakfast, and a can of sweet corn, two tins of tuna and some Milo, the latter of which he decided was the best treat so he polished off half a tub, spoon by spoon, dry.

He had met up (for a second time) with Alex Matthews a few days before, who arranged to give him a bed for the night and take him to the Enterprise

Hotel in Charters Towers to do some fundraising. Cad found that the publican, 'Moorey', was 'a legend' who put $200 into the bucket collection to start the fund before one of the barmaids took it around and rustled up enough attention and support with the loudest female whistle Cad had ever heard. By the end of the night, thanks also to a raffle, there was another $800 for the Leukaemia Foundation ... and Cad hadn't had a beer.

DAYS 482–489, 21–28 APRIL CHARTERS TOWERS TO TOWNSVILLE (130.5KM) – DOWNTIME IN TOWNSVILLE AND CAIRNS

After farewelling the Matthews family it was time for Cad's compulsory visit to the bakery for a meat pie, then off to Salvos to buy a 'flanno'. The old lady behind the counter, after chatting to him, hugged him and said he was the nicest young person she had met in a long while. 'You have all the jewellery [earrings, lip and chin piercings] but I suppose I just have to accept it in this day and age,' she told him. She asked him to treat himself to something else from the store and he grabbed another 'flanno' and board shorts. On his way across the road he was bailed up by another endearing old dear, who gave him a long hug and $50.

His mood changed later in the day when he couldn't get away from a strange character who rambled on, warning him about political unrest that was in the Book of Revelations and how he'd met a High Court judge the day before at a petrol station who told him that President Obama was starting to build a military presence in Australia and around the world, and it was soon going to turn into a one-nation world run by the Americans who were going to unite with the Catholic Church and start implementing Catholic ways, and the church would run the Australian government: '*&###% fruitcake!'

That evening he devoured two steaks that were given to him, spoke to Choli in Thailand, and heard from good mate Dobbsy, who was celebrating the birth of his first child (a girl), whom his wife, Lucy, had delivered that day. He slept well, a rare stint of eleven hours, only to be woken by a guy who emptied the garbage bins at the rest area. Hours later Cad's tolerance of opportunistic religious fanatics was given a new test. A woman pulled up and left her car, walked towards him, asked if he was the guy walking for cancer and explained that her brother, who maintained the rest areas (and had woken Andrew up), had told her about him. She announced she was a Jehovah's Witness and unleashed a sermon about her religion and what it could do for him, abating only to Andrew's carefully constructed verbal repellent about being a devout Catholic-school raised Christian. 'So you don't want any material?' 'No, thanks.' Worked again! Still, Cad was mightily pissed off that 'some bin-emptying hillbilly' could call his sister to prey on him while he was alone on the back ways of Queensland.

Soon after, Cad arrived in Townsville; he'd walked to the top of the country to Darwin and now the width of the country and was back on the east coast. In four weeks he'd had only half a day's break (other than walking 9.5 kilometres into Mount Isa on Good Friday) at an average of almost 56.5 kilometres a day. It was an astonishing effort, considering the headwind he had to contend with and the heat for most of that month. It matched the daily distances the Ride2Rescue crew were achieving on their bicycles.

However, the pace he'd set from the Stuart Highway to the Pacific Highway, as incredible as it was, was about to be surpassed as he had one thing dominating his thoughts: 'Get this mission finished!'

14

THE SPRINT HOME

Andrew's five days in Townsville and Cairns were to be his last bender of the trip, and he didn't miss an opportunity to enjoy himself with the period coinciding with Anzac Day 2012. He had to buy going-out clothes, get a haircut and pay a visit to a doctor because of an infection in an ear piercing that he was told needed cosmetic surgery – so all in all it was an expensive diversion.

After two nights in Townsville he'd caught a bus to Cairns for two nights before returning to Townsville for the regular maintenance and shopping activities. No one could begrudge him an extended break after having just four days off in fifty-five, and none for the last thirty days, meaning he'd averaged 49 kilometres a day for nearly two months.

But his penchant for partying hard matched his on-road work ethic, and he only had twenty-four days to get to Brisbane – 1400 kilometres away – on the day he'd nominated to fly home to attend the Sink One For Simmo festivities in honour of Chris Simpson (and to dispose of the belongings of his that were stored at our place, which we were about to move out of). It also meant he didn't have time to detour to Airlie Beach further down the Queensland coast, a break he'd earlier planned. Fortunately his mates at home had taken up a collection to fund his airfares so he could be there to honour Simmo; he was in the middle of the Nullarbor the previous year when the first anniversary fundraising event took place.

After leaving Townsville there were very few days when he didn't walk until well after dark. He had one day off (in Gladstone) before reaching Brisbane, and twice had his arm twisted to have one beer but otherwise did not have one alcoholic drink, even during his days back on the Central Coast. His preferred liquid consumption had become coffee in excess to give him energy, and water. It saw him somehow get to trudge almost 1400 kilometres to reach Brisbane on the twenty-fourth day – averaging 56 kilometres a day!

DAYS 490–494, 29 APRIL–3 MAY 2011 TOWNSVILLE TO PROSERPINE (272KM)

After leaving Townsville Andrew was in familiar territory for the first time after almost 12,700 kilometres travelled, as he'd cycled the Sydney–Cairns section of the national highway four years earlier. Memories of many of the places came flooding back to him.

His new pet hate became the constant roadworks he had to navigate in many sections, his attitude to not missing one metre of the journey from Sydney to Sydney often putting him in conflict with lollypop-stick holders and even the on-site managers, as their concern for his safety was paramount. Many offered to put Cad and Redge on a ute and transport him through the hazard areas but he would not have a bar of that.

A bigger hazard, he found, were trucks travelling too fast. A few hours out of Townsville he came very close to being hit by one and killed. It was about an hour after dark and he had his head torch on, putting his hand up to his face to avoid being blinded when cars came at him with high beam on; I assume he had also crossed the highway to walk with the traffic rather than against it. With his hand shielding his eyes from the oncoming headlights he had ventured slightly off the shoulder into the car lane when a road train pulled out to overtake the car on the other side of the road. Cad had music blaring through his headphones and could not hear the road train's motor. Suddenly, as Cad recorded, 'I just sensed the extra light as he pulled out, took my hand away and truck was right there at over 100 kph. I had to push on the handlebars and get on two wheels, just turned the thing into the grass and he just missed me – I should have dived out of the way. It just brushed me, it was so close. That was in the top ten closest calls on the trip.' I'm glad he didn't document the nine others!

He had never seen so much truck traffic on the walk and I could hear the constant loud whirring of the passing vehicles on his voice memos (he did not continue his written diary past Townsville, but recorded daily events into his phone). One truck roared past, causing the beloved but badly worn hat he'd owned since Port Headland in Western Australia (day 300) to missile into a 'filthy little swamp'. He was hit with the dilemma of whether to part with the now putrid, dilapidated hat or keep it for sentimental reasons. He explained next day in witty Cad style: 'I wasn't going to let it drown, but it's like watching your baby drown in a swimming pool and turning around to your wife and saying, "It's alright, we'll have another one next year." I had to get him out.'

After four successive 60-plus-kilometre days, he made Proserpine on the fifth. By this stage had quickly begun to rely on taurine tablets (a natural stimulant), Guarana (a Brazilian plant extract used in energy drinks) and coffee to rev him up for the constant big days.

DAYS 495–502, 4–11 MAY 2012 PROSERPINE TO ROCKHAMPTON (471KM)

He was woken in Pioneer Park, Proserpine (where he'd also camped on his bike tour) by a groundsman on his leaf blower but had had his first solid eight-hour sleep in a long time. That day he walked until 11.30pm and those long shifts became common. A minimum 60 kilometres a day became his mission, something he would achieve twenty-four times in the thirty-six walking days from Townsville to the Central Coast.

He woke next day not far off the highway but just over a sugar train track, on the front yard of a cane property, trains and trucks breaking his sleep. Kane Foley called and said the boys had raised $250 for his airfares to come home and a few other mates also called, lifting his spirits enormously. 'A few of the boys rang and made my day. I had some funny conversations.'

The next day he heard from his cousin Matt Ruff who ribbed him, asking, 'Are you finished with the "waahs" yet?'

'What are the "waahs"?' Cad replied.

'The noise cry babies make,' Matt advised, pointing to Andrew's perceived whining on his video blogs.

Josh Simpson called later the same day and made a similar observation.

That evening Cad made the announcement that there would be no more whingeing on his blogs.

He did an interview with the local paper in Mackay and was almost stumped by the most unusual question of the many interviews he did en route: did he think he would have trouble socialising again and forging relationships? He replied, 'No, I haven't become a hermit yet; I'm looking forward to it.' It wasn't included in the article.

Later that day came another one-off for the trip – he was shot by a paintball gun! 'Some dickhead shot me with blue paint and I had a big welt on my finger. I didn't see where it came from – not sure if it was someone in a car or someone hiding.'

On Day 497 Cad passed through Sarina. He'd already seen monuments such as the big mango (in Bowen), the big crab (in Cardwell), the big lobster (in Kingston) and the big prawn (in Learmonth), but he couldn't understand why Sarina displayed the big cane toad. 'I couldn't believe how they could make a monument of a national pest.'

Next day Sean Conway, a Zimbabwean living in London, pulled over on his pushbike for a chat. He explained he was part of the World Cycle Racing Grand Tour, which was a race covering 18,000 miles (the designated cycling distance – geographically, it was over 24,000 miles from point to point) from London back to London through America, Australia, Asia and Europe to claim the Guinness World Record for cycling around the world. Sean had been hit by a truck in Arkansas in the United States, and been forced to spend three weeks recovering (much of it in hospital), but was still completing the course for his own benefit, even though he had no chance of winning. (The winner was Englishman Mike Hall, who completed the race in ninety-two days.) Two days later Cad received an email from Sean, saying his mum had just donated $100. It was yet another gesture that blew him away: he was in awe of Sean riding around the world, yet his mother was so impressed with what Andrew was doing that she donated that large amount.

A couple of days later Cad came across other cyclists with a cause, the Tour de Cure ride, which is best known through the involvement of Mark Beretta, the Channel Seven *Sunrise* sports presenter (and a mate of mine), who has been a participant for the past two years. Around sixty riders travelled from Brisbane to Mission Beach south of Cairns, fundraising for cancer research. The Channel Seven crew, when they became aware of Andrew's mission, sent a camera back to capture Cad (Beretts sent me a tape much later), and after he'd completed the shoot one of the crew was impressed enough to suggest Andrew do some motivational speaking – which was ironic, because Cad recorded: 'I should have hyped it right up and said how I fought ferocious storms, wild bulls, locust plagues etc.'

Next day Cad showed his humane side yet again when he came across an injured hawk that he thought was close to death. He called the RSPCA to see if they could help his feathered friend, who he called 'Henry the Hawk', and gave him a free ride until he could pass him over for treatment when he approached Rockhampton. He was more impressed with the lifeless bird than the lifeless locals, who afforded him far more curious stares than hellos let alone any donations, and he relayed this without any ambiguity about this on his video blog.

DAYS 503–509, 12–18 MAY 2012 ROCKHAMPTON TO HERVEY BAY (168KM)

In a really special show of support, a good mate and former cricket teammate of mine, Greg Nicholls, who'd known Andrew since he was six, drove 320 kilometres from Emerald to a little place called Bajool, south of 'Rocky', to personally pass on a donation and tell him how awesome his effort was. Cad and 'Nicko' had lunch at the local pub, where Cad was treated to a free pizza and a beer he didn't want but the owner insisted he accept. They laughed about the crap cars Cad and I owned, which Greg, a mechanic by trade, often helped us fix up over the years.

Next day he saw another familiar face in Scott 'Garlo' Garlick, a mate from back home who was living in Gladstone. Scott picked him up on the highway and took him near town to stay with him at a mining camp; Cad was ecstatic when he won a small trifecta on the greyhounds and $1350 in poker machine jackpots at the local pub.

The joy subsided next day when he had to contend with 20 kilometres of almost continual roadworks and confronting new stop-go staff at each section. One female worker followed him in a ute as he almost sprinted past, insisting he put the pram in her truck and get off the road. After he argued that he was causing no hazard, a bloke in an excavator turned up, then a third worker demanding he quickly get on the shoulder side of the witches hats. I can imagine the conflict, with Cad refusing to give in. In the end, he walked on the newly laid bitumen with a ute trailing him all the way, the driver explaining, 'Mate, we're just trying to look out for your welfare, bad drivers come through and ignore the speed limit, we don't want you to get killed.' It was a lecture that would be repeated at least six more times before he'd left Queensland. The funny side of the episode was that, as he walked through the long roadworks section, he received constant donations from other workers who had no issue with his presence.

By the time he'd reached the next section three kilometres further ahead, it was obvious that the workmen had been warned of his pending arrival via two-way radio. He spoke to the 'stop-go lady' and asked if it was alright to walk down the outside of the works and she saw no issue; neither did the traffic controller at the next section.

The following night came another treacherous encounter. For a long stretch in the night Cad was watching YouTube videos, checking Facebook or listening to music and was walking with the traffic rather than into it. His concentration had lapsed and he wasn't wearing his high-vis vest and, because his batteries had run flat, did not have his head torch on. He was inviting disaster. As he walked around a bend he wandered onto the road and a truck driver coming around the corner swerved at the last second to avoid him. 'It scared the shit out of me – gee, my heart was pumping. It must have been millimetres away from the side of my pram; it would have broken the handle or ripped my arm off. After that I thought maybe I better pull up for the night.' He saw a farm gate soon after and bashed through it and called it a night, just near Miriam Vale.

He was back to constant roadworks again next day but met a series of accommodating traffic controllers and foremen – except one, who explained, like his predecessor days earlier, that it was all about Cad's welfare and the safety of people working there, and he could be endangering people's lives if he continued to walk close to the works and the traffic. Andrew wouldn't budge in his mission to walk every step, and at one stage traffic in both directions was stopped while he walked an 800-metre section. Ironically, drivers of the stationary cars loaded him with donations as he passed.

As another works vehicle pulled up in the same section of work and Cad braced himself for an additional verbal onslaught, out jumped a mate from his from Gosford skate ramp days, 'Ads' (presumably Adam). Adam's cousin, who also worked on the road gang, had heard on the two-way a walker was coming through and, as he had been tracking Cad through the YouTube blogs, knew it was him. The foreman, whom Cad had just abused, suddenly had a change of heart and advised Andrew he was going to chaperone him through the works and raise some money along the way. Ad's cousin turned up with other workers, and handshakes and high fives were happening everywhere.

As Cad walked through with his new-found posse, he could hear dialogue on the two-way radio between the truck drivers and excavators, like, 'I've got a visual on the walker, geez, he's moving, he's walking quick,' and, 'He's come from Sydney, he's been all around, he's got a bit to go.' 'Ads would knock on every excavator's door and say this is my mate walking around Australia, I picked up over $200. There were heaps of legends, lots of Kiwis among them too.'

Cad ended up staying at the home of the head surveyor, and going out for dinner. The next morning he was asked by the project manager to address the staff at the morning's briefing. He was introduced with: 'This young man is walking around the country; he was sitting down yesterday having something to eat and I pulled up and asked if I could give him a lift through the works, but he was pissed off and he was ready to kill someone; he had this look in his eyes. He told me straight up he's walking every single metre and I'm not putting this in the back of your ute because I'm doing this for my dead mate. I thought straight away, "This is a bloke not to mess with."' Cad departed with more donations, a 'sick' jacket from a young Kiwi ('which is exactly what I needed'), new rain gear, a new high-vis vest and a photo with the Leighton gang (pram centre-front).

After climbing what seemed endless steep hills, Cad walked until 12.45am, meaning he'd been awake for seventeen hours after only six hours' sleep. He was thinking of pushing on to Childers as he wanted to get into the 90-club, having only recorded an 80 kilometres and one 100-kilometre effort to date. But after a car crossed double yellow lines to overtake a truck and missed Andrew by less than a metre, he knew it was safer off the road than on it and pulled into a rest area.

Next day my sister Narelle picked him up at Torbanlea and took him to Hervey Bay, where she lived, as did my other sister Denise and her husband, Peter, and Cad's cousin Ryan Hunt and family. They had a good family catch-up before Narelle took him back to the highway the next morning, his departure unfortunately delayed by her battery going flat while they unpacked his gear and said their goodbyes. (Finally, a motorist stopped and provided a charge.)

DAYS 510–520, 19–29 MAY 2012 HERVEY BAY TO BRISBANE (241KM); CENTRAL COAST, SINK ONE FOR SIMMO

It took Cad three days to traverse the 167 kilometres to Kenilworth where a former schoolmate, Adam Broomhall, lived and worked in his family's café, which had raised $920 for Andrew. The pretty town of just 300 people, nestled in the foothills behind the Blackall Ranges north-west of Brisbane, contributed another $260 while Cad was there overnight and for breakfast the next morning.

Adam dropped him back to the Maleny–Kenilworth Road, from where Cad took the 'back road' to Brisbane as pedestrians were not allowed to walk on the Bruce Highway. Walking without the pram, as 'Broomy' had agreed to transport it to an agreed point on the main road, he was pointed to a shortcut that involved a gravel road and monster hill climbs; one stretch was a 10-kilometre ascent up a mountain range, with cliff falls on each side. But Cad was taken by the beautiful countryside of green rolling hills below, dairy farms and 'cool Queensland cottages'. He was surprised he'd averaged six kilometres per hour despite the rugged terrain; shedding the more than 45 kilograms of Redge's weight was a major factor.

It was Chris Simpson's birthday on 22 May, and Cad had a good long chat with Josh, who was obviously struggling emotionally. Josh, who knew better than anyone how taxing Andrew's daily existence was, couldn't understand why he was in such a hurry to get home and why he was putting so much physical stress on himself. Cad could only answer that he just wanted to get it over with and start the next phase of his life. (As it happened, Josh offered me the same advice while I was trying to finish this book on a self-imposed deadline for the same reason.)

After he'd cleared Maleny in the Sunshine Coast hinterland, altitude 425 metres, Cad felt he was on the downhill run to Brisbane. A woman he'd never met (named as 'Mel McD') but who had followed his trek on Facebook arranged to meet him and offered a bed for the night, but he was determined to get as close to Brisbane city as he could and walk until midnight. Mel, whose husband had lost his battle with cancer, brought him a goodies bag including toothbrush, socks, deodorant and heat balm, which he greatly appreciated; it was yet another gesture of kindness from strangers.

Hours later, he hit the wall as he approached Caboolture. Feeling that he was so close to the northern perimeter of Brisbane, he made a call to his sister, Nicole, who lived in the southern suburbs. He explained that he really needed a bed, a good meal and some friendly faces, and begged someone to come and pick him up a night earlier than they'd organised. He laughed at Nicole's first reaction: 'But I don't have enough for dinner!' His mother was staying there too, but Nicole's husband, Glenn, was happy to drive the hour each way to rescue him.

Andrew was disappointed that his five-year-old niece, Kayla, and two-year-old nephew, Max, whom he had hardly seen, were asleep when he arrived and when he left early next morning. Nicole had to leave at 5am for a flight to Sydney for a conference, so Chris dropped her off and continued, taking Andrew back to Beerburrum, where he'd finished the night before. From there he motored into the city the next day, sans pram, pulling up stumps 15 kilometres short of his target for the day, the Storey Bridge, before Glenn drove him back to their place. It was State of Origin clash number one of 2012 that night, the biggest rugby league event of the season, but while Glenn was glued to the television, Chris and Andrew were off to bed before halftime, neither being footy fans.

Cad loved spending time with the kids that evening and next morning, and he loved that Max insisted Andrew take him to his preschool. ('I could hardly keep him in my arm – he weighed more than a bag of cement!' Cad commented.) After breakfast at Wellington Point with Chris, Andrew was off to the airport for his flight to Newcastle. I was there to pick him up and take him back to the Central Coast, where he was reunited with his trusty old mutt, Redge, and caught up with friends and family (including Nicole, who stayed down overnight) over the next five days.

There was a very social par-three golf day for Simmo followed by a fundraising night in a factory at West Gosford. Beforehand, Cad enjoyed dinner with Chris Simpson's parents, Wayne and Kim, whom he had previously met only briefly, and Josh. 'It was pretty special; we all got a bit emotional and teary. I had a nice dinner and a really nice night. Wayne pulled me aside and said how he was really proud of what I did, not just doing it for Simmo but that I had guts and determination to pull it off, and it was very special what I'd done. It meant a lot to me.'

Four days later he was back in Brisbane, refreshed and ready for the final 1000-kilometre leg.

DAYS 521–526, 30 MAY–5 JUNE 2012 BRISBANE TO COFFS HARBOUR (430KM)

After arriving in Brisbane late afternoon, Andrew had another night at Glenn and Nicole's and again enjoyed time with them and the two kids. There is a wonderful photo of Andrew, Kayla and Max on the lounge taken that evening that is a very special memento of what was to be the last time the kids and Glenn saw Andrew (that photo is now the wallpaper on Chris's iPad). Nicole, Kayla and Max said goodbye just after they woke, and Glenn did when he dropped Cad back to resume the walk north of the city. Nicole did see Andrew again – sadly, in hospital.

Cad hit showers almost immediately, and the rain rarely let up for the thirteen days it took him to reach the Central Coast. After embarking on an involuntary 6-kilometre detour in the southern part of Brisbane, he walked to Coomera on the northern edge of the Gold Coast the first night and made it to Tweed Heads the second night – after taking a wrong turn and heading west at Burleigh Heads, meaning he had to backtrack to the coastal highway.

When he was on the highway outside Coolangatta Airport, in pouring rain, a bolt on the wheel snapped and the pram bounced violently before collapsing, a wheel rolling down the road. He sat on the road's edge contemplating what he could possibly do, then fortunately realised he should call Glenn's father, Grant, who had just moved to Burleigh Heads with his wife, Heather. Glenn relayed Cad's dilemma to Grant, who came to the rescue with a bolt from his pushbike that quickly saw Andrew back on track.

He felt a massive sense of relief when he crossed the border into New South Wales and saw his first signpost to Sydney for almost eighteen months. He pitched his tent in the mud just off an on-ramp.

After next morning catching up with family friend of thirty years Debra Jeffery, who had immediately gone out searching for him after seeing his Facebook post from Tweed Heads, Cad walked all the way to Bangalow, where he desperately needed to restock his food supplies. After 76 kilometres for the day, at 12.45am he camped under an overpass in the midsection of roadworks on the Ballina bypass.

It took him just three days to travel the 213 kilometres to Coffs Harbour, where he attempted to camp behind a twenty-four-hour service station in town after a sixteen-hour shift, only to be ordered away by an overzealous employee (yes, a very vocal argument developed) forcing him to continue until he found a well-grassed oval – at 1.30am. When he left Brisbane Cad had said he would do seven straight 70-kilometre days; he did better, averaging 73 kilometres, with his biggest haul 82 kilometres.

DAYS 527–531, 5–9 JUNE 2012 COFFS HARBOUR TO BULAHDELAH (329KM)

Next day came his biggest single donation on the road when a truckie named Mark gave him $50, then doubled back with another $20 before retracing his steps again and handing over $50 more.

A strange encounter happened soon after when an overbearing insect-repellent salesman bailed him up and offered free product (which Andrew rejected as he said he was nearly home and the bloke was a year too late), and that he had 'contacts' to give Cad extensive promotion. Half an hour later a woman approached Cad and said she'd just heard about him on the radio; the salesman had been true to his word and got on air to alert Coffs Harbour residents to Cad's cause, but apparently also took the opportunity to plug his repellent offer. Next day the bug repellent guru left several phone messages saying he'd been trying to get hold of Andrew and had several more radio stations who wanted to talk to him. His last message was: 'Turn your phone on, buddy. I've lived up to my end of the bargain and got you some publicity, good luck, buddy.'

Cad wasn't too concerned about the missed opportunities – his focus was simply to get to Sydney.

By lunchtime he had made it to Urunga, where had lunch with his cousin Josh, who had driven in from his home at Bellingen. Cad really enjoyed their rare catch-up. Incredibly he was able to continue walking until 4am, reaching Clybucca; an 82-kilometre day. He'd planned to do a twenty-four-hour 120-kilometre stretch but dropped in for a shower at a roadhouse, his first since Brisbane eight days earlier, and couldn't convince himself to start again. He did his video blog before he went to sleep boasted of his first 500-kilometre week with: 'I reached the 500-club for the week, pretty stoked about that. Everyone talks about getting in the mile-high club but 500-club shits on getting a squashy root in an aeroplane dunny, I'll tell you that for free. Anyway, see you tomorrow.'

After only four hours' sleep, he was back on the bitumen at 9.30am in surprising good spirits, and a truck driver pulled him over to say he had just heard about him on Ray Hadley's radio program on 2GB. I gather another truckie had called in after seeing Cad on the road, and Ray put to air an enormous 'rap' on his efforts.

As he became closer to home Andrew was overwhelmed with the amount of people offering accommodation and requests for media interviews. He recorded: 'After doing it by myself for so long I'm a bit overwhelmed now by people wanting to get involved and help me out. It's great everyone wants to help, but there is too much going on all of a sudden and I just want to get home next Wednesday. I don't want to slow up or get distracted; it's starting to get on top of me a bit, all the attention.'

At that stage his goal was to finish on the Sydney Harbour Bridge on Wednesday, 13 June. When I realised that coincided with the second State of Origin match that night, I quickly called contacts at the NRL to see if it was possible for him to walk into a packed stadium to a massive roar, which would have been an amazing moment for him and good public relations for the sport and Sydney, considering he was raising money for the Leukaemia Foundation. Unfortunately, it was too late to make an alteration to the night's pre-match run sheet. If only I had considered the coinciding of events and thought of the idea weeks earlier...

He'd targeted reaching Port Macquarie in the driving rain, but at 1am he pitched the tent under an overpass on the Pacific Highway at Telegraph Point, on the Pacific Highway 17 kilometres short of 'Port' (which was 8 kilometres east of the highway, so he saved a 16-kilometre round journey). He woke up to sunshine for the first time in ten days but desperately needed more sleep and wasn't underway until 11am.

It started to hit Andrew how close he was to the finish line, and how special that would be after having no permanent home other than what was packed in his pram for the last year and a half. But, like other times when he had too much time to think, he wasn't sure who and how many he wanted to be there or walk in with him. He'd spoken to Kane the night before, which sparked him to record this: 'I spoke to Foley last night and it got me thinking. Wednesday is going to be the most special day in my life, except for the day my baby is born. I thought about reaching the bridge and I only want people there who really want to be there. From where I was last year, the lowest point of my life, one of the only things that would make me feel better was when I spoke to the boys or family when they would ring me. I didn't want to speak at times and wouldn't answer the phone, but the point is when they rung it made me feel like someone cares that I'm out here and made me feel better. They're the ones I'd like to be there.'

As he approached Taree a young bloke hopped out of a car and screamed, 'Are you Cad?'

'Yeah, mate,' Andrew replied.

'I know you – you're famous!'

It turned out he was a good mate of Redmond and Leon Stephens, among Cad's best friends. Jack asked Cad back to his house to sleep but Andrew was determined to make it to Taree, and that that would not happen until early the next morning. Jack said he'd still be awake and remarkably picked him up at 2am and dropped him back to the highway at 10am next morning, after getting bags of ice for Cad to have an ice bath to try to ease the pain in his left knee. Andrew had a profound discussion about fate with Jack, who had had a fascinating life and once lived on the street, and recorded: 'A year ago I believed everything was planned out for us, but it makes more sense what Jack said – sure there's fate but fate puts forks in the road in front of you and you chose your own path, and you have to make your own decisions. I think deciding to do the walk was a fork in the road for me. I don't want to get too deep but there's something there.'

Later that day Cad decided he was doing his 'Triple Marathon Madness' – walking the equivalent of three marathons, in one hit, in an effort to create a spurt of donations. He hit Facebook seeking pledges for donations and several responded with promises of $1 per kilometre, while others committed to doing celebrity walks with him along the marathon route. The most special commitment came from Steve and

Jessica Browne, his friends who he was going to join in Karratha for work after his walk; they offered ten cents for every kilometre he walked from Day 1 to the finish – over $1500! And they came good – an exceptional gesture from a couple who supported Cad all the way.

Josh Simpson was heading up the coast to Forster for a birthday party and arranged to walk part of the leg with Cad – his goal to do 100 kilometres. Billy Holloway, back living on the east coast, completed the reunion of the crew from Western Australia, and Cad's mate Kaine Dobbs and uncle Ken, in Newcastle for Ken's cousin Gary's fiftieth birthday that weekend, also joined in for some part.

Before that he had a family celebrity walk session from a rest area 10 kilometres south of Bulahdelah, which he reached at 2am on Day 530, with his aunty and uncle, Alison and Wayne Woodward, and their daughters, Kylie and Megan, and Megan's partner, Matt, who had worked with Andrew as a carpenter for a while, all joining hm. That night Matt Delaney and his son Lincoln were to camp overnight with Cad at Karuah, from where he was to start his Triple Marathon Madness effort.

Andrew woke at 9am in a bad way, very fatigued and his knee extremely sore, but didn't want to let on to his fellow walkers who had made such an effort to join him. With Wayne driving behind, the others walked with him until 3pm, although having some breaks (except Matt, who walked the whole way with Cad). Kylie eventually rode a pushbike with him until her husband, Scott, picked her up. Cad limped in alone to Karuah with Matt Delaney picking him up at the nominated spot which was 128.2 kilometres from the Kariong turnoff of the F3 motorway, starting point for the triple-marathon distance set for the next day. At that stage Cad still thought he could walk the motorway, only to find, quite dramatically, that he couldn't. It appears he calculated the distance incorrectly – a marathon is 42.195 kilometres; three times that is 126.6 kilometres.

At the end of the day Andrew could feel he was almost home with all the sudden company. Andrew, Matt and Lincoln slept in Matt's tent, Lincoln in fits of laughter at how quickly Cad slipped into a megaphone-like drawn-out snoring routine. A potential good night's sleep was further complicated by the air mattress Matt brought going dead flat, despite Cad trying to inflate it before daybreak. Let's just say he hadn't had a particularly appropriate preparation for a sixteen-hour, 128-kilometre slog when he woke at 6am!

DAYS 532–533, 10–11 JUNE 2012 TRIPLE MARATHON MADNESS: KARUAH TO OURIMBAH (127.4KM)

It was Sunday morning, 10 June, on the Queen's Birthday holiday weekend 2012. After bacon, eggs, sausages and spaghetti with the Delaneys, Cad ditched his tent, mattress and whatever was not needed in the pram for Matt to take to the Central Coast as this had been his last night of camping out. The 'marathon madness' started at 8am. After doing a phone interview with the *Newcastle Herald* and posing for a photograph, Cad walked for five hours by himself in brilliant sunshine until he was joined by Josh and Billy, well equipped with wet-weather gear.

They walked uninterrupted for two hours down the F3, joined by Ken and Dobbsy. By dark Bill was limping badly, and sipping beer through a tube was unable to temper his pain. Two policemen pulled over and questioned whether it was safe for so many of them walking on the freeway because they weren't visible in the dark, which resulted in some 'attitude' from the boys as Cad was wearing a high-vis vest and had reflectors and torchlights. After driving off and allowing the boys to continue, the police returned ten minutes later, and the least sympathetic one relayed that his sergeant had told him to order them off the freeway immediately. Despite Cad pleading for them to be allowed to walk 2 kilometres to the next exit (Freemans Drive), the cop refused to accommodate them and told them to backtrack to the previous exit (Palmers Road), adding an extra 8 kilometres to walk. That fired everyone up, but after continuing for a couple of hours along the dark Freemans Drive their spirits improved, thanks to Billy entertaining the others with his funny stories.

By 2am Billy was done and called his partner to rescue him; he'd walked just under 60 kilometres (59.2, but there was no way Cad would not let him claim a 60-club membership). Ken, who showed enormous resilience for a fifty-year-old, was next to drop off, at Morisset, so it was down to Josh, Dobbsy and Cad. It started to pour rain and, as Cad recorded, 'things started to get a bit solemn'. 'Josh was struggling but he wouldn't pack it in. I said to him, "You have done 70 kilometres, mate, that's an awesome effort, it took me a long while to get up to 70 kilometres. How about you pack it in?" He told me, "Don't start blowing smoke up my arse, I'm doing 100."'

After reaching Wyee (via Wyee Road), Dobbsy told Cad he didn't have many more steps in him so he called Lucy to pick him up, and Josh reluctantly made the call to also quit; it was 16 kilometres to Wyong and they didn't know what was in between. They were in awe that Andrew was able to keep going, considering he had started about 28 kilometres before them.

'I was surprised they lasted so long,' Cad said. 'I said, "Thanks, boys, and goodbye," and pretty quickly put my game face on – this is the mental bit. It was pissing down and I had to get focused. I'd done around 100 kilometres by this time, and was getting a bit sore but wasn't too bad. I walked into the pitch black and thought I knew where I was going. It was nearly 5am.

'By this stage I was soaked through, I was cold and I could feel my singlet, shirt and flanno sticking to my skin. It was too wet to get the iPod out so here I was left with my own thoughts, no music and no one to talk to. I was digging deep. It wasn't my legs killing me, I was just exhausted. My eyelids were getting really heavy. At times I was walking through ankle-deep torrents of water, I could feel it splashing up my legs, and water was running over my feet and my shoes were squelching. Dawn started to break and I hit the wall big time, almost falling asleep while walking. I could feel my eyes closing and my head would drop and I'd snap and wake myself up, just like when you're on the lounge watching TV at bedtime or on a plane. I kept thinking, "I'm going to wake up on the ground with a smashed face in the gravel."

'I'd yell top of my voice – "C'mon ... yaaah ... keep going ... c'mon!" I kept doing it every thirty seconds. Sleep deprivation was setting in, I thought I was seeing people and hearing dogs and cars but there was nothing there; I was wigging out pretty hard. I stopped and had three No-Doze tablets but they didn't help much. I just kept trudging along, slapping myself in my face, but I was struggling to stay awake.'

That's when a car pulled over: it was Wayne and Kim Simpson, with Dobbsy and Josh in the back. Kaine hopped out to see how Cad was but Josh wasn't capable of moving. 'Kim came up to me and said, "Gee you're a strong man." I was delusional by then; I was laughing to myself over nothing. They gave me a pie and coffee. My hands were frozen. I had wet gloves on; I put them on after the boys had left. I found Josh's glove in the back of the pram; he thought he'd lost it when he'd had a piss. All I could say to Wayne was, "Tell Josh I've got his glove," and I kept laughing and just repeated it again and again. Wayne gave me another coffee. Dobbsy said, "I thought you were going Sparks Road?" I said "Yeah, I am," but he said, "Well, you've missed it, man."' Cad had stayed on Hue Hue Road, west of the motorway, instead of joining the old Pacific Highway to the east.

Wayne pointed Cad to the freeway, where he was going to run the gauntlet for about 3 kilometres from the Wyong Road turn-off to Ourimbah, probably halving the distance compared to sticking to the back roads, but Cad was so disorientated he kept walking over the freeway along Wyong Road, past Westfields Shoppingtown, to Tuggerah and had to walk down the old highway to Ourimbah. Being forced to take the non-freeway route since the night before had at least seen him cover enough extra distance to achieve his desired kilometres in Ourimbah, although he had no idea how far he'd walked until he stopped at McDonald's at Tuggerah.

With no phone battery left, he searched for a payphone and I can only guess at his frustration when the first he found was out of order. The second phone gave him no dial tone, but it accepted his money and he called me, hoping I might be able to hear him while he couldn't hear me. Fortunately, I could and he said that if I could hear his voice could I pick him up at the Mobil service station at Ourimbah. His words were: 'Dad, I don't know if you can hear me but I'm really fucked. Can you meet me at Ourimbah? I'm wet and cold and need some dry clothes.' I hitched the trailer onto the car and headed for Ourimbah.

About the same time, my sister Alison, who lived nearby, had decided to look for him and she was trailing him in her four-wheel drive when I arrived. Alan Shaw (we were staying with the Shaws after selling our place) came too, and dropped me off to walk the last couple of kilometres with Cad; I was thinking it would help lift his spirits and get him to the finish line. I was wrong; he was in no mood for any conversation, and certainly told me so. He was on the edge and it gave me my first real-life taste of the condition he must have often been in many times, and it was confronting. At 10.15am his triple dose of madness came to an end, after twenty-six hours of nonstop walking.

Just after I took him to my mother's place, where he was about to hop into the shower, an NBN Television reporter called saying he was on the F3 looking for Andrew; they'd gone on the *Newcastle Herald* report that he would arrive on the coast mid-morning. They were insistent that they get an interview and vision of him walking with the pram, so he relented and had to get back into his saturated clothes and walk along the main road, Brisbane Water Drive, several times. 'I was surprised I made any sense at all after how I felt earlier in the morning.'

All Andrew wanted to do was have a shower and then a sleep, but when he went back inside my mother's place my sister Robyn was there and had run herself a bath and – can you believe it? – the hot water had run out! (My mother has a habit of turning the hot water switch off if she's away for any length of time.) Andrew called me to pick him up and take him back to the Shaws at nearby Koolewong. He enjoyed a long hot shower and a snack, then went back to my mother's and staggered into bed. What a day ... make that a day and a half.

DAY 534, 12 JUNE 2012 FILLING THE GAP IN SYDNEY: BLAKEHURST TO THE BRIDGE (21KM)

By next day the media interest had stepped up and Andrew was looking to join a panel on the late-night

Channel Ten news, hours after finishing his walk, but decided it was too late to keep going. Channel Seven's breakfast show *Sunrise* also wanted him to go on the program the morning after he made the finish line and they were happy to provide accommodation the night before, so he elected to do that as it allowed him more rest (Channel Ten still covered him crossing the finish line).

Mid-morning I dropped him back to Blakehurst on the Princes Highway in southern Sydney, the spot where it all began 534 days earlier, from where he back-tracked to the harbour bridge where he wanted to finish the walk in glory; this leg necessary so he would cover every metre from where he'd started almost eighteen months earlier.

When we arrived I said to him, 'I remember this spot like it was yesterday.'

Andrew replied, 'Me too, and I was stressing out.'

'I certainly remember that too, Cad, don't worry,' I smiled.

He walked, without the pram and thus without the stares, to halfway along the Sydney Harbour Bridge, where he made a red line with electrical tape that would be his finish mark two days later. Then he jumped on a train at Wynyard and headed back north to continue from where he'd left off. He was planning to walk 11 kilometres from Hornsby to Berowra, the northern point of Sydney's sprawling suburbs, in order to fill in another gap and make the next day shorter, but was far too tired. After waking on the train with the driest mouth, he was sure he'd snored all the way to Woy Woy.

DAY 535, 13 JUNE 2012 OURIMBAH TO HORNSBY (69KM)

I picked Cad up at 6am and took him Ourimbah, where he'd finished his Triple Marathon Madness. From there he had 91 kilometres to the finish line overlooking Sydney's glorious harbour. This was to be his last long day, but he could at least do it without pushing Redge once he cleared West Gosford; he thought he'd have it with him, for show only, until then to attract some donations. He did an interview on local radio station Star FM, which prompted a few donations along the way.

After offloading the pram to me and climbing the hill from West Gosford to Kariong, it was back to the old Pacific Highway through Mount White, Cowan and Berowra to Hornsby. On the northern outskirts of Sydney he called Thai Airlines to check flights and prices after finally deciding that he'd definitely head to Thailand the following Monday – four days after finishing his walk – to rest and convert his diaries into book form.

He caught the train back to Koolewong and had dinner with Chris and me and the Shaws, and I took him to

Point Clare, where he stayed at his grandmother's retirement villa (she was still in hospital) to prepare, alone, for the 452nd day en route around the vast continent of Australia. (It would actually be Day 536 of walking, but he'd also had eighty-four days away from the trek: in Thailand, in Fiji and back on the Central Coast for the Dobbs' wedding and Simmo's fundraiser.)

DAY 536, 14 JUNE 2012 THE FINISH: HORNSBY TO SYDNEY HARBOUR BRIDGE (22KM)

Cad was entitled to be absolutely exhausted. He had been wanting this day to come for so long. As it drew near, the distress and weariness caused by the torturous journey had largely subsided and was overtaken by pride, satisfaction and exhilaration at what he had achieved. Only he truly knew what an achievement this was – to be facing his final few kilometres almost eighteen months after he'd taken his first steps.

He'd endured the army of flies near the Victorian border, terrible shin pain in Tasmania, the isolation and endless horizon of the Nullarbor, where his mind first started to show more frailty than his body, the bitter cold and rain of southern Western Australia, the months when he had the company of old mates and new to give him enjoyment in Perth and further north, the detours to Fiji and Thailand either side of the arduous and life-sapping Kimberley, the near misses with speeding road trains, and the single-minded sprint home from Darwin.

The stats of his three and a half month 'get home quick' journey from Darwin provide compelling evidence of a super-human effort. He walked 2493 kilometres from Darwin to Townsville in fifty-five days, averaging a tick under 49 kilometres a day with only four days off; he increased that to 54.3 kilometres a day for the twenty-five days it took him to travel the 1359 kilometres from Townsville to Brisbane (with only one day off), and then somehow managed an epic 62.4 kilometres a day from Brisbane to Sydney (999 kilometres) over fifteen days without a day off (except for an afternoon sleep after completing the Triple Marathon Madness). That was the equivalent of a marathon and a half a day!

I think it was Josh Simpson who drove him to Hornsby, where he met Kim and Wayne Simpson, his cousin Matt Ruff, Redmond Stephens, Kaine Dobbs, Adam Martin and Tristan Norris. Along the way to the bridge, they were been joined by Chris and me, and later by Matt Delaney. A few others who wanted to join him couldn't get out of work.

Of those who were there, Josh held a special place. For all the people who had said they were in awe of what Cad was doing and pledged that they would try to join him en route for days or weeks, his father included, Josh was the only one who had actually followed through. He'd walked over 500 kilometres by Cad's side, first crossing the country to do so on the west coast and now for the second time on the east coast, right by his side at the emotional ending. He was the only one had witnessed what it took for Andrew to get to the finish line. Cad understood, respected and appreciated Josh's commitment; I know this because he told me.

Wayne and Kim were hurting near the end, with Wayne's Achilles tendon really tested, but there was no way in the world they were not going complete every step of the way to repay Cad for going through his pain barrier in honour of their son Chris.

It was a special few hours; lots of banter – mostly aimed at Andrew, telling him to slow down – and just a heap of admiration for what we had, briefly, been allowed to be a part of (Chris's sister Lynne joined for a short while as we went past her workplace at Gordon). It should remain such a happy memory for all of us, and those who were there to greet Cad at the finish and celebrate afterwards – and it is. But it is also bittersweet now.

We stopped so I could take a group photo in the shadows of the bridge, at the bottom of the stairs that climb the northern pylon. Then we followed Cad to the finish – the red line he had fixed to the eastern walkway two days earlier – to the applause from friends, family and Leukaemia Foundation representatives and the only media contingent, Nick Lockyer from Channel Ten, which was disappointing considering how epic an event it was. A lovely touch was Lucy Dobbs meeting Cad and Kaine at the finish line with their six-month-old daughter Lyla, who was wearing an Oz On Foot T-shirt.

Having the Leukaemia Foundation representatives there was fitting. Andrew's cousins Luke and Megan, his aunty Alison and their friends Mark and Kim Ella were also there. Cad's reaction at finishing his classic trek seemed to be a combination of being overawed and understated. He didn't know how to feel, and relayed that to me next day, and it certainly hadn't hit home that the life he'd had for almost a year and a half was about to change. He looked remarkably fresh, fit and happy, and very controlled emotionally.

Some of us adjourned to the Australian Hotel in the Rocks, Cad refusing to accept an alcoholic drink to celebrate. I asked Josh to say a few words and he was brief but perfect, and then I spoke, which would have embarrassed Andrew. I mumbled about how no one in our family, in any generation, had ever done something as incredible as what Cad had just completed, and how in awe and very, very proud we all were of his extraordinary achievement.

Chris and I left him with his mates, Cad drinking lemon squash so he was in the right condition for his breakfast interview on *Sunrise* the following morning. He was able to defy the encouragement of others to kick on (close mate Todd Bailey had also joined later), and he and Josh retired to their hotel about midnight. Josh joined him at the Channel Seven studios early the next morning.

His mission was completed. Circumstances and distractions – injury in Tasmania, attending two weddings and spending a week longer than he'd planned in Perth – had added a month alone and contributed to him having to add a further two months sitting out the Top End's wet in Thailand. But the job was done, his commitment met: Simmo had been honoured. Cad had walked 15,109 kilometres.

He was home.

Just not for long enough.

After only three and a half more days in our presence, he was gone. To Thailand. I think he felt he just had to get away from the fanfare – he genuinely couldn't handle being the centre of attention for too long – and he wanted to escape the temptation to party too much. He had a big network of friends and loved his close mates, many of whom had shared experiences and adventures with him home and abroad and were tight and loyal, but he was also a bit disappointed more friends had not taken an hour, or a day or half a day, from work to join him on his last few days of walking or be there at the finish line.

In many ways, though, he seemed more settled, and more at ease with himself, than ever before when he'd always seemed to be searching for fulfilment. His trek ended up being, for him, as much about the miles he travelled in his mind as the miles he'd travelled on land, his brain too often in overdrive while looking boundlessly at his life past and present during all those hours he had to himself. Despite being seen among his peers as the one who had done so much and who would take on any challenge, no matter how hard or how stupid, Cad had come to think he'd wasted too much of his time and could have achieved more (which I think was unfair). And he'd finally realised how much he wanted to settle down and become a partner and father himself, although he laughed to us that week that he might soon be too old for that and might have to get a Thai wife!

He had his next plan – to work at the mines at Karratha in a few months and stack away some cash, although he truly didn't know, just then, how to handle what might come next – other than writing a book about the walk, which has become this book, as a means of closing that chapter of his life and moving on.

I wasn't the only one who couldn't understand why he so urgently felt the need to escape. Then again, none of us could truly know how the previous 540 days had affected him.

And so Cad and I were at Sydney Airport on the Monday, just the two of us, exchanging an embrace and sharing the last words we would speak face to face.

'See you when I see you.'

15

THE SPLIT-SECONDTHAT CHANGED EVERYTHING

14 JULY 2013, CHIANG MAI

At the beginning of this book I touched on what happened next, just four weeks later, and the phone call I received from the Australian Department of Foreign Affairs and Trade. The phone call every parent dreads but never expects to receive.

The saying is so, so true: one split-second can change your life forever. But I had no idea how real and confronting that cliché could be until Chris and I arrived in Chiang Mai just over twenty-four hours after I had received that chilling telephone call notifying me that Andrew had been involved in a motor accident. I wrote this and the next chapter as I sat next to Cad's bed in Thailand (the rest of the book followed after we'd returned home). How that split-second in the early hours of 14 July 2012 changed everything forever for Andrew, his family and closest friends still didn't seem quite real.

After dropping Andrew at Sydney Airport, my first contact from Thailand was an email four days after he'd arrived in Chiang Mai, telling me he had again (a repeat of his first week in Thailand earlier in the year) left his card in an ATM, and asking if I could get a new one organised from his bank and send him $1000 via Western Union to get him by.

I didn't hear from him much after that. Most of that time he was immersed in transcribing his diaries onto his laptop and emailing them progressively to me. I think I had just two brief phone conversations and a few emails from him in the twenty-four days after I dropped him at Sydney Airport. The last email I received from Cad, the last conversation we had, was when he informed me he wanted to get a tattoo of his grandmother, pictured in her younger days, to be done by Jaclyn Rehe, the tattooist in Melbourne whom he'd struck up a good relationship with. Cad's email was typical of his sense of humour (if that's what you call it!), and I shared it as part of my eulogy at his service:

> *Hi*
>
> *Your daily annoying, pesky email has arrived!!*
>
> *I have commissioned my tattooist in Melbourne to do a painting for me of grandma's wedding photo, and then she will tattoo it on me at a later date.*

She is a brilliant artist in high demand and has just finished some paintings so need to grab this opportunity while she is free.

I need to send her a photo ASAP for the painting, but obviously don't want to send her some to choose one and have to send back in case it gets lost ... SOOO ... when you get time – ha! can you scan all the wedding photos you have of her and granddad. It doesn't have to be their wedding photo, it just needs to be one of them together a bit dressed up.

Grandma looked ugly in the wedding photo that she showed me, and while that is fine for a painting I don't want a ugly chick tattooed on me – grandma or not.

Jaclyn could easily make her hot but I want to keep it as realistic as possible.

I know you are busy and lost a day taking Redge, thanks for that by the way. But whenever you can would be good.

Something that might be good enough is just to take pics of the photos with your phone and email them straight from your phone. (I think I remember you saying you had some there from the family tree thing, hopefully one of them will be cool.)

Attached are some of her photos showing the style it will be in to give you an idea.

Glad Redge was OK with a male husky!

Grandma might like to have the painting up for a while until I settle again.

Cheers

I'd left home two days before receiving his email, to Queensland's Sunshine Coast to join Chris, Nicole, Glenn and the grandkids for a week's holiday (and go to Brisbane to watch State of Origin II while there). On the way I'd dropped Andrew's dog Redge to his new home at Chris's cousin Leonie's home at Lismore; since Andrew was planning to be in Thailand and then Karratha, and with Chris and me temporarily without a house, he needed a new home. I was back only a day before heading to Port Macquarie to attend the national open schoolboys rugby league titles as part of my agent accreditation scheme manager's job, then detouring for a day and a half to Grafton for the annual Grafton Cup and Ramornie Handicap carnival to join good mate Craig Brown.

The next time I would set eyes on Andrew, days later, he was barely recognisable from the son I said goodbye to at Sydney Airport twenty-seven days earlier.

As we entered his ward in Chiang Mai's Maharaj Nakorn Hospital, Andrew's bed was second on the right. He had the ventilator hooked up to his mouth and his head was severely swollen, with the scalp bandaged. Both his eyes were black and closed over, and there were stitches in his right eyelid. Chris let out a gasp and had to turn away.

A doctor was there and he tried to explain to us the seriousness of the injuries, but we couldn't understand him very well. He said until the swelling went down he could not fully determine how Andrew would end up, but it was not looking good. He said that if Andrew survived he could be unconscious for weeks, even months, and when he did awake he would have little brain function and would need ongoing care; he wouldn't be able to walk or talk or do anything for himself for the rest of his life. Chris and I looked at each other and broke down.

I asked the doctor if he had seen anyone recover from such a prognosis and have a better scenario than he had just explained, and he said no. I thought, 'Well, you haven't met anyone like Andrew Cadigan before.' Also going through my mind was that perhaps the expertise wasn't great here and they could be wrong; this was not a big Australian hospital or the Bumrungrad or other hospitals in Bangkok that had been recommended to us by DFAT, if we could eventually move Andrew. I immediately asked about transferring Andrew to Bangkok but the doctor said it was too risky; Andrew was not capable of being moved.

We didn't know if Andrew was on life support; when I asked the doctor that, he didn't seem to understand me. I assumed that was the case as I think he said Andrew couldn't breathe without the mechanical respirator. (I honestly didn't know about these things at this point, and was in a state of shock anyway.)

We went to the apartments where Andrew was staying and told them what had happened, asking for the keys to his room. It was surreal walking into his apartment; the first thing I saw was a small round table with his laptop on it and a single white chair, where he had obviously been typing out his diaries for the book. The apartment was quite large and had a small kitchen, separate bedroom and bathroom. Looking in the wardrobe and seeing his clothes, and the shelf where his iPod Nano and other things were, was hard. He had a Lonely Planet guide to Cambodia, which he was so looking forward to seeing more of, along with Burma and Laos; he'd been talking about this to Chris, who had gone to Cambodia in 2004. He was actually planning to cross the border within the next three days, and return to Chiang Mai, as his visa was only for thirty days. It broke my heart to know he would never get there now.

Nicole arrived on the Tuesday evening, and we were so worried about how she would cope when introduced to the nightmare we had confronted. I'll never forget her reaction, her shock and disbelief, when I led her to Andrew's bed: here was her brother, unrecognisable with a swollen, distorted head and half his skull missing. She didn't believe it was him at first, until she saw the tattoos on his legs, which were sticking out of the sheets. She showed such bravery in the forty-eight hours she was in Chiang Mai, but we insisted she return to Glenn and their two children, who she needed to be with. I thought it might be the last time she would see Andrew alive.

In our first few days in Chiang Mai I became determined to find out how all this had happened – to put together the pieces of what would either be the last days of Cad's life or the last days of his life as he knew it.

With Chris's brother Ken, who arrived four days after the accident after deciding without notice to head to Thailand to help out, I went to the gym where Andrew had been training. I contacted names listed on his Thai phone and checked his email and Facebook messages, desperately trying to contact someone who was with him that night. I found out he came back to the hotel after a big shop on the Friday morning, the evidence of which of which was in his fridge – chicken, bread, eggs and protein shakes. And he left to go out late that evening. That's all I could fathom. After reading his emails and Facebook messages, I also learned that the previous Friday was the only time he'd gone out for the night during his month in Chiang Mai.

I contacted the motor scooter hire company to advise them of the accident and that one of their bikes was obviously banged up. Within an hour I left the hotel for the hospital, and the proprietor of the hire company, without having advised me of his intentions, was in Andrew's ward asking questions when I arrived; I found that very off-putting. But he ended up being quite helpful and told me he was going to the police station, and that I should follow him. There I was told details of where and how the accident had happened. I was taken to a rear yard and shown Andrew's bike and the other vehicle he collided with. There was little damage to either.

I had to return to the police station the next day; an Australian, Laurie Simmons, a volunteer 'tourist police officer', was there to assist (he also ran a motel/guesthouse). We went back to the yard, where investigators tried to piece together the impact point of the vehicles. What I gleaned is that Andrew was riding his scooter in the direction of his hotel when the driver of a motorbike with a sidecar full of vegetables, on his way to the markets just after 4am, pulled across in front of Andrew to enter a street that was clearly marked 'no entry'. It was purely the other driver's fault. However, it appeared Andrew had not been wearing a helmet; in fact, the helmet was still clipped onto the bike under his knees.

I visited the crash site many times, which was on one of the main roads that traverse the boundary of the old city of Chiang Mai in a square shape. There were two lanes going one way, two lanes the other way, and they were separated by a canal and, in some parts, the remains of the wall that had surrounded the old city. There were no right-hand turns allowed; drivers could only do U-turns at the designated breaks in the canal and merge into traffic going in the other direction. It was like many Thai road rules – as they were rarely policed, motorists were used to ignoring them. At this particular U-turn point, to enter the road a vehicle had to go slightly diagonally and into the path of the oncoming traffic to get into the street the other vehicle was entering.

Of all the breaks in the roads that formed the square-shaped boundary of the inner city, this was the most dangerous, because drivers were obscured from the entering traffic on the right because the old ruins of the wall ran right up to the U-turn lanes. Also, the east-facing lanes in which Andrew was travelling took a slight left bend from behind the wall, making vision more difficult. If you wanted to pick a likely black spot for such a collision in Chiang Mai, this was it.

On the Thursday after the accident, hours before Nicole was to return to Brisbane, Laurie arrived at our hotel and asked to see me. Gathered outside were the offending driver, his wife, his daughter and a family friend. Laurie said he had tried to contact me (but was getting the busy signal) to ask if we were prepared to see them, as the family insisted they come to apologise and beg our forgiveness, which is extremely contrary to Thai culture, where people tend to walk away and not confront such issues or experiences. We agreed to meet them.

Laurie opened by saying the father wanted to relay that he was entirely responsible for the accident, that he could not forgive himself and that he was not rich but would do anything he could to help. They said they had been to visit Andrew twice in hospital. I vaguely remembered seeing the man and his wife leaving the ward as I entered one day, but was unaware they had been there to see our son.

It was little comfort that the wife confessed her husband's eyesight was poor and that he shouldn't have been driving. They obviously persevered with him steering the old bike and sidecar to the markets in the dark every morning in order to survive. She told us her husband would drive no more and they would rely on family or friends to get them there.

Chris, Nicole and I did not know how to feel, beyond the shock that the family came to visit us without notice. But, strangely, I did not feel any anger. It was surreal to look directly at the man who had caused such pain although he could not make eye contact because of the shame and regret he felt, and most of the time had his head buried in his hands. Yet, in the haze of confusion and emotion, I had some appreciation that he had the courage to come to us to pass on his regret.

As time went by in Thailand and the nightmare of waiting, waiting, waiting and feeling trapped and helpless continued, my thoughts on that elderly man swung erratically. My initial feeling was of resignation and acceptance that the accident was just inherent in the ignorance of road safety that plagues the country, but it swung to anger then just a nothingness to be honest.

My most vivid memory from the family's visit is of his daughter: as her parents and family friend walked away from the alcove where we met at our hotel, she doubled back, going down on her knees and bowing before us, hands gripped, begging forgiveness or understanding.

It became unnerving that they continued to frequently visit Andrew in hospital. I ran into them a couple of times later, and they would leave food or drink or lucky charms and written messages by Andrew's bed. One day, I entered to a mounted card beside his bed with the message: 'I apologize for accident. Get well soon.'

We were not comfortable with their regular visits and I feared they would one day be there when Chris arrived at the hospital, which was an experience she would not have been able to handle. I was about to, through Laurie, insist that they no longer visit Andrew when, late one morning, the father, his wife, daughter and friend arrived as I was crying after sitting with Andrew alone for a couple of hours. The father had shaved his head and was wearing saffron monk's robes. Their arrival tipped me over the edge and I immediately left, glaring at them in a way that undoubtedly signified that I was not comfortable with them coming into the ward whenever they liked. As far as I know, they did not come again.

Although I knew the circumstances of the accident, I was resigned to never knowing where Andrew had been, who he was with and how he was feeling that night; whether he was content, or lonely and unhappy.

About five weeks after the accident I logged on to Andrew's Facebook account and found a message that had been sent three weeks earlier from George Guthrie, an Australian from the Gold Coast who was trying to get in contact to tell me he was with Andrew that night and was riding a motor scooter behind him when the accident occurred. They'd met only hours earlier and Andrew offered his Christian name but said, 'Call me Cad, everyone does.' George left Chiang Mai three days later for London, and while there his brother (who lived in the UK) somehow tracked down stories about Andrew's walk on the internet. This enabled them to discover his identity and make contact through Facebook. I am very glad George took the trouble to do so; it was a breakthrough that provided the missing piece in the puzzle of what happened that night.

In his email I found that George had only met Andrew that night and, both being Australians away from home, got along well. He was on a motor scooter behind Andrew when the accident happened, and ran to his rescue, trying to comfort Andrew, who was unconscious. Later in the day he contacted his father in Australia to ask him to contact the Australian embassy to offer assistance. After leaving for the UK, he wasn't able to get any information about what happened to Andrew.

I spoke with George by telephone a few days later when he'd returned to Australia and found that he'd run into Andrew just before midnight on the street near the Thapae Gate on the city walls. It was near Starbucks, where Andrew drank coffee and went to work on his diaries and to get on the internet. I had already learned that Andrew was Facebook messaging until nearly midnight.

They talked and decided to go to a bar to have a few quiet drinks and a chat. About 4am, George followed Andrew's motor scooter on his. They were riding along the main road and were approaching the Chiang Mai Gate when the collision happened.

It seems, in a freakish case of centimetres determining his fate, Andrew's head hit a vertical steel bar holding up the canopy on the sidecar, so there was no chance to brace himself or cushion the impact. It must have been horrifying for George to witness the accident involving a bloke he had only met that night. He immediately stopped and cradled our bloodied son in his arms, screaming for onlookers to stay away and yelling for someone to call an ambulance.

The wife of the other driver had told us said she also cradled Andrew's head and when the first of two ambulances arrived she insisted that he was taken away and that her husband, also injured, could wait for the next.

Closely observing the traffic in Chiang Mai for all those weeks I was there, I was left with an overwhelming feeling that these sort of needless occurrences and tens of thousands of road deaths a year have to be greatly reduced; surely someone has to take responsibility. There has to be more policing, greater penalties and thus far more serious deterrents for motorists in Thailand. The roads are simply mayhem, unsafe and especially so for foreign drivers who subconsciously expect those around them will follow the road rules because that is just second nature at home.

The real story of how many deaths there are on the roads in Thailand is somewhere between what you read and who you listen to. The government figures are around 12,000 a year but other sources told me the real figure was certainly upwards of 20,000, and one person told me it was as high as 70,000, which seems almost unbelievable. Certainly Thailand is regarded as having the highest per population rate of road deaths of all Asian countries. Motorbike accidents account for 70 per cent of road deaths and the level of riders and/or passengers who do not wear helmets is the highest in Asia. One official figure I saw was that only 47 per cent wear helmets.

I hardly saw a policeman on the road, and when I did they seemed disinterested in any traffic control. I would often count the bikes and the ratio of those wearing helmets and those who did not. It wavered between 40 per cent and 60 per cent. Sadly, tourists seemed less inclined to don a helmet than the locals. My theory was that they were in an environment where the strict traffic rules they were used to did not exist, so they relaxed their compliance, and their sense, too. It's a potentially fatal mistake.

Local motorists would ignore the basic road rules. If a light was red and there was no traffic crossing, they would turn left anyway or, at times, just drive ahead. Pedestrian crossings meant nothing; in fact, pedestrians were at the very bottom of the totem pole on the roads. Often we would walk across a pedestrian crossing having waited for the green 'walk' light only to have to stop suddenly as a bike ploughed through. On our second day there I had to pull an unsuspecting Chris back to the kerb as this happened; she would have been hit for sure. Another time I was crossing the road on a green 'walk' light at the two-lane each way main road; the car on the inside lane stopped at the red light; the car on the next lane did ... then a motorbike whipped along the parking lane closest to the curb and missed me by centimetres.

This was the environment in which Andrew placed himself when he elected to get a scooter as his mode of transport while in Chiang Mai; so he had to take responsibility for that. But after talking to George, at least I know now that Cad was happy and relaxed that night, when his life as he knew it ended.

What I also knew was that we were in the heart of a nightmare we never envisaged, and for a long, long time there just seemed no escape.

16

TRAPPED IN THAILAND

15 JULY–19 SEPTEMBER 2012

Words cannot explain the pain and the helplessness a father feels when, day after day, he sits and watches his son – always active, energetic and full-bore into life – lie in a hospital bed staring blankly ahead, not responding to words, touch, music played through headphones or any stimulus I could think of providing. Andrew was alive but had no life. Lying on the bed in front of me was a slowly diminishing body, but no working mind.

Day after day, week after week.

Trapped.

The weeks Chris and I spent in Thailand watching him in this state was the most disturbing and difficult thing I will ever do in my life.

I forced myself to enter a zone of numb stoicism every time I walked, always with a knot in my stomach, into Cad's hospital ward but it never got easier to watch him. I just pretended it did to help those around me, especially Chris.

The cruel reality was that, according to all the doctors we consulted, there was hardly a miniscule chance that the once exciting, often adventurist and rarely dull life of Andrew Cadigan would continue in anything but this terrible state and it seemed there was nothing I or anyone could do for him. After all the close calls with road trains during his around-Australia walk and after surviving all his mad antics over the years, which left him seemingly bulletproof in the eyes of so many, some poor, small, feeble old Thai man driving a patched-up old motorcycle and side cart had destroyed him. How the hell could this be – how the hell could his life be ripped apart like this in a flash of time?

This existence went on for almost nine weeks in a Chiang Mai hospital where only a few of the nurses, as helpful and polite as they were, had even basic broken English. Any information from the doctors came in the form of brief responses to my questions, responses that were rarely clear, often contradictory and almost always forcefully extracted from them. Don't get me wrong, they were, I can only hope, fine neurologists, but for all those weeks in Chiang Mai Chris and I battled to understand what was truly going on. Andrew could not tell us how he felt. He could not tell us anything at all, and the doctors seemed intent on providing little commitment (or perhaps they had no real idea) about how long he might stay alive, or alternatively how long he might take to get 'better'.

Twice Andrew looked like he would be well enough for us to get him out of the crowded public hospital, where there wasn't even the facility to put him into isolation in his own room, only to have to abandon the plans as he was beset with complications. Pneumonia then swelling and bleeding of the brain on his good (right) side were detected, so he required further surgery the week we were first due to fly him home (6 August – twenty-three days after the accident). He continually sparred with infections which threatened to end his life, amazing us and the doctors by winning each battle. Naturally, I prayed for a miracle, trying to believe that just maybe there was some hope he could defy everyone and lead some sort of normal life, but I was told from the outset that that was very, very unlikely. At the other end of the scale, I'd often hope he would pass away in that lonely bed so that we didn't have to take his living corpse back to Oz for a life that he would have been shocking.

All the while Andrew's well-trained spirit and natural toughness and fitness kept defying the odds without him realising it. Or maybe he did.

Even though the first opinion we received from the hospital in Chiang Mai was dire, Chris and I naturally wanted further medical opinion. So, through some contacts of great friends of ours, Ian and Joy Heads, I was put in contact with a leading neurosurgeon in Sydney, and sent him Andrew's report and scans. The Australian consulate in Bangkok had also referred me to an Australian, Dr Peter Morley, who worked at the highly regarded Bumrungrad private hospital in

Bangkok, to whom I also sent all the information on Andrew's condition, which he passed onto all his neurology department specialists. The message came back from both sources that every indication was, as advised by the Maharaj doctors, that Andrew had little chance of progressing past remaining in a vegetative state if he woke from his coma. If the accident had happened in Australia, I understand his life support would have been turned off, but the culture and religion in Thailand dictates a different attitude.

The doctor in Sydney asked me to find out what Andrew's Glasgow Coma Scale score was. It was a term I had never heard before, but after googling I found it was what the medical profession regards as the most accurate measure of likely brain damage, taken during the telling hours after trauma occurs. It relates to the person's eye-opening response, verbal response and motor response. The scale goes from three (the least responsive and thus most serious damage) to fifteen. Andrew's rating was four.

Before Nicole left, we had been advised by one of the neurology team that Andrew may not live more than a few days. He surprised so many and hung on for over two and a half months. Every day of that period was an emotional roller-coaster that, truly, we would have battled to survive without the incredible support of family and friends, fifteen of whom came to Chiang Mai to comfort and support us, or more specifically Andrew, over the two-month period we were there.

Cad was taken off life support five days after the accident and was able to breathe independently, albeit with the use of an oxygen mask. He emerged from his coma after five and a half weeks, as far as I can ascertain, as there was no definitive announcement of this by the doctors. His right eye progressively opened wider and he would stare blankly ahead; eventually it would open fully and his head would move laterally at random; he would look back at us, never acknowledging he was in any way aware of our presence, making it confusing about whether he could digest some of what anyone was saying. It didn't matter. I knew I had to keep talking to him just in case he could take any of it in. His left eye was badly fractured (although we weren't made aware of this until we moved him to Bangkok weeks later), stopping it opening.

I encouraged him, continually telling him that I loved him; I told him about the day's events, that we wanted to get him home. Other times I became so dejected at the lack of progress; because his fight seemed so in vain, I begged him to give up and put himself out of the misery. Eventually, so inspired by Cad's refusal to give in to the constant threats thrown at him, I made a vow that I would get him back to Australia, telling him that every day, and I begged him to hold on. Thank God, if there is one, we were both able to honour that commitment.

I (and Chris and whoever else may have come to Chiang Mai) spoke to Andrew endlessly, praying for a response. I stroked his arms, moved his feet and legs and arms and fingers, and wiped the sweat from his forehead; I watched as his heart rate and body temperature fluctuate widely. I watched him breathe through his neck after he had a tracheotomy. When he closed his eyes, I would be relieved that he seemed asleep and at peace. I looked at him and thought, 'How tragic; how bloody unfair; how meaningless – is this nightmare ever going to end for him?' Then I would snap and think, 'This is reality; man up and show the toughness and single-mindedness that he always showed.'

Needless to say, those fifty-eight days Chris and I spent in Chiang Mai were the toughest of our lives, which includes thirty-seven years shared as husband and wife. Yet it was special for the support we received from home, and especially from those who travelled to Thailand: Nicole; Chris's brother, Ken; Andrew's close mates Matt Delaney, Todd Bailey and Adam Martin; Jaime and her mother, Mandy; Ken's wife, Llewellyn, and daughter, Nicala; my sister Alison and her husband, Wayne; my nephew Luke Naividi; Matt's mother, Kerryanne, who headed up for a few days from a holiday in Phuket; and Chris's sister, Lynne, and their mother, Maureen. We shared many tears, we accepted the silence between us, and we laughed at and revelled in some of the memories of Cad. Having each of them there gave Chris and me the strength that we so desperately needed, even though at times we had to detach ourselves when we needed time just to us.

Matt and Todd, schoolmates of Andrew's and very close ever since, were desperate to fly over within a day of the accident, but we begged them not to until Chris and I could digest the seriousness of Andrew's condition and get ourselves together. We also needed to consider whether we could endure having someone witness firsthand how Andrew looked and was, and whether he would indeed even be alive when they arrived. I'm glad they came; we spent some heartrending and special moments together (as we did with the others).

Jaime, who we still get on great with and who will always have a place in our hearts, just as desperately wanted to come over (and we asked her, too, to hold off), even though she and Andrew had been apart for about twenty-one months. She obviously still had strong feelings for him, and I have no doubt he did for her. Fortunately, they had communicated by text messages the day he flew out for Thailand (on his prompting). While in Chiang Mai, Jaime was able to cope with longer stints at his bedside than any of us, which Chris and I were thankful for and which was very special to us.

Apart from the hotel Andrew had stayed at, our home away from home became Maharaj Nakorn Hospital, where I felt very much felt like a *farung* (foreigner) every time I stepped foot into the always frantic ground level of the hospital. Getting out of the 'red car' or tuktuk at the hospital was a daily challenge, and it never became less confronting as the weeks went on.

The Maharaj is the larger of the two major public hospitals in Chiang Mai and was a beehive of activity on weekdays, with the emergency department and the administrative section on the ground floor heaving with people. The care appeared good, although basic, but it was obviously an overutilised and underfunded facility – third world, really. It was only when we had Andrew transferred to the Samitivej Srinakarin Hospital in Bangkok that we really understood how basic the facilities, and communication, in Chiang Mai were by Western standards. I won't mention the most basic, yet still inadequate, 'comforts' that we had to pay cash for.

However, the nurses always appeared pristine in their light blue uniforms, and seemed very efficient and happy in their work. There were two nurses in the ICU neurology ward who had a little English, and Andrew became their favourite patient. Maybe it was because he was the only foreigner in the ward, or maybe it was because that natural Cad charm could still be seen in the glint in his one starry eye that could open. They would speak to him calling 'An-rew ... Hello, Anrew' (or 'And-ew') to see if there was any hint of a response.

Andrew's regular neurologist, the young Dr Khemmachat, was always courteous and generous with his time, even though I had to start the conversations and ask all the questions. However, when he wasn't on the twice-a-day rounds with the other doctors (many of them interns, as it was the country's chief teaching hospital with a university next door), they would often walk to Andrew's bed, look at his chart and totally ignore me. The bizarre situation we'd found ourselves in, while receiving little clear information from the doctors in Chiang Mai, was that we had to ask questions of those in Bangkok and Australia and have them relayed to the Chiang Mai doctors on our behalf, because too often we couldn't get explanations from the Maharaj team. Too often they either wouldn't tell us, couldn't tell us or the information varied so much from day to day or doctor to doctor it left us totally confused, but more so stressed and frantic. Sometimes I felt they were telling us whatever sounded plausible just to save face, which is a big part of their culture, or they felt threatened that I had sought advice from elsewhere.

After a few weeks the staff seemed unhappy if we were there outside of visiting hours, so we had the task of enduring the many empty hours away from the hospital. There were the meals and massages (desperately needed to relieve the body tension), contact with those back home, and for me the transcribing of his diaries and writing these pages.

And there was the walking ... hour after hour of walking. During the first day at Andrew's hotel we asked how far the hospital was away and if we could walk it. 'Oh no,' the woman shrieked with a smile, 'too far.' The hotel was just inside the north-east corner of the old city area, while the hospital was just outside the south-western corner. Almost every day we walked the thirty-five minutes one way or the other, often finishing in a lather of sweat on the hottest, most humid days, but as we had so much time to fill, it became somewhat therapeutic. Then I would walk around the canal and ruins of the city walls alone with my iPod playing in my ears, in my own world, hour upon hour, sometimes with Chris.

Back home in Australia was another world altogether, where hope sprung eternal, where support from people we either knew dearly or never knew at all but who were very familiar with Cad's story, was just overwhelming.

Facebook became the most expedient and convenient way of communicating beyond our inner circle of family and friends. But knowing there were well over a thousand people in Andrew's, Oz On Foot's and my own friends groups, I couldn't bring myself to spell out the degree of his terrible diagnosis for all to see and share. And things changed so dramatically from day to day; it would have only been spreading a potentially unclear situation anyway. But I knew a few days after coming to grips with the prognosis, when it appeared Andrew was going to live past the first week or two, that I couldn't sugarcoat the severity of his condition. So, after an initial post advising people of his accident, I announced that he had suffered 'permanent severe damage from the brain trauma suffered in the collision, so we have effectively lost the Cad we knew'. I thanked everyone for the overwhelming love and support that had been expressed since his accident.

Andrew had no travel insurance, although even if he did have the standard cover, he would not have been covered because he was riding a motor scooter, and with no helmet. I implore anyone travelling overseas to ensure they have insurance, and to check its details, as it can make such a difference in emergency cases like this.

Soon after my Facebook post I learned that, in a gesture that was a godsend and absolutely unexpected and overwhelming for us, a fund had been set up to help with expenses by Andrew's friends and family; it raised an amount that Chris and I could never have envisaged. We are forever grateful to Fleur Lloyd for starting that fund (and Haidee Hines, a former workmate of Cad's, for later refining and administering it), and to those who contributed; it made a massive difference to our lives having that money to reimburse our extensive costs during the whole ordeal. Sadly, Fleur lost her brother Aaron less than a year after Andrew's death; life is unbelievably cruel sometimes.

It was weeks after Andrew had died before I gained (through the records of donations), the full picture of how many people contributed and I still get quite overcome when I consider this – why us? Close to $90,000 was donated ... I'm still lost for words. Any surplus after all our costs in Thailand and back home was used to continue Cad's charitable spirit in his memory; the fund has been named Cad's Cause.

I was advised that Channel Nine promoted the fund extensively through their rugby league coverage, no doubt organised through my lifetime mate Steve Crawley, who is head of sport there. Several websites also published something, and supportive column items appeared in the newspapers. (I found all this out later.) I was stunned but so thankful to the people responsible. To all those who donated, messaged us and said those kind words, please accept a massive thankyou from our family.

As I went through Cad's diaries and starting writing this book while in Chiang Mai, it was difficult to reconcile that the person I would bring to life in these pages was a very different person to the one lying lifeless beside me.

Great regret hit me as I sat there telling Andrew of the admiration I had for things he had achieved in his life, blurting out all my inner thoughts; neither of us had ever created an opportunity to share such things before. I so wished I had taken a week out of my life, as I had planned, to walk with him on his around-Australia trek, instead of finding myself trapped in the mindset that I was too busy with work. There's a lesson for all of us there: while it is easy to say 'I'll do that another time', you can so unexpectedly find that 'another time' may never arrive. Time, especially with those you love, is indeed precious.

After being in Chiang Mai for just over six weeks, I had to get home for four days to do a job changeover (I had resigned from the agents' accreditation scheme), and just to have a brief break. Chris had had one a week and a half earlier, returning to be with Nicole and Glenn. Chris's mother, Maureen, and sister, Lynne, had offered to come over and stay with her while I was away.

A week after I returned from Australia, Andrew's condition (after deteriorating for days) had improved enough to plan another attempt to fly him home. I can't explain the trauma that Chris and I, who were alone in Chiang Mai by this time, felt when this again had to be aborted the day before the scheduled departure because of further infection and other complications; it was the second cancellation of a scheduled escape back to Australia, five weeks apart.

Thai Airways' medical evacuation specialist ruled that Andrew was not safe to travel to Bangkok, although authorities in Bangkok and Australia had deemed him fine to fly home. I was at the end of my tether and asked – well, I virtually demanded – that surely it was safe for Andrew to at least be taken to Bangkok by road ambulance, a tenhour journey. We didn't want to stay in Chiang Mai a day longer. Fortunately, he was ruled fit enough for this.

So, on the evening Cad had been due to fly home, he instead was in an ambulance bound for Samitivej private hospital in Bangkok, where he could be assessed and hopefully made well enough for the longer journey. We were one step closer to home.

Samitivej was a stark contrast to what we had become accustomed to in Chiang Mai; it was like we had entered a new world. Andrew was admitted into his own private luxury room, with a nurse allocated to each of the mostly foreign patients in his ward. The hospital had three staff members whose sole roles were liaison with foreigners. It was just absolutely first class. The hospital was new, roomy and as extravagant as any I had visited, with three cafes, hairdresser, mini-mart, donut and juice outlets, a vast crèche and children's playground area, wi-fi access and a department to service foreign patients and families.

I cried upon first entering Andrew's private room (we had to put on a gown and mask and wash our hands when entering and exiting – no such precautions were ever requested in Chiang Mai); so starkly different was it to what we'd had had to endure in what seemed another world, a third world, away in Chiang Mai.

We were flattened when told it could be two weeks at least before Andrew might be able to go home but, thankfully, it took only eight days before doctors somehow got him in a good enough condition to fly him to Sydney – on 19 September, eight weeks and five days after his accident. It was at Samitivej that we learned Andrew had contracted meningitis in Chiang Mai, although he no longer had pneumonia.

The big thing was that we were going home. Hallelujah.

We were very fortunate that the Australian embassy had introduced us to Dr Morley at Bumrungrad very early in the piece. He became a valued confidant as I struggled with the cultural and language issues at the Maharaj, and he had been trying for six weeks to organise Andrew's repatriation to Sydney. 'Dr Peter' cannot practise in Thailand so he manages the international affairs at the big private hospital, but he goes beyond his normal job description to help others like us. I never met Peter in person but we had several phone and email conversations.

Then there was the contact I received through Dr Glenn McKay, managing director of Air Rescue Australia (and Air Rescue New Zealand), who had heard that Andrew had just walked around Australia raising money for charity and the dilemma he was in by having no travel insurance coverage. Glenn offered his or his company's services at no charge to escort Andrew home, plus cost-only access to an air ambulance if needed. I was overwhelmed by his generosity, and he worked hard to borrow equipment from other organisations and arrange for Dr Harley Hunt and also nurse Stephen McNally to accompany Andrew home on a Qantas commercial flight, bringing the cost of taking Cad back to Sydney down by thousands and thousands of dollars. Chris and I are forever indebted to all three men, and I have got to know the Gold Coast-based Glenn in the past year.

Qantas amazingly also came to the party through the representation of the National Rugby League, after I made contact with my long-time mate John Brady at the NRL. The hard work of Matt Raward at the NRL (and later Glenn McKay) in gaining the support of Qantas in greatly reducing the repatriation costs is also something for which we will always be grateful. Such an exercise requires at least two rows to be removed for medical equipment and apparatus, and more seats need to be assigned for accompanying medical staff, and Qantas were just magnificent; thank you.

I am extremely grateful too for the assistance we received from the DFAT staff in Bangkok – David Costa, who we had the most contact with, Amanda, Trudy and Calum, who were very supportive and co-operative. Those who watched Channel Nine's documentary series *The Embassy: Bangkok* would have seen Trudy McGowan and Calum Starr and what they go through in their jobs, and how many cases like Andrew's they deal with.

Chris flew back on her return ticket with Thai Airways and I boarded a Qantas flight for Sydney with Andrew, Dr Hunt and nurse McNally. I felt drained and overcome but relieved that the first long chapter of the nightmare was ending. As Andrew was brought onto the plane separately to me (I was already seated), I couldn't hold back the tears.

I looked at him and told him that we had done it; we'd kept our commitment to each other that he would go back to Australia. At the same time it was heart-wrenching to consider his condition compared to when he'd flown the same route in the opposite direction three months earlier – the people's hero, albeit an exhausted one, four days after completing his walk; a young man so full of hope, ready for 'the rest of my life'. I wish he had never boarded that plane from Sydney.

I had no idea what we were going home to, just that we were leaving this hell and the confusion that fogged our every day and that we were at least returning to an environment where, for the first time for over two months, we might get a clear, true indication of what lay ahead – in plain English.

17

HOME ... AND THE END

20 SEPTEMBER–12 OCTOBER 2012

I could hardly sleep on the way back to Australia. I was nervous, tortured by the uncertainty Andrew was about to enter into, but relieved that someone was at least now going to give us a precise insight and understandable explanation of his injuries, and his likely future. I was expecting, however, that he was facing a life of months to years of permanent care.

We were home now, at least, and that brought obvious comfort and relief. But it was like a whole new journey was about to begin.

We elected to have Andrew admitted to Westmead Hospital, in Sydney's west, where both Chris and I grew up. But there was an eleventh-hour issue, relayed to us by Glenn McKay hours before we left Bangkok, because the public hospital system dictated that a patient had to be allocated according to his place of residence, and despite Andrew's acute type of injuries suffered overseas, and the fact he'd had no fixed address for almost two years, he was no exception. I had chosen Westmead because it was accessible and recommended as having a very good neurology ward. Fortunately, the problem was somehow overcome, which I was glad about as in the end it meant the last two weeks of Andrew's life were to be played out right across the road to where Chris went to high school (Catherine McCauley) and my grandfather grew up, at Westmead Boys Home, and near the heart of where we both were raised (and Andrew was conceived). It ended up being a symbolic pilgrimage back to our roots, and over the next two weeks we drove and walked around the area when we needed a break from the hospital, which had a nostalgic effect on me.

Within twenty-four hours of Andrew's admission, after tests results were examined, we learned that the extent of Andrew's terrible injuries had been complicated by the fact he had contracted a methicillin-resistant staphylococcus aureus (MRSA) infection. This, in short, is a 'staph' infection that is basically immune to just about all the common antibiotics, and is potentially fatal for someone in Andrew's condition. On top of the pneumonia Cad had somehow fought off in Thailand, meningitis and the deteriorating condition of his much-damaged brain, he would not be capable of beating this.

Doctors at Westmead also confirmed that the initial injuries most certainly were as terrible as we had been told. The head of the orthopaedic section at Westmead, Dr Andrew Dexter, uttered one word that finally gave us a true validating impression of what happened from the impact on Andrew's head the night of the accident, describing his brain injury as 'catastrophic'. It also got back to us that the staff at Westmead were generally stunned that Andrew had even survived long enough to get back to Australia.

I, and others who knew him, could believe this, though, because it typified the incredible fighting spirit of Cad. I don't know what I believe any more – that there is a God, that there is a true spirit and soul within us, or that the brain, of which so much is unknown, is such a powerful thing that it can defy what we consider impossible. What I do believe is that somewhere in his mangled mind was a power that determined that Cad wasn't going to surrender his life in Chiang Mai and that he had to get back home. And I'm so grateful now that he didn't die in that lonely, faraway place.

Nicole happened to be in Sydney for a work conference and came to the hospital the day after Andrew was admitted. I was worried about how she would respond to seeing him; when she was in Chiang Mai soon after the accident his head was bandaged and he was swollen, bruised and beat up, but now he was more skeletal and, well ... no more detail. But she was fine – and brave.

Over the ensuing two weeks, the people at Westmead Hospital were wonderful. Our first mission was to give Andrew's relatives and closest friends the opportunity to see him and say their goodbyes. News of his fatal scenario so soon after his return would have been a shock to most, as there was a wide hope that he would come home and miraculously recover – this was Cannonball Cad, the most determined, resilient, immortal person they knew.

We spaced visits over the next few days between family and his closest friends. It was hard to watch the shock and sadness on their faces but we shared tears and laughter and I will be forever grateful that Cad, and they, had that time. They were very intimate, deeply personal days for Chris and me.

Did Cad sense anyone was there? We'll never know for sure, but I wasn't the only one who believed that he could. It didn't stop him being the receiver of many confessions, vows and reminisces. Cousins and their partners, aunties and uncles, grandparents and his close friends came in small groups. Kim and Wayne Simpson, in a very emotional experience for them and us, came down; Josh was back in Western Australia working, and struggling with what had happened. Who could have envisaged that, just months from the day we met for the first time on the last leg of Andrew's walk, we would share their grief of losing a son so young?

As Andrew's condition deteriorated, Chris and I made the decision to stop other visitors after Nicole had made a second trip from Brisbane to see her brother for the last time. Enough pain had been shared with others. We then bunkered down, most nights staying at the hospital and others close by with Chris's sister

Lynne or our great friends the Leabeaters. It was terrible. It left me with such a strong belief that euthanasia, in appropriate circumstances like these, is a right Australians should have. It was, I felt, unnecessarily traumatic watching Andrew slowly die.

It was the following Friday, at 5pm on the dot, that Andrew finally left us. It was a relief; a blessing that the nightmare had ended and Andrew's ordeal was over. We could now celebrate his life and somehow try to wipe out the past twelve weeks with memories of how he lived and the many things he achieved, instead of him lingering on and on in a horrible state.

He had not spoken a word in the eighty-three days since the accident. We'll never know whether he heard or understood a word spoken to him. But it didn't stop me having the longest, most revealing (as one-sided as they may have been) conversations with him.

As Chris and I walked to the car that night, the thing that hit me was that I had witnessed both my father's and my son's last breaths; my dad had died at age sixty-three from cancer in 1987 (just before I had turned thirty-one; Andrew was six), at home under the care of my sister Robyn, a nurse. You naturally expect to outlive your father, but not your son. You certainly don't expect to watch them both slowly die.

As we drove back to the Central Coast, to Mandy and Alan's, I instantly switched to funeral mode, another example where my surreal daily existence was on autopilot and I couldn't consider beyond the next necessary duty. Another vow I'd made to myself and to Andrew was that we would have the best damn celebration of someone's life that anyone on the Central Coast had seen. With the help of Cad's mates, who rallied to put together a most amazing, emotional tribute video that was played to about 650 people at the service, it was a mission that was accomplished.

I didn't want it to be called or to feel like a funeral, so we communicated it as a celebration of Cad's life. And rather than conduct it in a church, which would have been hypocritical, considering Andrew's beliefs, or a chapel that could not have coped with the attendance, we elected to use the auditorium at the Mingara Recreation Club. We could not have hoped for the event to be better.

The central theme for the day was the saying we adopted in Chiang Mai from a card Chris found in a peculiar shop – 'we live in deed, not years'. Rather than the traditional funeral program that is handed out as people arrive, we provided laminated bookmarks designed by good mate Craig Loughlin-Smith, who was my art director at *Big League* (and still is), and whom I would have worked beside at the Olympics in July that year. On one side was Rik's classic shot of a shirtless Cad walking into the sunset, literally in the middle of nowhere, with the words:

WE LIVE IN DEED, NOT YEARS

You'll always walk on in our hearts and our memories

I wrote the main eulogy but, despite having too many experiences of reading them myself, including at Dad's funeral, I knew I was no chance of doing it this time, so I handed the duty to outstanding celebrant Tony Thorington. Tony, a kind man with a soothing, deep voice who in a former life was a tough cop, had to take an emotional pause near the end of my eulogy, forcing him to reach for a gulp of water. I knew then I'd hit the spot with my words. There was humour that (thankfully) drew laughter, but also emotion, and when Tony finished there was a massive ovation.

Cad's cousin Luke read a wonderful eulogy too, and Wayne Simpson faced the very tough task of delivering his tribute. Andrew's close mate Kane Foley had asked to read a eulogy 'on behalf of the boys', but I talked him out of it, as I knew how difficult it would be for him to do and I thought a video tribute would be more memorable. I'd asked the boys to make a video using Cad's blogs from his walk and his bike ride to Cairns three years earlier, and some of the more tasteful grabs from his Cannonball Cad DVD compilation, along with tributes from mates (and from Jaime, which was wonderful) to the camera. In the end, Kane was happy to anchor that. I knew it would be the standout memory of the day, and it was, and a far easier task for Kane.

The video tribute, brilliantly edited by Blake Copeland, was just unbelievable, to the song 'Kick Push' by Lupe Fiasco, so appropriate due to Cad's love of skateboarding. I could sense Cad would have been looking down from above saying, 'Great shit, Dad; pretty good show.' There is no such thing as a good funeral, but to have many, many people say it was the best service they had witnessed, and that the video was just so powerful in emotion, humour and providing an insight into Cad's character, made me feel proud that I had honoured Cad as best I could. It was unexpectedly special to have so many young people on screen so naturally and sincerely saying they loved him and thanking him for his influence on their lives. Those who knew him well said it captured him so aptly; those who didn't know him well, or at all, said they left the service feeling they did. Just as comforting was that Chris got through it; in fact, she loved how it went.

The attendance that afternoon was, like so much of the love and support we received during those tough three months, almost overwhelming. Many, many friends who came from all over, so many family from both Chris's and my side, my cricket mates and partners, so many of Cad's friends, people who knew him only from the walk, friends of Nicole and Glenn who wanted to support them, former work colleagues and many from the rugby league community, which has been such a big part of my working life.

The toughest part was when Andrew's casket was taken out – by pallbearers Matt Delaney, Todd Bailey, Kane Foley, Leon Stephens, Luke Naividi and Matt Ruff, representing four good mates and two cousins – to the Foo Fighters' song 'My Hero'. Some of the boys broke down as the hearse drove away. I had to fight very hard not to as well, while holding a crying Chris in my arms.

The most touching moment of the day for me came when Nicole's five-year-old daughter, Kayla, who only joined us after the service, wanted to send a balloon with Andrew's name on it to him in heaven, as she had volunteered to Nicole days before. The experience (and particularly the photographs) of family and close friends lined up with balloons, waiting for Kayla's bossy prompt to release them only after she had let go of hers, is something I'll never ever forget, even though I expect Kayla and Max will have little memory of their uncle, something that has really saddened Nicole and Glenn (and Chris and me); he would have been an 'interesting' uncle!

I knew I had to be upbeat for the occasion, to pull off my theme that I wanted it to be a celebration and not a funeral, and thus I talked openly and enthusiastically to all I could greet. But I know now that I was existing purely on adrenaline, and keeping it together for the benefit of Chris, Nicole and all those around me. I was obviously still in some degree of shock after almost three months of navigating daily through a nightmare that was too real.

Soon after, all the daily helter-skelter, the publicity and the dutiful daily commitments that had seen Andrew be wholly the centre of the universe for Chris and me for what seemed an eternity, were gone. The mop up after the devastating cyclone had to begin. Chris and I were homeless and jobless, but that didn't matter a lot just then.

I knew, however, that when I woke up from whatever sleep I would get that night, it was my turn to adopt the words Andrew said to the camera from the centre of the Sydney Harbour Bridge, with that satisfying smile I'll take with me to my grave. Those thirteen words still run round and round my mind:

'Tomorrow will be day one: getting on with the rest of my life.'

EPILOGUE

WE LIVE IN DEED

10 NOVEMBER 2014

It is just over two years now since Andrew's death. I wrote most of this book in 2013 and self-published it, distributing primarily to friends and family of Cad and our family, or those who had heard about his story. The response, like so much I have experienced since Andrew completed his walk, was quite overwhelming, and so I decided to release the book to a wider audience.

It has been incredibly evident to me that Cad has left a legacy that will endure for a long time, judging by the hundreds of messages I have received from those who met Andrew, some for just minutes during his trek. They all tell me what a difference he had made to their lives, and I've also received many other messages from those who have read about his story. It has truly blown me away.

We have held two memorial fundraising walks (in October 2013 and 2014) in Cad's honour, from The Entrance to Terrigal on the Central Coast, the route of the fundraiser he had started to plan on his homeward leg but aborted. It seemed the right way to launch what I hope might remain an annual event, and become a way of sustaining his memory, of raising money for Cad's Cause and of drawing together Andrew's friends, family and admirers once a year. We had about 180 walkers both times, and many more donated to Cad's Cause. We have raised close to $12,000 from the two days, and other fundraising events are now planned. We had Cad's pram with us, and inside it was much of the gear he'd carted around Australia. I thought it was appropriate that Josh Simpson led us out, pushing the pram, on the first year, while my wife, Chris, and Chris Simpson's mother, Kim, took it out the second time.

Another significant event, coming just weeks after the first memorial walk, was when Cad's mate Adam Martin combined with Chris's brother, Ken Knight, to complete the 111-kilometre Hawkesbury Canoe Classic paddle race from Windsor to the F3 motorway, in honour of (and to complete) Cad's aborted attempt in 2009. It was a great show of determination by Adam, who carried a crook shoulder into the event and had never paddled before he began training two months earlier (much like Andrew in '09). They completed the course in fourteen hours in the canoe bearing 'Cannonball Express' signage (in reference to Andrew's 'Cannonball Cad' alias), with Matt Delaney, me and Adam's partner, Natasha, acting as the support crew. It was a wonderfully rewarding experience.

Inspired by Cad's story and his wish for his funds raised to go specifically to MDS, the Leukaemia Foundation in early 2014 launched a three-year PhD scholarship to research myelodysplasia, named 'The Andrew Cadigan–Leukaemia Foundation PhD, in honour of Chris Simpson'. When he first aligned with the foundation, Andrew's hope was that his money would go directly to an MDS research program and be named after 'Simmo'; now it is a reality. The Cadigan and Simpson families are very touched, not just that the boys' names are being recognised but equally that from this undertaking there might be better understanding and hopefully a breakthrough in treatment that might help many people avoid the fate Simmo confronted. We will commit, through Cad's Cause, to raise as much as we can of the $60,000 a year that is required.

Chris, Nicole and I spent a very emotional few hours in Melbourne as guests of the Leukaemia Foundation, where we met the research team and were given an insight into MDS and the breakthrough in treatment they are hoping to make. If this research creates a much greater chance for sufferers of MDS to live longer, or if a cure is found, and Cad's and Simmo's names are attached to it, it will be the proudest moment of my life.

I also heard from an electronics worker Andrew had met briefly in the Kimberley region, Daniel Walker, who was so inspired by Cad's mission that he organised a roadside memorial that was erected at a truck stop near Halls Creek; so look for it if you travel that way. Another memento is a portrait sketch of Cad done by Indy, one of the crew from Melbourne Andrew had struck up such a wonderful friendship with, which hangs on our bedroom wall.

In a very different 'memorial', but appropriate considering Cad's fondness for ink, Matt Delaney had another of Andrew's great mates, talented tattooist Todd Bailey, draw a masterpiece on his calf depicting Cad giving a peace sign with a cheeky grin, with the walking shot from the front cover of this book in the background. Cad's cousin Matt Ruff also (just as this book was being completed) had his calf inked with the Arnotts parrot – one of Andrew's tatts that I actually liked – below Cad's name as another personal memorial.

In another incredible tribute, way earlier in the weeks after Andrew's death, we were contacted by the producer of 2DayFM's 'Kyle and Jackie O' program, Kim Czosnewk, who had been alerted to our fate by another of Cad's mates, Ben Hansen, and we were absolutely stunned when, on air (after I was interviewed) they pledged $10,000 courtesy of Sony Music to go towards a family holiday. This enabled Nicole, Glenn, Kayla, Max, Chris and I to go on our first cruise, to the Pacific. It was just another example where kindness given to us was so unexpected and touching, as was the gesture by Craig Brown, who I was with in Grafton two days before rushing off to Thailand, in offering Chris and me an opportunity to join his 'Rugby League Experience' supporters tour to the 2013 World Cup in England, with me as a (very much non-celebrity) tour leader. We had a great trip, at a time when the break was invaluable.

Queensland rugby league legend Trevor Gillmeister, a mate of mine to whom I gave a copy of the initial version of this book, was so inspired by Cad's walk that he embarked on his own walk from Townsville to Brisbane in October 2014 to raise awareness of asbestos-related diseases. He also wished to raise money for a Queensland support group that helps families affected by the dreaded form of cancer that took Trevor's father, Ron. It was another powerful legacy that Cad created, and I was so touched that Trevor completed the journey and raised close to $150,000. I was proud and amazed that he carried a stress fracture in one foot through most of the thirty-one-day trek.

Chris and I moved to the Gold Coast three months after Cad's death, as we had been hoping to do for some time, which means we're only an hour or so away from Nicole, Glenn and the grandkids in Brisbane. We enjoy the lifestyle there although it means we are away from many friends and other family. It's been a new start, one that we needed.

As I said in my eulogy at Andrew's service, it is accepted that it is a father's role to teach his children valuable lessons in life, but perhaps Cad taught me as much as I did him. There are many days that I call on those qualities as my life goes on – his determination not to give in, his resilience, his strength and his innate ability to dust himself off and get done what he had to do, no matter what issues he may have been hiding inside.

On the testimonial video his mates put together for Andrew's funeral, Matty Hansen recalled something that has stuck with me. His story, about kicking stones in life, was just one of several amazingly emotional and genuine tributes to Cad on the video, which is a life's treasure for me: 'I just want to say thanks to Cads for being an inspiration to all of us growing up in Killcare and trying to train us to do what we wanted to do and not what other people wanted us to do. I'd see him down the beach in the arvo and I'd say, "What are you doing, mate?" and he'd say, "I'm just kicking stones around the car park at Killcare ... Don't get stuck kicking stones around Killcare car park! Do what you want to do and make what you want to make out of your life."'

To have read hundreds of messages from people whom Cad touched, even briefly, has been truly remarkable and almost incomprehensible, considering that those closest to him knew his frailties. Here are some that were posted on Facebook after his death:

> *'I will forever tell my children about the time I picked up a man on the highway and he was walking around Australia, I will tell them how he dropped everything in his life to see out a*

challenge that had called for him, I will tell them that sometimes you just have to go your own way, and you taught me that, Mr Cadigan. But more importantly I will tell the story of Andrew Cadigan.'

'You touched our lives so very briefly but left a lasting and indelible mark. You will have touched the lives of so many

who also travelled those roads. Your strength, humour, determination, commitment and apparent love of your friends and family will be missed by many, many more people than those of your family and inner circle will ever know about.'

'This world will miss his heart and energy, his smile and determination to make a difference. Having said that, he is one of most

inspirational people I have ever met and admired. He leaves behind a beautiful legacy and footsteps of a giant.'

'No one can ever accuse him of not living his life to the fullest, making the most of every situation and taking advantage of everything life had to throw at him. It is one of the saddest moments I've experienced in life, having to say goodbye to such a bloody legend.'

What I have so harshly observed is that what happened to Andrew and our family is not isolated. While we so naively think such a tragedy will never ever touch *our* lives there is nothing to suggest we may be exempt; there have been too many examples of that since Andrew died, involving people I knew well losing their lives, or those of sons or daughters, brothers or sisters, husbands or wives.

I found out in recent months that, on average, one Australian a day dies in Thailand, most from motor accidents. That is a staggering statistic, and we must try to change it. I recently heard from Julie, the mother of Nicole Fitzsimons, whose death in a motorcycle accident generated much publicity just weeks after Andrew died in 2012; Julie's daughter Kate has devoted much time to educating teenagers in schools about travel risks and dangers.

Janette Doolan, a wonderful woman who has transcribed tapes of interviews used in many of the books I have written, left me with a thought that, as succinct as it may be, has really hit the spot as much as anything said to me this past year. Janette lost her son Tom at age nineteen in November 2011, in tragic circumstances in Britain. She relayed some advice she received that goes something like this: 'You can keep asking "why" this happened to us, but the real question is "why not" – why should this happen to other people and not us?'

She's right. And that thought has given me more strength.

I hope Cad's story has moved you, entertained you and enriched you, made you laugh, cry and perhaps marvel at how he survived navigating Oz by foot. He was no angel but I loved him dearly. He may not even be among angels now, but he certainly is in the hearts of many in our world, even though he is no longer physically in our presence.

If you have had a Cad or a Simmo in your life, I hope you learn to understand that that is a blessing. To lose them is tragic, but you must be thankful that at least you've had the wonderful pleasure of having had them in our presence.

I hope mostly that these pages have triggered a recognition that many of us 'ordinary' people, like Andrew 'Cad' Cadigan, are capable of doing things that can be truly perceived as 'extraordinary'. I hope you have learned from his incredible determination and commitment that saw him defy extreme hardships at times to finish what he had vowed to finish.

Cad preached to so many of his mates, long before his grand walk, that we should aim to achieve and not have any regrets by failing to follow our dreams or our search for happiness or, simply, our niche in life. We may never get to our destination, we may always be searching, but it is better to be on the path to fulfilment and perhaps fall off than it is to be stalled in a bog of 'if onlys' and never step onto the trail.

However, we can do all the planning and have belief in fate, religion, destiny or our own apparent immortality, but none of those things may necessarily be our salvation. It is how we live our life that matters: 'We live in deed, not years.'

Lastly, I just hope you at least admire what Cad achieved, and how he did it; how he never surrendered.

If it so happened that you noticed him somewhere on a lonely road or in a town he passed through somewhere in Australia between late December 2010 and mid-June 2012, and you saw him as some heavily tattooed, pierced young bloke to whom you might have been tempted to give a wide berth, perhaps you have now discovered that Andrew was more than what he may have first appeared to be.

As could anyone we pass, on any day of our lives.

Whatever Makes You Happy

As I began writing this book's epilogue, the Powderfinger song 'Whatever Makes You Happy' came on my iPod while on shuffle. It was one of Cad's songs, which I'd copied from his library. The timing was a little eerie, and it felt as if he had some sort of presence in the room just then. Maybe it was a message he wanted me to relay. It seems an appropriate way to end this book.

If we never make it back to how far we've come along this way
We search around for solid ground that will help to carry us away
If the memories I left throw the light that helps to guide you through
We trickle down to our goodbyes but a part of me will stay with you
What we've spoken over time
Never broken or compromised
Dream on together
Leaning against each other
However it happens I hope it's
Whatever makes you happy
Whatever makes you happy.

'Whatever Makes You Happy' (Fanning, Mushroom Music Publishing). *Reproduced with permission.*

If you would like to donate to Cad's Cause, or to the PhD scholarship to study MDS, please visit www.ozonfoot.com.au.

BACK COVER MATERIAL

In late 2010 Andrew 'Cad' Cadigan quit his job, sold his home and set out to walk around Australia. He was doing it in honour of a mate, Chris Simpson, who had recently succumbed to a rare pre-leukaemia condition.

Over the next eighteen months Cad walked over 15,000 kilometres, pushing a three-wheeler pram that held all his provisions. Along the way he met hundreds of people from all walks of life, making new friendships and collecting donations for the Leukaemia Foundation. He battled extreme weather, injury, loneliness and depression, but refused to surrender.

Four days after triumphantly crossing the Sydney Harbour Bridge to complete his trek, Cad left for a holiday in Thailand, where he planned to turn his journals into a book. Tragically, within a month he suffered horrific injuries in a motorcycle accident, dying twelve weeks later.

Cad's father, Neil, vowed to his son that he would finish his book. *With Every Step,* which is by turns irreverent, entertaining, tragic and inspirational, represents the completion of Andrew Cadigan's mission. It is an emotional story that only a father could tell.

NEIL CADIGAN is a journalist and author who lives on the Gold Coast with his wife, Christine. He has written or co-written many bestselling books, including Andrew Johns' *The Two of Me,* Greg Page's *Now and Then* and *Danny Buderus' Talent Is Not Enough.*